Operational
Cash Flow Management
And Control

Operational
Cash Flow Management
And Control

Morris A. Nunes

Prentice-Hall, Inc.   **Englewood Cliffs, N. J.**

Prentice-Hall International, Inc., *London*
Prentice-Hall of Australia, Pty. Ltd., *Sydney*
Prentice-Hall of Canada, Ltd., *Toronto*
Prentice-Hall of India Private Ltd., *New Delhi*
Prentice-Hall of Japan, Inc., *Tokyo*
Prentice-Hall of Southeast Asia Pte. Ltd., *Singapore*
Whitehall Books, Ltd., *Wellington, New Zealand*

© 1982 by
Prentice-Hall, Inc.
Englewood Cliffs, N.J.

Library of Congress Cataloging in Publication Data

Nunes, Morris A.
    Operational cash flow management and control.

    Includes index.
    1. Cash flow.   2. Cash management.   I. Title.
HG4028.C45N86   658.1′52   81-8688
                                              AACR2
ISBN 0-13-637470-0

Printed in the United States of America

To my mother,
Betty Ann Ecoff Nunes,
who predicted and believed.

Acknowledgments

Many, many thanks to:

Mr. Haig Revitch for his volunteer work as an excellent sounding board;

Dr. James J. Busse of the U.S. Dept. of Energy for his advice on statistical methods;

Mr. W. Bert Effing, formerly of the Embassy of the Netherlands to the U.S. for his hospitality and assistance in the European research;

Mr. Richard W. Keene of Lloyd's of London for the special courtesies extended by Lloyd's;

Mr. G. L. Clarke of Midland Bank Ltd., Mr. Henry H. Weiser and Mr. Hans Schaerer, both of Union Bank of Switzerland and E. J. van der Hagen of Amsterdam-Rotterdam Bank, N.V. for their insights into foreign exchange and international business procedures;

Mr. James Agee of First American Bank of Washington, D.C. for data on domestic banking practices;

William C. Taylor of the U.S. Social Security Administration for his good humor; and

My wife, Janie, for her endless patience and support.

About the Author

Morris A. Nunes is an attorney and financial consultant in suburban Washington, D.C. He serves on the Board of Directors of many of his client companies, with whom he has promoted the successful application of the techniques included in this book.

A graduate of the University of Pennsylvania and its Wharton School of Business, he holds degrees in finance and accounting. He spent several years in controllership positions before obtaining a law degree from Georgetown University.

He is the author of a number of business articles for publications including the American Management Association's *Management Review, Public Utilities Fortnightly* and *Commercial Construction News.* He has also written mini-computer financial analysis programs published by Hewlett-Packard Company.

Mr. Nunes teaches finance and tax courses in college and continuing education programs and is a frequent speaker to business and professional groups. He is admitted to the Virginia, District of Columbia and federal bars, and is licensed before several appellate courts, including the U.S. Tax Court and the U.S. Supreme Court.

An avid racquetball sportsman, he lives with his wife Jane and their Yorkie, Valentino, in Northern Virginia.

What This Book Will Do for You And Your Company

You are a Financial Manager. In the final analysis there are two resources you use in the application of your managerial abilities: TIME and FUNDS.

Time needs no definition. Funds repose in various forms on the asset side of the Balance Sheet, constrained by their corresponding source liabilities and equity investment.

Whatever your organizational position, whatever your assignment, wherever your attention is directed, deep in the subconscious of your Manager's brain, in its most elemental state, always your motivating maxim is: "Maximize Funds in Minimum Time."

Why then should you invest either in this book?

Because this is a book for thinking managers; for doers who plan. If you are doing a lot, but getting little done, you probably know your planning is deficient. This book will help you shortcut your financial operations planning. If you are planning a lot but getting little execution, this book will propel the translation of plan to action. And if you're *the* manager who already plans and does, this book is tailor-made for you.

Take a look at 48 ways this book will help you manage cash flow:

1. Conceptualize and nail down your FUNDING NEEDS using Trapezoidal Analysis.
2. Prevent the ACCOUNTING TRAP from distorting your understanding of FUNDS FLOW DYNAMICS.
3. Develop the SEVEN TYPES OF ACCOUNTING DATA your company needs.
4. Establish a "KEY INDICATOR SIGNAL SYSTEM" to stay on top of your operations.
5. Prepare and USE an INTERNAL FINANCIAL POLL.
6. Use INTERNAL AUDIT AS A BALANCE WHEEL to keep your operations of informational programs on track.
7. Design a NORMATIVE OPERATING PROFILE for the company and each of its profit centers, to objectively PINPOINT PROBLEMS AND SUCCESSES.
8. Develop a COMPREHENSIVE AND FLEXIBLE CASH ACCOUNTS POLICY.
9. Create, monitor and operate a LOCK-BOX AND REMOTE DISBURSEMENT SYSTEM with maximum efficiency.
10. Verify and utilize FLOAT to IMPROVE CASH FLOW.
11. Define the ELEVEN PARAMETERS of MARKETABLE SECURITIES in terms of your requirements.

12. Implement seven ways to PROTECT PROFITS FROM FOREIGN EX-CHANGE RISKS.

13. Establish a flexible CREDIT POLICY THAT PROMOTES SALES.

14. Utilize ACCOUNT GROUP SPLITTING TECHNIQUES to make your credit policy work in every case.

15. Gain positive action techniques from PROBLEM CREDIT ACCOUNTS.

16. Manage with a READY CREDITWORTHINESS SCREENING PROCESS.

17. Get the EXTRA DOLLARS IN YOUR BILLING.

18. Calculate and interpret the FOUR KINDS OF RECEIVABLES AVERAGE AGE.

19. Recognize problem receivables using MOVING AVERAGE PAYMENT SCHEDULES, CUSTOMER SCHEMATIC CREDIT REPORTS and EX-CEPTIONS INDEX REPORTS.

20. Organize a WASTELESS COLLECTIONS PROGRAM.

21. Administer NINE WAYS TO PUT TEETH IN COLLECTIONS PROGRAMS.

22. Use the "magic" THREE EXTERNAL COLLECTION ALTERNATIVES.

23. Draw the line with your BAD DEBTS POLICY.

24. Develop an INVENTORY CONTROL SYSTEM minimizing conflict among finance, sales, procurement, warehouse and traffic functions.

25. Create a SELF-ADJUSTING INVENTORY BUDGET.

26. Evaluate and administer an ITEM-BY-ITEM INVENTORY PERFORMANCE REVIEW.

27. HOLD DOWN INVENTORY LEVELS: Nine money-saving ways.

28. Make your inventory accounting system contribute to POSITIVE PRICING.

29. Become a WINNING INVENTORY MANAGER: Seven steps for success.

30. Use a RISK ACCEPTANCE FLOW CHART to manage your insurance program.

31. IDENTIFY, QUANTIFY AND CLASSIFY RISKS for pinpointing insurance needs.

32. Employ TWENTY TECHNIQUES to REDUCE INSURANCE AND LOSS COSTS.

33. Apply SEVEN STEPS OF ASSET ACQUISITION.

34. Organize vertical ASSET EVALUATION DATA.

35. Profit from your CHOICE OF ASSET DEPRECIATION METHOD.

36. Turn your BANK into a multi-dimensional EXTERNAL RESOURCE.

37. Weigh the EIGHT FACTORS IN BANK SELECTION.

38. Develop an ATTRACTIVE AND EFFECTIVE LOAN REQUEST.

39. Select from SEVENTEEN OPTIONS FOR STRUCTURING the most desirable LOAN.

40. Build a BALANCED LIABILITIES STRUCTURE.

41. Choose among the FOUR PRINCIPAL BANK DEBT ALTERNATIVES and their FOURTEEN VARIATIONS.

42. Have answers to the key questions in FUNDING PERMANENT CAPITAL.

43. Calculate, interpret and apply the ACCURATE COST OF CAPITAL.

44. Tap the FIVE BASIC CAPITAL MARKETS.

45. Use an INVESTOR MOTIVATION TALLY to zero in on the optimum capital market.

46. Discover SIXTEEN ways to structure EQUITY KICKERS to improve DEBT ATTRACTION.

47. Apply TEN tactics to ATTRACT EQUITY INVESTMENT.

48. Develop, implement and control a COMPREHENSIVE BUDGETED BUSINESS PLAN covering the seven COMPONENTS OF BUSINESS OPERATIONS.

What this book contains is only part of its value. HOW it contains will be just as important to you, as the book is sequenced like an eleven-chapter balance sheet, sandwiched between two strategic control chapters.

Each chapter is a focused program concentrating on one sector of the balance sheet designed to improve its quality by improving the operations that affect it. With that concept in mind, you can determine your priorities, flip to the appropriate chapter and begin attacking the problems now, head-on, not two weeks from now when you reach that section of the book.

Or, you can take your organization and balance sheet and start redesigning, restructuring and refining your operations, step-by-step and chapter-by-chapter.

Start planning and doing now to make the most of your managerial abilities and those two precious resources: TIME and FUNDS.

Morris A. Nunes

Contents

Operational
Cash Flow Management
And Control

Chapter 1

Effective Funds Control: Key to Ready Cash and Capital When You Need It

THE FUNDING BUDGET CONCEPT

Classic business doctrine posits that the manager's elemental responsibility is the optimum allocation and application of scarce resources. These resources break down into land, labor and capital. Some commentators maintain that management itself is a fourth scarce resource, distinct from labor, which must also be allocated and applied.

Of these elements, capital (referred to here as funds) is the only one of the elements readily convertible into all of the others. It is the common denominator of management decisions and business measurement.

Yet, too many managers gloss over the elementary planning critical to laying a foundation for the proper relationship of a given business to its capital. Common thinking on the subject often consists of just two statements:

1. "Let's get as much money to work with as we can, at an acceptable cost, of course."

2. "Let's make the most money we can."

Managers then proceed to act on these scanty premises, calculating their actions based on their particular set of perceived circumstances.

Inherent in both those statements are some definitions and assumptions that may or may not be fitting for the given business.

The biggest problem with Statement 1 is that there always comes a point when the cost is no longer acceptable. No minor problem is the corollary of determining where that point is to be fixed.

As for Statement 2, it lacks a time frame. The "most" money today may mean bankruptcy in the long run (or even the short run). Waiting for the "most" money for the long run can tax the patience of the most patient manager, not to mention the hungry shareholder.

So let's look at a way to conceptualize your proper relationship to funds and the need for them. This is the foundation for the Funding Budget Concept.

At any particular point in time there are four competing demands on the funds of a business:

1. *Capital Servicing Demand:* This is the demand for funds to maintain the firm's capitalization and set the stage for future capital attraction. The funds allocated to this demand are called interest, dividends, sinking fund payments, etc.

2. *Operations Demand:* This is the demand for funds to support the day-to-day business of doing business. Payroll, materials, advertising expense, etc. reflect allocation for operations demand.

3. *Growth Demand:* This is the demand for funds to expand. Capital expenditures or research and development are examples of allocation here. However, there are some businesses with no allocation to growth and others whose allocation in theory is something else in fact.

4. *Contingency Demand:* This demand is two-edged. On one blade sufficient funds are found to protect the entity against unforeseen problems and failures. On the other blade lie the funds to capitalize on the unexpected opportunity. Lacking funds for the former can be fatal, for the latter heart-rending.

While these demands are dynamic, sometimes dependently and other times independently, it is still useful and indeed necessary, to examine how they relate at a static point in time. If a trapezoid can represent available funds, their allocation to the four demands may be represented this way:

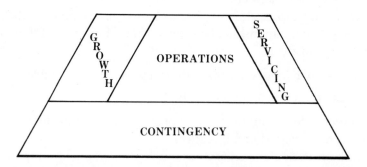

The area allocated to each demand within the trapezoid graphically shows the approximate relative percentage of funds expectedly devoted to that demand.

While contingency funds might flow to satisfy a failure or opportunity arising from any of the other four demands, the actual allotment of the contingency sub-trapezoid to the other three demands will probably not reflect the same proportions as in the rest of the figure, but will look more like this:

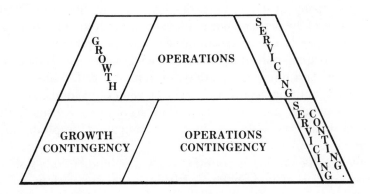

Making a gross determination of these real dollar relationships, just by eyeballing from management experience, can help establish a basic philosophy on which the specifics of building a complete budget can be accomplished. Knowing that not more than 25% of all the budget should be allocated to growth can be very useful in setting priorities among competing projects.

Before looking at the parameters for specifying that budget, we need to examine the information system by which the parameters will be evaluated.

THE INFORMATION NETWORK

In terms of funds relationships, the prime information system is the accounting system. However, in too many situations, the typical accounting system is responsive to only one kind of information need. In fact, there are at least six kinds of needs in every company and seven in many:

1. Book Accounting
2. Cash Flow Accounting.
3. Budgetary Accounting
4. Management Accounting
5. Tax Accounting
6. Operational Accounting and
7. the "optional" Regulatory Accounting

Book Accounting encompasses the activities attendant to the production of financial statements. Because of the standards imposed by Generally Accepted Accounting Principles (GAAP) and the conventions necessary to developing financial statements (e.g., the somewhat arbitrary assignment of lives to assets for the purpose of charging periodic depreciation), Book Accounting can distort what is actually happening. It can also be particularly unsusceptible to certain types of requisite financial analysis, as the limited number of accounts frequently mix transactions that preferably would be separated. These shortcomings are often especially exaggerated in companies, such as public utilities, whose charts of accounts are prescribed in detail by regulation.

Yet, every company must have its set of books, whether in a 5″ × 7″ notebook or on a floppy disk. Because of the permanence of these books, they are too often paramount in, or even constitute all of the company's accounting scheme, despite their problems, when they should be just one coequal share. The strong financial manager will take care to look behind and beyond the standard monthly, quarterly or annual P & L Statement.

Cash Flow Accounting details the actual movement of funds. As a required part of today's certified financial statements, cash flow accounting is usually the number two system, although cash flow is derived in many companies simply by manipulating the historic information contained in the books.

The challenge in cash flow accounting is the development of a system that will both monitor sources and uses of funds in terms of the initiating causes of funds flow, and forecast the results of transactions to permit the balancing of cash needs with cash availability. While some may argue that availability is more appropriately balanced with need, the sad fact is that in the short run, the overall availability of funds for any business is fixed by its power in the capital markets. Hence, the needs are ultimately the thing to be recast.

Budgetary Accounting consists of two equally important phases. The first is the futuristic planning and establishment of goals and spending targets designed to achieve those goals at least cost. The second phase is the measurement of results against those goals and targets.

A serious problem in many organizations is the distortion of results that occurs when budgets are measured against book accounting. The credibility of the company budget system can be destroyed by the bickering of the manager charged with meeting the goals and the accountant charged with measuring the manager's achievements.

A key factor in the creation of this unfortunate situation is that budget systems are usually designed around the company's book accounting system with the format of the budget process determined by the financial and accounting arm of the company. The manager responsible for developing his own budget is then behind the 8-ball in trying to translate his perspective into the appropriate tables and columns. That disadvantage is in turn frequently exaggerated by the differences in budgetary accounting needs among the different company segments. For example, the concentration on personnel and payroll budgeting in a labor intensive company may yield rather insignificant value for the department in that company with relatively few personnel, even though a department, such as insurance with its budgeting for co-insurance and self-insurance, may have a major and direct impact on the company's profits and cash.

Zero-based budgeting (ZBB) is in part an attempt to address these problems, but its pitfalls, particularly for the manager (whether proposing or approving the budget) who is inexperienced in ZBB, can be devastating. In attempting to expand the budget system to compensate for the variety of budgeting needs found throughout an entire organization, ZBB too often destroys the integrity of the budget process by entangling its participants in a mire of detail. Whereas many budget systems tend to be ineffective by slighting some desirable aspects of analysis, ZBB tends to be ineffective by overwhelming the same aspects with layers of superfluity.

Another frequent criticism of budget systems is that once the budget is in place it becomes an immutable force, stolidly disregarding developments that may render some or all of it obsolete.

These and other budget questions will be explored more fully in a later chapter. The point is that the effectiveness of the accounting function is critical to the effectiveness of achieving meaningful and well-directed budgetary control. When dealing, then, with the budget process, the astute chief will:

1. Include non-accounting managers from a cross-section of the company in budget *process* design;

2. Seek to tailor performance measurement to each company operation so that the responsible manager can relate real decisions to the standards of measurement;

3. Synthesize both budgets and variances into terms that give top management a common frame of reference for evaluating different company segments with and against each other;

4. Translate budget information into profit and loss and cash effects so that management can successfully guide each area in relation to overall company direction; and

5. Demand flexibility to keep both budget and performance measurement in tune with the dynamism of events.

Management Accounting concentrates on analysis of corporate activities for management decision-making. The sine qua non of such analysis is good input data. The function of management accounting is to provide that data in a form that lends itself to cogent manipulation.

The nature of much of the analysis complicates the accounting job by requiring extensive detail. Like the budget process, the results of this analysis should be reconciled with profits and cash reporting.

Management accounting requirements vary greatly from company to company. In a sense, as the goal is decision-making, all company accounting is management accounting. Hence, the prime attribute of a good management accounting setup will be the ability to draw on all aspects of a company's information system and sources, and then meld the individual pieces of information into a logical, comprehensive and comprehensible whole.

Tax Accounting focuses, of course, on the determination of the minimum legitimate liability, the development of the documentation to defend and support that determination and the timely preparation and submitting of returns in compliance with requirements. In addition to these de rigeur activities, additional facets of tax accounting that should not be ignored are the inputs to decision-making (including the budget process), as few transactions will be devoid of tax consequences.

Operational Accounting is the "statistical" and non-financial recordkeeping that is absolutely essential to relating pure dollars to operations. Included in such accounting are human resources and industrial management data.

While much of this kind of information is often considered outside the traditional accounting bailiwick, the progressive firm will still monitor it with its accounting unit, taking care to assure that the financial information systems are returning results that are both reliable and useful. These needs will also vary substantially by company.

Regulatory Accounting is simply recordkeeping in compliance with the requirements of any governmental unit. While often thought to be the concern of only utilities, transportation concerns, communications companies, etc., it is a growing problem for a great number of companies. From the Securities and Exchange Commission to individual state licensing bureaus, more and more demands for pre-formatted information are being made on businesses.

The greatest problem with regulatory requirements is that they usually do not conform to management's own preferences. The second great problem is simply the cost of tracking and reporting the same information in so many ways with so little value for the reporter. Accordingly, the goal of regulatory accounting is often the minimum output to satisfy regulatory authorities. The additional goal that should be considered, as in tax accounting, is input to decision-making to assess the impact of alternatives on regulatory reporting, and, thence, on regulatory judgment.

The concept the financial manager must keep in mind is that each accounting type has its own applications. Communicating their differences in methods and goals is as important as using them to provide answers. One of the best ways to facilitate that communication is to reconcile and relate to book accounting, which is the most commonly used and recognized of the types. By reconciling, the differences in perspective can be underscored with minimum risk of mistrust of the results.

Because all of the accounting types are pulling information from the single transactional data base (i.e., one set of transactions) it is sometimes difficult for the non-financial manager to conceptualize the differences. Therefore, the presentation of the accounting results, including a reconciliation, can be as important as the data itself.

Using a simplified example, assume it is year end and mythical Company Z is about to consider buying a new $100,000 production line machine. Exclusive of this transaction, the year's profit and loss figures will be:

Revenues	$1,000,000
Expenses	−900,000
Profit	$ 100,000

The transaction could be analyzed like this:

	BOOK	CASH FLOW	BUDGET	MANAGEMENT	TAX	OPERATIONS
Calculations for this Yr.	Rev $1,000,000 Exp −900,000 Pretax $ 100,000 Machine purchase is capitalized.	In. $1,000,000 Out: Exp. −900,000 Mach. −100,000 Net In −0−	Has this machine purchase been contemplated in capital budget?	What impact on yearend ratios, credit rating & market acceptance?	Investment tax credit and minimal depreciation reduce tax by $10,000 + (10%), increasing net.	No impact on present year
Impact on Future Years	Increase pretax expenses by depreciation. Choose deprec. method.	Add back deprec. to eliminate effect of non-cash expense.	Increases in maintenance and carrying charges for responsible unit.	Calculate expected annual incremental profit from use and determine return on investment.	Depreciation reduces annual tax liability. Local personal property tax increased.	Determine productivity increases expected, including learning curve. What impact on break-even? Should prices be adjusted?
Reconciliation to Book	NA	Capital expenditure is not expensed creating this year's difference. Future years differ by depreciation.	Depreciation is "non-controllable" expense & therefore not in area budgets.	Show impact on selected accts.	Show impact on tax accounts.	Show impact on selected revenue and expense accts.
Conclusions	No effect on this year's pre-tax profits. Depreciation in future years will reduce profits unless offset by gains due to operation. Control expenses carefully during test period.	Cash shortage may result while awaiting payback. Short-term borrowings may require consideration; possibly lease or finance machine.	Purchase may generate cost pressures in maintenance budget. Can temporary cutbacks be made in other areas until machine is proven?	Machine will yield sufficient ROI if operated properly. Monitor downtime closely and be sure sales are absorbing production.	Tax consequences mitigate real cost.	Productivity management crucial to project success. Be sure sales is kept aware of cost profile to determine pricing and discount strategies.

Schematically, the accounting types can be summarized this way:

ACCOUNTING TYPE	GOALS	REPORTS	EXAMPLES OF OUTPUT	PITFALLS
BOOK	Determine profitability and net worth of entity.	Financial Statements.	Profits, Net Worth.	Constrained by GAAP, etc. Can lack specificity. Strictly historic data.
CASH FLOW	Understand changes in cash positions and determine cash needs and match availability.	Cash Flow Statement; Cash forecast; Cash Reconciliation.	Cash Balances; Cash Needs; Cash Available.	Fails to elucidate commitments, obligations and non-cash transactions.
BUDGETARY	Control expenditures. Set targets and provide performance motivation and measurement	Budgets; Variances.	Targets; Performance.	Lines of authority do not necessarily follow functional logic.
MANAGEMENT	Analyze activities to plan and improve.	Special purpose reports.	Investment decisions, etc.	Relation to book and other reports can be distorted.
TAX	Compliance and liability minimization.	Tax Returns.	Tax payments and refunds.	Artificial requirements not useful for non-tax decisions.
OPERATIONAL	Control and planning of non-financial aspects of activities.	Special purpose reports.	Units of output Employment, etc.	Not always subject to accurate quantification.
REGULATORY	Compliance and best case to receive regulatory approval.	Special purpose Reports; Required Filing.	Rate Base; Compliance Reports.	Artificial requirements distort and not useful for non-regulatory decisions.

KEEPING AHEAD OF RESULTS

The manager's job is future oriented, yet the heart of the accounting system is only a commentary on the past. Individual financial statements are valuable, but they have three drawbacks in relation to day-to-day business:

1. There is a lag from time of transaction to time of report.
2. The financial statement is necessarily not detailed enough, as it covers such a broad spectrum of activities. It is a summary.
3. By internalizing certain assumptions and conventions, the real story can be distorted.

The U.S. Government issues a monthly report of Economic Indicators, which includes several factors that economists have decided generally foreshadow the direction of the economy. A similar "early warning" device can be utilized to overcome the shortfalls of the financial statements of any company.

To help give such a system instant recognition and appeal among management, consider using an acronym like KISS (for "Key Indicator Signal System") in the establishment of the program. For such a system to work, the data developed must receive prompt attention from those managers who will govern response.

There are four decisions to be made in establishing KISS:

1. What information is truly indicative?
2. How much information should be included?
3. How frequently should the information be reported?
4. Who should receive the reports?

The hardest part of the exercise is the determination of the data that is appropriate for the reports. There are at least six criteria of evaluation:

1. *Forecasting Value:* Each indicator should foreshadow business performance in one or more areas of activity. A simple example is that sales volume correlates with profits.

Regression analysis is a useful tool for testing potential indicators. A related and simpler technique is the comparison of graphs of various suspected indicators against graphs of sales, profits, cash balances, employment, etc. Management intuition and experience that favors one indicator or another should not be disregarded. Rather, that indicator should be investigated for statistical confirmation of its validity.

External data (stock market averages, government data, trade statistics, etc.) should be considered as potential indicators. Caution is advised, however, in using more than one or two external figures, as the system could become more reflective of the economy than of the company. As the fortunes of many companies tend to swing with the economy, this is an easy trap to fall into.

Also to be avoided are data, either internal or external, that receive or require frequent revision or adjustments. Maintaining comparability is essential to a tool of this kind. The other problem with revised data is that adjusting to retain comparability is time-consuming and may be confusing. Late data is also to be assiduously avoided, as its forecasting value may be expired by the time it reaches the managers. This is a major shortcoming of much government or trade association data.

2. *Reliability:* Each chosen indicator should be as free as possible from the likelihood of containing extraordinary transactions that will create "glitches" in the data or demand arbitrary adjustment in reporting. For example, while total assets on hand may be a good indicator of profit potential, the time of acquisition of new assets can be an extraordinary period, as training and installation may cause a dip in fortunes, when greater assets on hand might ordinarily presage increases in sales or profits.

The other, more insidious risk, is that data must not be misleading. For example, while the number of active salesmen might be important and statistically correlative to sales, this could be a highly unreliable indicator without modifying for experience, full-time vs. part-time, etc. Such vagaries, while possibly subject to adjustment (although "experience" is likely to be a highly subjective adjusting factor) will probably violate the timeliness and simplicity tests.

3. *Magnitude:* There should be a tendency to choose indicators that in and of themselves are informative on the status of major components of company health. For example, in a contract construction business with fixed contract revenues and high labor intensity, gross payroll hours are going to be very important for the present and the future, and reflect a large portion of all expenses.

4. *Coverage:* The system architect should seek those indicators that will illuminate a broad cross-section of the company. The indicators should lead managers to recognize opportunities and problems company-wide. If the indicators are unlikely to reflect activity in one or more areas, then the neglected areas are effectively relegated to time-lagged management. For example, in a retail business, given a choice between receipts for inventory and purchases, the latter would be likely to be the better indicator, as it will relate to all orders placed for all departments, rather than just expenditures for merchandise. In this case, it has the added advantage of being earlier in time. In any event, total purchases will include a monitoring of inventory, though not directly. Logically, however, if a bulge showed up in purchases, purchases for inventory would undoubtedly be among the first areas checked, as it is the largest single area of expenditure.

5. *Speed:* An early warning system requires early data receipt. Therefore, however well a particular indicator may meet the other tests, if the data is cumbersome to organize or slow in coming in, the indicator is not a good one.

For example, in a manufacturing environment, inventory values may be an extremely valuable set of figures. However, if it is known or feared that the "book" figures usually require extensive adjustment to account for shrinkage, then the effort and time needed to obtain an accurate count, price and extension make it an unrealistic item for inclusion in the system. That is not to say that inventory values will not be taken or confirmed, but that when done the information will form part of reports outside KISS.

6. *Simplicity:* KISS is also an acronym for the admonition "Keep Indicator System Simple." That admonition is fitting here.

KISS should be designed to be readily grasped and subject to quick response. The more complex the less likely KISS will be accepted or utilized effectively.

For example, while analysis may show a fine statistical relationship among use of credit lines, capacity utilization and labor productivity, such figures are likely to be too esoteric to accomplish the task of giving managers information they can act on in confidence. After all, how many production managers would adjust their schedules just because the company pays down a number of loans?

Having developed a list of satisfactory indicators, chances are the list will be a fairly long one, especially as availability of the data is generally controllable. Whether or not a lengthy list is useful is largely a subjective decision. The total system result should have a meaning as a single statement about the health and prospects of the firm. If too many indicators are combined, they may dilute each other or smother the manager with too much data, destroying the purpose of the system. On the other hand, if too few indicators are used, the system loses its effectiveness. It is conceivable that a series of indicators could be developed on different aspects of the business, if responsible feeling runs strong that too many of the items on the list cannot be ignored.

The frequency of the KISS report is also a matter for management judgment, constrained by the flow of corporate information. Consideration should be given to arranging for special handling of data requisite to KISS in order to expedite the output. The frequency should be great enough to allow maximum response time and minimization of the time in which problems can compound themselves or opportunities dissipate. The greater the frequency, the simpler the indicators should be in order to cut both preparation and review time. KISS should be a welcome management tool, not a grudgingly accepted burden.

Who should receive the report is also a judgment call. The greater the distribution, the more likelihood that important points will be noted and that pursuit of solutions and opportunities will be undertaken. Knowledge is almost always a boon to managers. However, where sensitive data is or might be included, or where a specified level of sophistication is required to properly assess the output, the distribution group should be so confined.

When presenting the KISS report, two approaches that may improve its value are:

1. Develop the indicator information into a composite index; and
2. Graph the index, both to catch its trend and to compare with graphs of actual results, so that the accuracy of the system can be consistently evaluated.

The following example illustrates the basics of a KISS:

A company engaged in manufacturing chemical cleaners for industrial sale has developed the following 8-piece KISS, based on regression analysis, management input and graphic analysis:

Item 1: Salesmen Customer Calls (Week's) as an indicator of sales.

Item 2: Average Age of Accounts Receivables as an indicator of cash flow and, with Item 8, profits.

Item 3: Back orders as an indication of sales and operating efficiency.

Item 4: Water consumption (Week's) as an indication of inventory levels and production, since almost all inventory items are made with water, which is metered.

Item 5: Dow Jones Spot Commodity Index, which is used as an indicator of price and cost pressures, particularly for raw materials.

Item 6: Gross Payroll (Latest Week) as an indicator of expenses and profits.

Item 7: Purchase Order Values written (Week's) as a measure of expenses, inventory levels and profitability, especially cash flow profits.

Item 8: Cash on Hand as a measure of profitability, as the business maintains a fairly stable amount of fixed assets, so that cash, assuming fairly stable receivables age (Item 2), is a good indicator of profitability.

The following report is issued on a weekly basis:

COMPANY
KISS REPORT

Date Issued: Oct. 7, 19XX   For Week Ending: Sept. 30, 19XX

Item No.	Item	Item Date	Amount This Week	INDEX			
				Week	Wk. Ago	Mo. Ago	Yr. Ago
1	Salesmen Calls	9/23-9/30	219	109	112	111	110
2	Avg. Age Receiv.	At 9/30	43 days	96	96	98	100
3	Back Orders	At 9/30	131 Orders	134	130	123	118
4	Water Consumption	9/23-9/30	18,433 gal.	162	160	144	132
5	DJ Spot Commod.	At 9/30	365.91	145	148	148	178
6	Gross Payroll	9/23-9/30	$6,743.13	166	166	164	158
7	P. O. $ Value	9/23-9/30	$ 68,944	187	143	161	164
8	Cash on Hand	At 9/30	$132,334	132	152	134	129
	Composite Avg.			141	138	135	136

Weekly Notes: Salesman Smith on vacation beginning 9/28. Most back orders are one item, Product V, awaiting delivery of Raw Material Q. Carload order placed last week for Materials. Drop in cash reflects month-end expenses, primarily rent and lease payments.

Report Preparer

A few comments are in order here on some of the finer points that may be apparent from the example:

An item like Accounts Receivable Average Age is on an inverse index; i.e., as the age increases, the index drops, as an increase in age is an unfavorable development. It is used instead of just gross receivables, as an increase in gross receivables would be a favorable development if due to sales growth, but unfavorable if due to a slowdown in collections.

Although the Dow Jones Spot Commodity Index is already in index form, it is re-computed to put it on a basis comparable in time for the company. The base period of the first report issued under KISS is given a value of 100 for all items. In the event that the index number gets too large, the easy thing to do is divide by a common denominator to bring the indices back into reasonable values.

A comments section is certainly appropriate if meaningful information can be quickly conveyed. For the most part, however, the numbers should speak for themselves.

In this particular example, it appears that the company is experiencing a moderate uptrend, on the whole, comparable to previous periods. The one problem that appears to require some thought is the receivables age, as the decline in the index indicates the age is stretching out.

OTHER FORECAST METHODS

In addition to mathematical and statistical techniques, there are people. An interesting, but too infrequently used approach, is the management or employee survey as a regular and ongoing forecast tool. While this may seem to some to be a subject more in line with industrial psychology than finance, the finance man can find real value in this technique. The perception and/or the fact of success, opportunity or problem in one area can have major impact on surrounding areas or the company as a whole. Of course, such a survey may have other purposes, such as measuring employee morale, but *that* is beyond the finance function.

Whether a sampling or a universal poll is superior will vary by company. The appeal of the sample is speed and cost saving. For companies testing the polling technique, it would be wise to analyze the poll's projections against future results, and against mathematical indicators. Consultants might also be retained in this area, to help determine the best format for the poll.

If sampling is to be used, care must be taken to be sure that the sample is properly chosen. In this case, that does not necessarily mean a representative sample in relation to the entire company, because only a select employee group (e.g., supervisor or above) or a select area (e.g., headquarters staff only) may be found to be the most accurate in its aggregate opinion.

The good financial pollster will be alert for these problems:

1. Responses based on what the respondent believes management or the poll taker wants to hear, as opposed to what the respondent really thinks. While anonymity will reduce this danger, it also may weaken the value of the poll, because it will be difficult to trace where opportunities or problems are perceived. The best defense is clear communication of intent coupled with a healthy management outlook. If that is not possible, then the poll is probably not a useful idea.

2. Misunderstanding of terms. For example, if asked, "Do you think the company will have a good year next year?" some managers may think a profitable year is good while others consider a year good only if earnings per share increase by at least 10%.

Again, the key is communication. Respondents may require some education in the ground rules of the poll. Care in the development of questions is also of equal importance. One way to determine the differences in perspective is to ask for an appraisal of a past or present situation, on which facts are generally known. Another more effective step is to avoid the use of questions that elicit subjective answers. The best way to ask the example question would be: "Do you think the company will increase its earnings per share next year by at least 10%?"

The frequency of such a poll should not be greater than monthly. Whatever the frequency, remember this is but one forecasting option, which should be viewed in the context of the entire forecasting/information network.

INTERNAL AUDIT AS A BALANCE WHEEL

In using the information network, periodic independent appraisal of its effectiveness is a tonic for insuring its integrity and vitality. The internal audit units of most companies are used almost exclusively for operational, internal control and financial auditing. The additional purpose they can serve in the use of the information network is as "decisional auditors."

This certainly does not mean evaluative review of management decisions or second-guessing; nor does it mean spying and fault-finding. It is not an examination of the "what" of decisions. Decisional auditing explores the "how" of decision-making with emphasis on information flow and utility. It scrutinizes what information is relied upon, how timely that information is, how accurate it is, how it is manipulated and how it influences the decision. An extremely difficult part of this process is determining what information is missing, why it is missing, how crucial it is and, most importantly, how it can be developed in a suitable fashion for future similar needs.

Although some internal auditors may feel uncomfortable with such a role, the financially trained auditor is an ideal candidate for this "balance wheel" function. His understanding of financial dynamics provides a valuable backdrop directing analysis at the bottom line thrust of decisions. Internal control audit procedures, including flow charts and responsibility write-ups are easily adapted to decisional auditing. No other unit will have the mandate or experience to cut horizontally across the entire company to trace information flow, information demand and information use.

In choosing which decisions or decision processes to audit, the audit unit should be careful to evaluate apparently good ones as well as apparently deficient ones. Each has its own lessons.

The basic steps of decisional auditing are:

1. Determine the players and their roles. Find out not only who is involved in the decision and information flow, but how they are involved in terms of:

   A. Responsibility for making the decision

   B. Responsibility for intentionally influencing the decision (e.g., as a staff man)

   C. Opportunity for influence (i.e., by providing or omitting information)

   D. Freedom from conflict of interest (i.e., how, if at all, will any outcome affect the role-player's status, budget, income, etc.)

2. Determine, preferably by flow chart, how information is requested and channeled. Evaluate efficiency of this flow.

3. Evaluate the quality of information in terms of:

   A. Is the information accurate? Is it devoid of errors, misrepresentations and biases? Does it state truth?

B. Is the information timely? Do you have the information soon enough? Is it received on schedule?

C. Is the information complete? Do you receive all the information you need? And not so much as to bog you down in useless detail?

D. Is the information consistent? Does it lend itself to comparison with previous periods and other like data? Can you compare apples to apples?

E. Does the information lead? Does it have a purpose? Is it devoid of useless trivia? Can you seize it and know whom to contact and what to do?

F. Is it readily susceptible to analysis? Is it orderly? Is it presented in both form and substance in as simple a manner as possible without dilution of meaning or oversimplification?

4. Determine if the information is properly used.

A. Does newer (or older) information receive disproportionate attention?

B. Does information from one source receive disproportionate attention?

C. Is information realistically accepted and applied?

This is no easy task, but the rewards can be substantial. The ability to perform decisional audits will vary to some extent with the authority granted to the audit team. There has been much discussion in recent years of the proper organizational role and positioning of the audit staff. It is generally conceded that the higher the source of audit's authority, the more effective the audit unit can be in proceeding with assigned tasks, whatever they may be. It is in keeping with the expanding role of the internal audit function to encompass this strategic analytical responsibility.

PROBLEM AND SUCCESS PINPOINTING

Too many outfits concentrate simply and solely on what's gone wrong. Many a Management-by-Objective program has been inadvertently converted into a Management-by-Exception program when too much attention has been devoted to seeking failures. While failure has its lessons, so too does success. The trick is to deduce the elements of successful operations and duplicate them.

The nuts and bolts decisional analysis of what makes this program or that system work will vary by company and industry. The merit of these analyses will be very much a function of what expertise is brought to bear on the problem by decision-makers and analysts. This cannot be completely controlled.

What is more subject to control, however, is where they devote their attention, which should be to the activities whose problems and successes offer the greatest potential for affecting the fortunes of the company. Having developed an efficient and effective information network, as free as possible from distortion, it is time now to put that network into operation tracking and deciphering problems, opportunities and successes.

The essence of this analysis is variance, i.e., pinpointing those programs, operations and activities whose measurable characteristics depart from the norm. In most cases, variances are thought of in relation to budgets, which are one normative value. However, the pinpointing under consideration here is broader in scope, examining performance in several different contexts:

1. Intraunit Norms: Analysis of the unit's own standards.

   A. Past History—Compared to present operations.

   B. Budgets—Compared to present actual operations.

2. Intracorporate Norms: Analysis of the unit against other company segments.

   A. Unit-to-unit comparisons.

   B. Comparison to corporate averages.

3. Extracorporate Norms: Analysis of the unit against external standards, such as industry standards.

For each unit, an analytical profile is developed, rating performance in terms of both input and output. In most cases, absolute values alone are not as useful as when related to each other showing cause and effect. To put this in an elementary example, comparing dollar profits in Company A against average industry profits is a futile exercise without reference to Company A's size, sales and resources against like industry averages.

The elements of the profile will vary with the type of unit under consideration. Carried to extremes, the unit could be an individual, whose output would be expressed as a function of several parameters, (e.g., salary, experience, etc.), and compared against other individuals. However, that's really a personnel function. Accordingly, the place to start is with the department, moving up through division, subsidiary and group (as applicable) to entire corporation.

There are three basic output standards, which can each be subdivided in a number of ways, again subject to company and industry circumstances. The three output standards and some sample subdivisions are:

Profits	Sales	Production
Gross Profits	Total Sales	Unit Production
Pretax Profit	Net Sales	Salable units produced
Net Profit	Total Accounts	Inventory Value Produced
Earnings per share	Total Transactions	Sales Value produced
Cash Flow Profits	Unit Sales	

Production can of course be in terms of service performed, such as area cleaned for a janitor, pages typed, calls taken by a receptionist, etc.

There are also three basic input standards, which can also be refined in a variety of ways. For example:

Assets	Expenses	Personnel
Total Assets	Total Expenses	Total Personnel
Tangible Assets	Direct Expenses	Manhours
Productive Assets	Indirect Expenses	Overtime hours
Type of Asset	Type of expense	Type of personnel
(e.g., engineers)	(e.g., machinery)	(e.g., advertising)

The norms used in the profile are ratios of these input and output standards. A sample form for this analysis is shown below:

XYZ COMPANY
DIVISIONAL PROFILE

Division: CUTLERY.   Period: Year 19XX

Row Item	Amounts	Col. 1 Pretax Profit	Col. 2 Total Sales	Col. 3 Total Accounts	Col. 4 Production Total $	Col. 5 Units Produced	Col. 6 Units Net Produced
		1,000,000	20,000,000	20,000	18,000,000	185,000	180,000
1 Total Assets	25,000,000	25.00	1.25	1,250	1.39	135.14	138.89
2 Tang. Assets	20,000,000	20.00	1.00	1,000	1.11	108.11	111.11
3 Total Expense	19,000,000	19.00	0.95	950	1.06	102.70	105.56
4 Direct Exp.	14,000,000	14.00	0.70	700	0.78	75.68	77.78
5 Indir. Exp.	5,000,000	5.00	0.25	250	0.28	27.03	27.78
6 Payroll Exp.	7,000,000	7.00	0.35	350	0.39	37.84	38.89
7 Supplies Exp.	3,000,000	3.00	0.15	150	0.17	16.22	16.67
8 Total Pers.*	500	2,000	40,000	40	36,000	370	360
9 Total Manhours*	21,000	47.62	952.38	0.95	857.14	8.81	8.57
10 Produc. Hours*	16,000	62.50	1250.00	1.25	1,125.00	11.56	11.25

Rows 1-7 are calculated Row divided by Column. For example, Item 1,1 is interpreted as $25.00 of total assets were available to produce $1.00 of profit. Rows 8-10 (marked with an *) are calculated reciprocally, Column divided by Row. For example, Item 8,1 shows profits of $2,000 per employee.

Having developed a profile, the contents should be individually compared in each of the contexts considered worthwhile. Continuing with the example:

XYZ COMPANY
CUTLERY DIVISION
Profile Element: ASSETS PER $1.00 PROFIT
Year 19×9 = $25.00

Past History:

	19×4	19×5	19×6	19×7	19×8	Average	19×9
	24.80	23.70	23.50	24.40	25.20	24.32	25.00

% change versus average: 2.80% Increase

% change against prior Year: 0.79% Decrease

Budget:

Budget: $24.65   Variance: 0.35 Over   % Variance: 1.42% Over

Divisional Comparisons for 19×9:

Divisions:	Flatware	Cookware	Tableware	Pottery	Utensils	Rest of Company Average	Cutlery
19×9:	21.30	18.65	24.90	19.35	26.40	22.12	25.00
Cutlery %:	117.4	134.0	100.4	129.2	94.7	113.0	

Industry Average:

Industry Average: 22.40   Variance: 2.60 Over   % Variance: 11.61 Over

---

Analyzing this profile element comparison, it appears that by most measures the Cutlery Division is substandard. It is the fifth poorest performance of the last six years, over budget, worse than current corporate and industry averages and fifth out of six divisions.

Each profile element is compared in turn. Management follow-up is aimed at upgrading those elements that are deficient in each unit and finding out what steps the successful divisions took where their performance is superior, to pass along to the deficient areas.

Looking a little more closely at the example to so follow-up, several questions could be pursued on this issue, to find out the "why" behind these apparently unfavorable statistics:

Is asset utilization proper?

Does the division have excess assets that should be disposed of?

Are assets kept in good operating condition?

How does the age of these assets compare with other divisions?

With past Years?

With Averages?

Are there extenuating circumstances that affected performance?

Are the responsible personnel adequately trained and capable?

There are, of course, many more questions that can be asked, and each question may lead to others. In any event, all the questions will fit into one of five categories:

1. *Conceptual*: Does the unit's mission fit with the general business plan?
2. *Operational*: Is the system logical, streamlined and efficient?
3. *Personnel*: Are the responsible people adequate for the task?
4. *Resources*: Have sufficient and appropriate resources been provided?
5. *Controllability*: Is the situation within the company's control? (e.g., affected primarily by economic conditions?) If not, how can control be gained?

These categories are useful and appropriate as a frame of reference for determining where actions should be directed. As questions are asked, their thrust should be categorized so that a pattern can be found, and the source of the problem or success can be traced.

The example given here is convenient, as sales, profits and production can all be allocated to a division of this kind. Unfortunately, meaningful allocation of all three standards, or even one output standard, cannot always be accomplished. For example, the work of the Legal Department is difficult to quantify in a sensible way. Cases won or suits instituted are hardly a measure of legal acumen or performance. In fact, the ideal legal unit may well be the one that prevents the company from ever needing to go to court as either defendant or plaintiff.

In such cases, two alternatives are available:

1. Use absolutes. Measure strictly in terms of input.
2. Use the output standards of the smallest unit in which the subject unit is contained. For example, if the Legal Department is part of a division, to which a specific amount of profit, sales and/or production can be allocated, then use divisional output standards with departmental input standards to develop the norm ratios.

The illustrative example given here is abbreviated. The actual comparisons that might be usefully developed in the real world will probably be substantially more detailed. With data processing equipment, they can usually be developed in fine detail with relative ease.

Once problems are pinpointed, the concentration for solution should be prioritized considering three principal factors:

1. Materiality in terms of:
   A. Unit size
   B. Net Cost
   C. Potential Gain

2. Anticipated ease of solution in terms of:
   A. Time to produce solution
   B. Resources to produce solution

3. Pressing need

Beware the last of these, lest the company find itself operating with crisis management, fragmenting its efforts every time a new report comes out. The specifics of arriving at these priorities will again be a function of management judgment.

The frequency of profiling may well be more frequent than annually. Some profiling should be strictly for monitoring purposes, because priorities can change with each report and could also produce fragmentation in correction and improvement efforts.

With the information network and profiling it yields, it is now possible to proceed from the strategic framework to the individual tactical problem solving, focusing on the components of company activity.

Chapter 2

18 Secrets of Successful Cash Management

Cash is the quintessential current asset. The goal of cash management is threefold:

1. Funnel cash into the profitable operation of the business; i.e., provide sufficient working capital.
2. Collect and conserve cash for future operational use; i.e., maintain sufficient reserves that will permit the company to seize opportunity and cushion the company against hard times.
3. Invest idle cash to make it productive; i.e., make the function of cash management a profit center in and of itself.

In examining these three goals, cash management must be correlated to overall corporate strategy. The various demands for funds enumerated in the previous chapter set the fundamental strategy of cash management. The sub-strategies and tactics examined here are designed to service the basic missions of cash flow, allowing an organization to do more within the constraint of its resources.

FOUNDATION FOR CASH ACCOUNTS POLICY

Working from the postulate that cash management is a support function, the matrix of accounts chosen should be that which best serves the organization. It should:

A. Maximize positive cash flow,
B. Offer sufficient accessability,
C. Provide security, and
D. Limit the cost of accomplishing these goals.

The components of the matrix are:

1. *Central Accounts*: These are the general purpose bank accounts which serve as the fulcrum of cash management.

2. *Collecting Accounts*: These accounts are strategically located to minimize collection time.

3. *Disbursement Accounts*: These accounts are designed to maximize cash retention time and to segregate funds to provide control and security.

4. *Reserve Accounts*: Used for funds storage and special purposes.

The character of the matrix (i.e., the number and complexity of accounts) will vary with:

1. Lines of business, both as to number and nature
2. Cash flow volume
3. Geographic trading area of the business
4. Organizational format
5. Corporate size
6. Regulatory requirements
7. Special needs

As each of the account types is explored, the impact of these parameters will be discussed.

GENERAL PURPOSE/CENTRAL ACCOUNTS

In the smaller operation, there may be but one account, which is used for all purposes. If the volume of activity is not large enough to support the cost of additional accounts, then a single account is sufficient. The kinds of costs that are generated by multiple accounts include reconciliation, check printing, bank charges and administrative time. Therefore, the fewer the accounts, the lower the costs.

Each unit that is entitled to any degree of cash autonomy needs a central account for overall control. Cash maintained in non-central accounts (i.e., collecting, disbursing and reserve accounts) should be kept to a minimum. The supreme account is the headquarters central account, through which final control is exercised over all subsidiary central accounts. Conceptually, the layout of accounts might appear like this:

CORPORATE ACCOUNTS LAYOUT

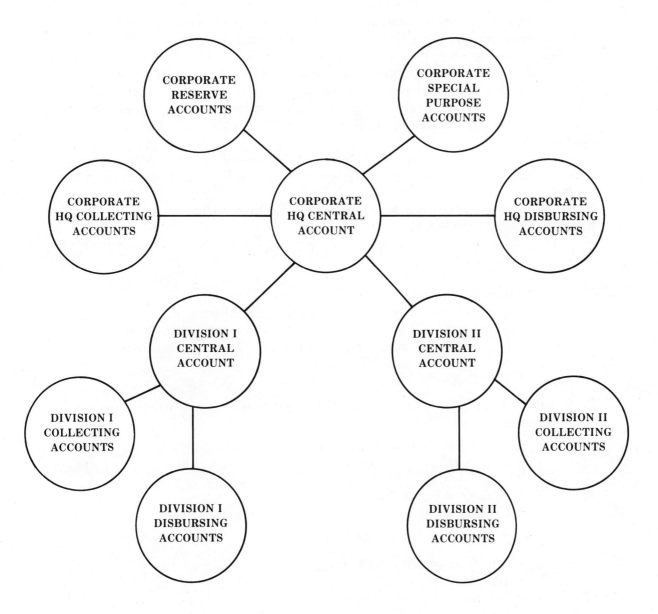

COLLECTING ACCOUNTS

Collecting accounts are located primarily on the basis of minimizing collection time, i.e. the time in which a check is cleared and converted into spendable cash. The frequent method for accomplishing the goal is the well-known lock-box setup. A lock-box arrangement is one whereby a bank is empowered to receive and process payments directly into the payee's account. The bank saves the payee the time involved in processing mail and depositing funds. An even greater savings is available if the lock-box bank is located near the customer, especially if the payor's bank and the lock-box payee are in the same Federal Reserve District.

Once the funds are cleared, they are wired to the central account, which is reported daily by that central account bank. The amounts wired will equal all the funds in the collecting account.

There is a fee for lock-box services charged by the bank, so that the volume collected must justify use of the lock-box:

$$F + W < (t) \, (i) \, (V)$$

where: F = Lock-Box Fees per month
      W = Wire charges per month
      t   = Time saved in days on the average transaction
      i   = interest rate per day earned on available funds (which may be considered to be interest saved on funds not borrowed because of the availability of lock-box moneys)
      V = Dollar volume collected per month

If the lock-box is not purely priced at a flat rate, but includes a transaction charge, the formula is modified to:

$$F + W + (T) \, (C) < (t) \, (i) \, (V)$$

with the additional variables:

    T = Number of transactions
    C = Charge per transaction

For example:

    F   = \$50.00 per month flat rate charge
    C   = 10¢ per transaction
    T   = 300 transactions per month
    W   = \$105 per month (\$5.00 per wire, 21 days per month.)
    t   = Time saving of three days on average
    i   = 12% per annum
    V   = \$300,000 per month collected through the account

Therefore:

$$\$50 + \$105 + (10\text{¢}) \, (300) < (3) \, (.12/365) \, (\$300,000)$$
$$\$185 < \$295.89$$

Savings per month:

$$\$295.89 - \$185.00 = \$110.89$$

Savings per year:

$$\$110.89 \times 12 = \$1330.68$$

Of course, the analysis is conducted for each lock-box account. If an account turns out to be unjustified, its activity should be routed to the geographically closest account in order to get the next best time savings.

A second part of lock-box processing is transfer control. In the preceding example, it was assumed that one transfer was made on every business day. In fact, less frequent transfers might be more economical. To be sure, a break-even level of deposits to be accumulated for transfer can be derived using another formula:

$$BE = \frac{(c)\,(f)\,(d)}{(r)\,(e)}$$

where:

- c = Cost per transfer (the wire charge)
- f = Marginal number of transfers per year
- d = Number of banking days per year
- r = Net annual Rate of Return on funds in the central account (For convenience, the same as i in the preceding example.)
- e = Incremental improvement in available balances resulting from each transfer.

Focus for a moment on the last variable "e." Assume that a lock-box bank is transferring funds twice a week, Monday and Thursday. Hence, funds deposited Monday are available the same day, Tuesday's funds are not available until Thursday, the next transfer day, and so on:

	Mon.	Tue.	Wed.	Thu.	Fri.	Sat.	Sun.
Transfer Day	x			x			
Days Til Transfer	0	2	1	0	3	2	1

Summing the days of idleness and dividing by days per week yields:

$$\frac{0 + 2 + 1 + 0 + 3 + 2 + 1}{7} = 9/7$$

Now consider three transfers per week on Monday, Wednesday and Friday:

	Mon.	Tue.	Wed.	Thu.	Fri.	Sat.	Sun.
Transfer	x		x		x		
Days Til Transfer	0	1	0	1	0	2	1

Summing:

$$\frac{0 + 1 + 0 + 1 + 0 + 2 + 1}{7} = 5/7$$

The improvement equal to "e" is:

$$9/7 - 5/7 = 4/7$$

Returning to the formula:

c = $5.00 wire charge
f = 52 (1 additional transfer per week, 52 weeks per year)
d = 260 days
r = 12% per year
e = 4/7

$$\frac{(c)\,(f)\,(d)}{(r)\,(e)} = \frac{(5.00)\,(52)\,(260)}{(.12)(4/7)} = \$985{,}833.33 \text{ additional deposits per year}$$

$985,833.33/52 = $18,958.33 additional transfers per week
$18,958.33/3 = $6,319.44 of additional deposits per transfer

Theoretically, one would prefer to check these calculations for each deposit. In fact, that would slow down the transfer process, negating the entire concept. Practically, a calculation is in order when interest rates materially change monthly.

While the marginal sum realized in transfer cost savings may be relatively small, the total savings per year over a number of remote accounts may add up to a healthy savings.

Point to Remember: *Make sure the system is flexible, so that a sudden need for all cash available can be quickly filled, at least in part, by funds awaiting transfer.*

If a particular lock-box turns out to be unjustified, there are some other alternatives. The first is the combining of several accounts into one. The savings on flat fees and wire charges may offset the costs of somewhat slower collection and still be better than ordinary processing.

For example, take these two lock-box accounts:

Account	#1	#2
Fixed Charge (f)	$50	$45
Transactions (T)	300	150
Trans. Charge (c)	10¢	9¢
Wire Charge (W)	$105	$84
Time Saving (t)	3 days	3 days
Interest (i)	12%	12%
Volume (V)	$180,000	$90,000

Formula   (t) (i /365) (V   )−(f) −(c) (T) −(W) =
Saving (Loss) #1 (3) (.12/365) ($180,000)− (50) −(10¢) (300) −(105) = (7.47)
Saving (Loss) #2 (3) (.12/365) ($90,000) − (45) − (9¢) (150) − (84) = (53.73)

Combining all the activity in either account will yield:

Account	#1	#2
(f)	$50	$45
(T)	450	450
(c)	10¢	9¢
(W)	$105	$84
(t)	2.6	2.5
(i)	12%	12%
(V)	$270,000	$270,000

Formula   (t) (i /365) (V   ) − (f) − (T) (c)−(W) =
Saving (Loss) #1 (3.0) (.12/365) ($270,000) − (50) − (450) (10¢)−(105) = 66.30
Saving (Loss) #2 (3.0) (.12/365) ($270,000) − (45) − (450) (9¢) − (84) = 96.80

Hence, consolidating the two accounts into #2 will be the most cost-effective. This particular example also demonstrates that the account with the larger volume or the larger time saving will not always be the best for use in consolidation.

As a rule of thumb when dealing with consolidation, it's usually a good idea to try to locate at least one collection account in each Fed District, and, if possible, in the same city as the Federal Reserve Bank or a Federal Reserve Branch for that District, as that will tend to reduce clearing time. These are the Districts and cities:

Dist.	HQ City	Branch Cities	Area Covered
1	Boston	None	New England except Western Conn.
2	New York	Buffalo	N.Y., Western Conn., No. N.J.
3	Phila.	None	East Pa., So. N.J., Del.
4	Clevel.	Cinn., Pitts.	West Pa., Ohio, East Ky.
5	Richmond	Balt., Charlotte	Md., Va., D.C., W.Va., N.C., S.C.
6	Atlanta	Birmingham, Jacksonville, Nashville, New Orleans,	East Tenn., Ga., Fla., Ala., So. Miss., So. La.
7	Chicago	Detroit	So. Mich., No. Ind., No. Ill., Iowa, So. Wisc.
8	St. Louis	Little Rock, Louisville, Memphis	West Ky., West Tenn., So. Ill., So. Ind., Ark., No. Miss., Most of Mo.

9	Minneap.	Helena	Mont., N.D., S.D., Minn., Peninsular Mich., N. Wisc.
10	Kans. Cy., Mo.	Denver, Okla. City, Omaha	Wyo, Neb., Colo., Kans., Okla., No. N.M., far western Mo.
11	Dallas	El Paso, Houston, San Antonio	N. La., Texas, S.E. Okla., So. N.M., S.E. Ariz.
12	San Franc.	Los Angeles, Portland, Salt Lake City Seattle	Pacific States except S.E. Arizona

A second method for upgrading lock-boxes is the establishment of collection accounts at the banks used by the largest customers. By making deposits at the drawee bank, clearing will take place immediately. Even the smallest company can make use of this cash production technique by studying the paying habits of the larger customers and acting accordingly.

DISBURSEMENT ACCOUNTS

The disbursement accounts follow the adverse logic. Stretch out as much as possible the clearing of drafts on the company.

An increasingly common strategy is the employment of disbursement accounts at small banks in Federal Reserve Districts farthest away from where bills are paid to. For example, pay bills to vendors in New England (District 1) from a bank in Hawaii or Alaska (District 12). To make the most of this system, the disbursement account bank must offer zero-balance disbursing, whereby it can draw on the payor's central account when checks are finally presented to the remote bank.

A "Remote Zero-Balance Disbursement System" like this requires tight control. The company has to keep track of checks as presented and ready for presentation, and is essentially required to reconcile all of these accounts each day. The value of such a system can be calculated using the same formula as presented for lock-box analysis.

> **A Related Point:** *When faced, as a collecting party, with faraway disbursement, consider revising your cash terms to allow discounts based on check clearance, not check receipt.*

If zero-balance is not cost-effective or is otherwise impractical, it's still a good idea to obtain daily bank reports on checks presented. Daily control of cash and daily reconciliation permit better cash planning. Many banks offer reconciliation service, which may be less expensive than in-house performance of the task.

PAYROLL DISBURSEMENT

A brief note is in order here about this special area. Payroll deserves separate consideration and separate accounts for these reasons:

1. *Safety*: Payroll checks should include a limitation on their face to minimize loss through alteration (e.g., "Not Valid For Amounts Over $1,000"). Such limitations are often impractical on most other disbursement accounts.

2. *Reconciliation*: The peculiarities of payroll and the uniformity among payroll checks makes reconciliation difficult when mixed with other checks and simplifies reconciliation to payroll journals when segregated.

3. *Data Purity*: Mixing payroll with other checks may distort information derived from accounts. For example, in calculating float (see below), payroll checks may improperly skew the data as most payroll checks will be cashed or deposited in a small part of a Federal Reserve District, that being where the employment center is located.

4. *Audit*: Segregating payroll checks by account saves audit time by reducing sort processes.

It may also make sense to have more than one payroll account, divided along one or more of these lines:

A. Type of payroll (e.g., Hourly, Piecework, Salary, Commission, Union, Non-union, Executive)

B. Frequency of payroll (e.g., Weekly, Monthly)

C. Payroll location (e.g., by plant, division or other employee unit)

D. Taxing jurisdiction (e.g., by state when different withholding rates apply or different reporting conventions are followed. Withheld taxes are readily segregated for payment)

E. Audit Subjection (e.g., government contract payroll where audit rights attach vs. payroll where no such rights exist)

> **Try This:** *Companies with thin cash flow might also use their payroll accounts as escrow accounts for withholding, by transferring gross payroll (not net) into the account plus employer contributions for social security. This will prevent the company from running afoul of withholding deposit requirements, which carry personal liability.*

THE MAGIC OF FLOAT

Maximizing float by use of remote disbursement accounts and other techniques is but half the battle. The cash manager needs to know what amounts of cash float produces in order to maximize its value. Additionally, the manager also needs to know what it costs to obtain that float to achieve optimum profitability on the process.

One way to keep abreast of float is by analyzing cancelled checks, using a matrix setup that looks like this (example assumes activity in only 4 Fed Districts):

```
                              RECEIVING FED DISTRICTS

                  ──────────────────────────────────────────────────────
                  Fed   Dist. 1   Fed   Dist. 2   Fed   Dist. 3   Fed   Dist. 4
                  ──────────────────────────────────────────────────────
                  DD   CD   F    DD   CD   F    DD   CD   F    DD   CD   F

   S  F  D   Fed
   E  E  I   Dist.
   N  D  S    1
   D     T
   I     R   Fed
   N     I   Dist.
   G     C    2
         T
                  DD = Deposit Date ... CD = Clearing Date ... F = Float
```

Into each matrix square (including each District clearing within itself) a sampling (or entire run, if computerization permits) of checks are entered and an average float calculated. Sample size should ideally be based on statistical sampling techniques, with the universe in each case defined as the total number of checks cleared between each discreet pair of Fed Districts over the sampling period. Sampling is best done not more frequently than monthly for "heavy traffic" pairs and not less frequently than annually for all pairs where transactions occur with some regularity.

> **Beware This Pitfall:** *Each pair (e.g., Dist. 1 to Dist. 2 and Dist. 1 to Dist. 3 are two pairs) requires its own sample, with each viewed as a separate universe. Unless so programmed, the peculiarities of statistical sampling are likely to yield insufficient data and hence imperfect results for some pairs.*

A refinement of float calculation uses predetermined samples, composed of color-coded checks which are sent at regular intervals. These intervals are calculated on the statistical sampling basis, using a scale of expected transaction volume. When statements are returned, the color-coded checks are recorded and analyzed for float as a part of the reconciliation routine.

Maintain a moving average record of float as well as a record for the latest transaction data. The average will permit discovery of seasonal trends and variations and offers the possibility of correlation with economic data. Also look for variations by deposit dates and days of the week, to take advantage of float during slower days.

To crystallize the basic technique, we'll use this example:

A company has two disbursement accounts, one in Fed District 1 ("Fx" will henceforth be used for Fed District x) and one in F2. Payments are regularly made into F1, F2 and F3. Float is calculated from a sampling of checks as shown in the following chart. (The following chart is abbreviated because of space limitations; a much larger sample size would usually be used to provide statistical reliability for the numbers of checks that would ordinarily be involved in a standard activity account.)

FLOAT CALCULATION DATA CHART
(Abbreviated)

Fed Dist Paid:	F1			F2			F3		
Fed. Dist. Paying:	Dep. Date	Clr. Date	FLOAT	Dep. Date	Clr. Date	FLOAT	Dep. Date	Clr. Date	FLOAT
	1/3	1/5	2	1/3	1/6	3	1/3	1/6	3
	1/4	1/7	3	1/4	1/7	3	1/4	1/7	3
	1/5	1/7	2	1/5	1/10	5	1/5	1/7	2
	1/6	1/10	4	1/6	1/10	4	1/6	1/10	4
F1	1/7	1/10	3	1/7	1/11	4	1/7	1/10	3
	1/10	1/12	2	1/10	1/14	4	1/10	1/13	3
	1/11	1/14	3	1/2	1/14	3	1/12	1/14	3
	1/12	1/14	2	1/12	1/14	2	1/12	1/14	2
	TOTAL		21	TOTAL		28	TOTAL		23
	# Trans.		8	# Trans.		8	# Trans.		8
	AVERAGE		2.63	AVERAGE		3.50	AVERAGE		2.88
	1/3	1/6	3	1/3	1/5	2	1/3	1/7	4
	1/4	1/7	3	1/4	1/6	2	1/4	1/7	3
	1/5	1/10	5	1/5	1/7	2	1/5	1/10	5
	1/6	1/10	4	1/6	1/10	4	1/6	1/10	4
F2	1/7	1/10	3	1/7	1/10	3	1/6	1/10	4
	1/10	1/12	2	1/10	1/13	3	1/7	1/11	4
	1/11	1/14	3	1/11	1/13	2	1/11	1/14	3
	1/12	1/14	2	1/12	1/14	2	1/12	1/17	5
	TOTAL		25	TOTAL		20	TOTAL		32
	# Trans.		8	# Trans.		8	# Trans.		8
	AVERAGE		3.13	AVERAGE		2.50	AVERAGE		4.00

Accordingly, best payment float is:

To Pay	F1	F2	F3
Use	F2	F1	F2

Where possible, all payments should be made using that routing, until and unless a subsequent study indicates otherwise.

By utilizing that routing, these results are attained:

TO:	F1	F2	F3	TOTAL
Per Month	$300,000	$600,000	$150,000	$1,050,000
Per Day	$ 10,000	$ 20,000	$ 5,000	$ 35,000
Float Time	3.13 Days	3.50 Days	4.00 Days	
Float Amount	$ 31,300	$ 70,000	$ 20,000	$ 121,300

(N.B. Some companies round float time down to whole days, both for the sake of conservatism and because they argue that partial days are not usable for calculating interest. However, the example shows the fractional days for calculation purposes, on the theory that *on average* this is the float that will be provided.)

Knowing that float provides approximately an additional $121,300 may lead management to:

1. Forego borrowing that additional amount; or
2. Pay down lines of credit by that amount; or
3. Invest that additional amount in marketable securities; or
4. Expand expenditures by that additional amount (including especially expenditures for capital goods); or
5. Employ any combination of the preceding alternatives that adds up to total usage of $121,300 of cash.

One refinement is that some companies calculate the exact amount of checks outstanding in each float category to develop a more precise measure of daily float, instead of using average float as our example. This refinement is recommended if sufficient funds are involved and if the time is available to make the calculations. Without data processing equipment, the cost of those calculations may well be prohibitive.

SHORT-TERM INVESTMENTS

Excess cash balances are, of course, available for money market investments. The number of alternative investments in this field continue to grow as the financial markets grow increasingly sophisticated. Our purpose here is not to examine specific alternatives, as such a perspective would be subject to constantly varying market conditions. Rather, we will briefly develop a framework for analysis of investment choices.

The overall strategy, foundation for the analytical framework, fulfills these principals:

1. *Diversified Portfolio*: Diversification minimizes risk and is accomplished by mixing security types as well as security issuers.

2. *Staggered Maturities*: Risk is also diminished when the cash will again become available at a variety of times rather than all at once. In general, maturities should be matched to cash flow budgets, with a contingency pool.

3. *Consistent Reevaluation*: While standardization is commendable for cost minimization, old sources and types of securities need to be regularly reviewed against goals and parameters to be sure that changing conditions do not compromise their desirability. At the same time, comparisons to new sources and types of investment offer a natural departure point for reevaluation.

4. *Demand Relationship*: Control cash investment to service operating, capital and contingency requirements as indicated by cash flow forecasts.

With that foundation in place, the particulars of tactical evaluation appear in order of importance:

1. *Safety of Principal* – The preservation of this temporary capital surplus is the number one objective of short-term investments. While conversion from cash obviously assumes some risk to obtain some return, strict limitation of that risk must be observed.

2. *Liquidity* – The wherewithal to convert the investment back into cash as quickly as possible without penalty is axiomatic for fulfilling the concept of short-term investment. There are three avenues for achieving liquidity, all of which are worth scrutinizing for investment, although the sufficiency of only one may not preclude investment acceptability:

A. Marketability is the ability to trade the investment for cash and is the usual standard of liquidity.

B. Fractionability is the ability to cut a single investment into a number of smaller pieces for different uses, so that only a part of the original (and profitable) investment can be liquidated if circumstances dictate. Fractionability becomes especially important in the situation where a large initial commitment is needed to obtain a higher return, but the ability to sustain that level of investment is questionable.

C. Collateralization is the ability to use the investment as security for a loan. Although borrowing involves additional costs, it is sometimes preferable to liquidation. For example, assume a contingency need for $10,000 in cash and a $15,000 short-term investment having 30 days left to run and yielding 9% annually. Liquidation of the investment will cost $30.00. The smaller $5,000 excess can be reinvested at only 8%. If liquidation is pursued, the 30-day cost will be:

$$\$30.00 + \frac{(9\% - 8\%)(\$5,000)}{12} = \$34.17$$

Borrowing $10,000 at 10½% interest for 30 days with the $15,000 investment as security produces costs of only:

$$\frac{(10\frac{1}{2}\% - 9\%)(\$10,000)}{12} = \$12.50$$

Hence, borrowing saves $34.17 − $12.50 = $21.67. When the investment matures, $10,000 of the proceeds are "invested" by paying off the loan producing an effective yield of 10½% at that point. The other $5,000 is simultaneously reinvested. This kind of short-term borrowing arrangement has these other flexible advantages:

If an additional need for cash arises during the 30-day period, additional borrowing can be accomplished by a larger takedown against the collateral, thereby avoiding whipsawing transaction costs. Conversely, if cash inflows rise unexpectedly, the loan might be paid off more quickly than expected (though not always, depending on the loan agreement, so the terms of the loan are another point to check) thereby preserving the original high yield. Look for investments that offer a higher collateral value. Your banker may be of some assistance in detailing the collateral value of various investments, although he may have his own axe to grind in steering you into bank investments.

3. *Maturity* — whereas liquidity is generally of concern as it relates to contingency demand, maturity relates to operational and capital demands. Maturities are arranged to match cash flow forecasts by screening new investments for maturities that will fill cash flow gaps. As more investments are made and cash availability is assured at more and more of the desired times, subsequent investments face tighter and tighter maturity screening.

4. *Yield* — While yield is the moving force behind the whole investment effort, it is not the primary objective. The definition of "Best Yield" is the highest yield that maintains safety of principal, while offering adequate liquidity and favorable maturity.

5. *Administrative Costs* — These costs are really a factor of yield, as they represent a decrement to the net. Administrative costs are necessarily included in yield calculations not only to maturity, but also to liquidation, as the act of liquidation before maturity is likely to carry its own administrative burden. The greater the chance of bail-out, the greater the weight to be given to net yield prior to maturity.

6. *Reporting* — Each kind of investment carries its own reporting requirements, which, in some cases, may be undesirable. Accordingly, the accounting treatment of potential investments is worth a look.

7. *Ancillary Uses* — Sometimes, short-term investments can be used as more than yield-producing parking places for cash. For example, by including foreign investments in the portfolio, perhaps proportionately with foreign activity, one may achieve not only additional portfolio diversity, but a foreign exchange hedge. Intercompany investments among affiliates may be used to shift income and expenses for tax and/or reporting purposes, while smoothing cash flows. The creative use of cash while pursuing investment objectives represents an opportunity for the cash manager to supplement yields, increase corporate profitability and satisfy all forms of cash demand for greater entity efficiency.

FOREIGN EXCHANGE

Turbulence in recent years in foreign exchange markets has prompted foreign exchange management to elevate these operations from sideline to first line defense of overseas earnings. The great swings in currency values, the sudden changes in the regulations governing currency movements and the sheer volume of transactions have created enormous risks and often tempting opportunities.

Bankers consistently maintain that the prudent course for international transactors is to hedge *all* transactions at the very moment a contract is made to ensure that the deal produces the budgeted profit, and that the calculations for that profit should include the costs of administering the foreign exchange operations spawned by the transaction. For the occasional trader, the frequent dealer or the multinational company, this remains sound advice.

The operative theory, as in short-term investment, is that the company is not in the business of foreign exchange trading and speculation. Its line of business dictates its operational profile and foreign exchange activities should supplement those operations by facilitating them and preserving their fiscal integrity.

Nonetheless, the urge to speculate (whether the speculation is termed "aggressive management" or otherwise euphemized) is often powerful, and the possibility that corporate personnel who are frequently "in the market" may develop a "feel" for it may offer a desirable opportunity. If so, three points:

1. To satisfy that urge (assuming a good case is honestly made for it) establish a "side-fund" for the speculative activities. Limit its size so that if all goes wrong, operations are not going to be impaired.

2. Closely control monies so employed, with the ultimate authority vested in someone superior to the foreign exchange traders. Require frequent, scheduled reporting, with full back-up documentation. Audit periodically. If trading does produce profits, pull some out of the side-fund, i.e. don't let it all "ride." But, if the trading produces losses, don't "punish" the traders, not only because of morale ramifications, but because punishment may encourage cover-up with greater incentive to gamble more to make up the losses.

3. Consider placing the handling of the side-fund on an incentive basis. The decision-makers must have something to lose as well as to gain to promote care in handling.

Recognize that foreign exchange risks attach to the values of all assets and liabilities overseas, but especially to:

1. Foreign account balances

2. Payable

3. Receivables

4. Inventories

In other words, the "short stuff" are the most vulnerable to the special risks of foreign exchange.

Alternatives for foreign exchange loss controls include:

1. *Currency Denominated Contracts*. If your home earnings are denominated in dollars (i.e., you're an American company) by getting the contracting parties to agree that the contract will be funded in dollars, all risk is eliminated from your standpoint. If your perspective is Italian, denominate in Lira, and so on. This is also the most difficult deal to make, as the other side is naturally going to be reluctant to accept all the risk.

2. *Currency Denominated Accounts*. Essentially the same as "1" except that the contract in question is the one with the foreign depositary bank. Beware, however, that use of such accounts may ultimately prove unwieldy for overseas operations and may involve extra charges by the bank to compensate for the denominative risk.

3. *Forward Market Operations*. These operations are very much like the purchase of insurance, using a bank as an intermediary. Say you've got a contract to sell merchandise on terms of Net 30 from the U.S. to Great Britain for £1,000, when the rate of exchange is $2.00 to £1.00 *and* you intend to repatriate the moneys as soon as the receivable is collected. You contract with a bank to deliver £1,000 in exchange for $2,000, 30 days hence, for which you pay what amounts to a fee, although your payment might be quoted as a less favorable exchange rate, e.g. $1,985. Even if exchange rates vary in the 30-day period, you deliver the £1,000 and receive the agreed $1,985, eliminating the risk in exchange for the $15 "premium." Were you purchasing foreign goods, you'd be on the other side of the transac-

tion, paying the bank for a contract to receive £1,000 (which you'd pass along to your vendor) for perhaps $2,015, 30 days hence. This is the most common kind of operation.

4. *Foreign Borrowing*. Take another look at our forward market example. Instead of purchasing a contract, *borrow* £1,000 (securing it with the receivable) and convert the funds immediately into $2,000. When the receivable is paid to you, repay the bank loan. You have substituted the interest cost for the forward market fee.

5. *Swaps*. At the point of contract, you agree to have the receivable paid to a British party, who in turn agrees to have an American receivable of like maturity and present equivalent value paid to you. Swaps are generally impractical for those who deal in this market irregularly. They become attractive where parties have pools of foreign exchange receivables that can be readily "packaged" to acceptable size and maturity.

6. *Barter*. By agreeing that payments will be made in goods (or services) of mutually specified quantities and qualities, the foreign exchange risks are avoided. Barter can be carried one step further, if your seller of, say, jute, doesn't want payment in your broadloom carpet, but would accept payment in nylon, you might purchase the nylon with dollars in the U.S. from a domestic manufacturer for shipment overseas to your jute supplier.

> **Point to Remember:** *Document barter transactions with great care, so that a disadvantageous value is not imputed by tax authorities in determining income and deductions.*

7. *International Monetary Market*. The IMM was established to sell fixed-size contracts in foreign currencies, and is, therefore, a sort of uniform forward market operation. The contracts are traded on the IMM, which is a subsidiary of the Chicago Mercantile Exchange, and which quotes daily prices for the futures, just as the Merc does for commodities. If a contract is purchased and the underlying currency strengthens, the value of the contract rises accordingly. That will offset the additional costs of making a payment in the foreign currency. Conversely, if money is due from overseas, shorting the currency contract provides a hedge. Some bankers argue that IMM is strictly a speculator's market and that it makes no sense to purchase standard contracts when custom-made contracts are available from the bank. There is, further, no significant transaction cost advantage with IMM, and there may even be extra expense. Still, it may serve these purposes:

A. Providing a ready-made "pool" investment to cover a variety of transactions.

B. Permitting combination transactions in more than one currency, effectively allowing a trading company to capitalize on internally generated arbitrage risk-matching possibilities.

C. Establishing a basic foreign currency position as an ongoing hedge.

D. For side-fund speculation.

E. Opportunity to buy contracts on margin permits the creation of a foreign currency position without the full investment of funds at the moment of contract.

The foreign exchange market is fraught with business risks. Fluctuations, controls, devaluations, embargoes, politics and international tensions make it an arena that demands specialized assistance. If your company is not large enough to justify its own full-time specialist, you can look for help from bankers, freight-forwarders, customs brokers, consultants, investment and merchant bankers and government agencies.

CASH BUDGETING

The cash management operations we have discussed—lock-boxes, remote disbursement, multiple accounts, foreign exchange, float control, marketable investments—largely support the last two goals of the three with which we opened the chapter. The fundamental responsibility of the cash manager is to funnel cash into the profitable operation of the business; i.e., provide working capital sufficiency.

The principal tool for achieving that goal is the cash budget, or, more specifically, a refined version called the "Rolling Cash Budget." While called a budget, it is also an essential forecasting tool.

Its basic form is:

Cash Received From	+
Cash Disbursed For	−
Net Cash Flow	+,−,0
Opening Cash Balance	+
Remedial Transactions	+,−
Net Cash Balance	+

If initial Net Cash Flow (adjusted by the opening balance) is negative, more cash is going to be needed and Remedial Transactions such as speeding up collections, borrowing or equity sales will be needed. Conversely, if that interim figure is positive, but excessively so, a productive use for the excess will be sought, such as paydown of debt or short-term investment.

The time frame for the budget is multiple:

1. As part of the company's forward planning, there should be a rough five-year cash budget, broken down by year. That budget is a guideline which should be updated at least semi-annually or whenever a significant revision is made to the company's strategic plan. (See Chapter 13 for the development and maintenance of such a plan.)

2. A detailed annual budget for the coming twelve months, broken down by month, is the central strategic time frame. It should be updated monthly or more frequently if dictated by circumstances.

3. An even more detailed monthly budget broken down by week is the central tactical time frame. The monthly budget is similarly updated weekly or as circumstances require.

4. At the beginning of each week, a detailed update for the coming week as derived from the monthly budget should be prepared. Variance and performance should be measured daily and revisions incorporated as they become apparent.

The budget "rolls" in the sense that each week, each month, each twelve months, the budget is subject to revision and the time horizon is continuously extended. In other words, a new budget is not prepared periodically, but one budget is continuously extended. The company is then routinely forecasting its immediate, intermediate and longer-term cash needs.

For the smaller company (particularly one without the benefit of data-processing equipment) it is possible to get by with the twelve-month and monthly budgets, as long as they are "rolled" on time.

WEAVING THE CASH BUDGET

A simplified one-month example will present the essential procedures for constructing and administering the Rolling Cash Budget:

Step 1: First calculate initial Net Cash Flow mandated by operations and existing commitments:

	WK. 1	WK. 2	WK. 3	WK. 4	TOTAL
RECEIPTS:					
Cash Sales	1,000	1,000	1,000	2,000	5,000
Receivables Cllctd.	25,000	28,000	20,000	32,000	105,000
Maturing Investments	-0-	-0-	-0-	25,000	25,000
Total Receipts	26,000	29,000	21,000	59,000	135,000
DISBURSEMENTS:					
Cash Purchases	500	500	500	500	2,000
Payroll (Net)	12,000	-0-	12,000	-0-	24,000
Tax Deposits	2,500	-0-	2,500	-0-	5,000
Payoff Payables	14,000	16,000	18,000	13,000	61,000
Mortgage Payments	-0-	8,000	-0-	-0-	8,000
Note Payments	1,000	-0-	4,000	-0-	5,000
Total Disbursements	30,000	24,500	37,000	13,500	105,000
Net Cash Flow	(4,000)	4,500	(16,000)	45,500	30,000

Step 2: Using the initial opening balance, calculate week to week surplus (shortfall):

	WK. 1	WK. 2	WK. 3	WK. 4	TOTAL
Opening Balance	6,500	2,500	7,000	(9,000)	6,500
Net Cash Flow	(4,000)	4,500	(16,000)	45,500	30,000
Closing Balance	2,500	7,000	(9,000)	36,500	36,500

Here we see two, possibly three, concerns:

A. In Wk. 3 we have a shortfall and will be unable to meet commitments unless it is remedied.

B. In Wk. 4 we appear to have an excessive surplus, so that some productive use for the excess has to be found.

C. The company has a policy of maintaining a "cushion" (i.e., contingency fund) equal to one bi-weekly net payroll, currently running at $12,000. Only in Wk. 4 is that goal met.

Step 3: Cover shortfalls.

Examine the options in order of lowest cost to do so. These options will probably reflect this pattern:

1. Cut expenses. In the monthly time frame, it may be difficult to achieve substantial savings.

2. Delay payables and expenditures that will not result in lost discounts or incurrence of late charges.

3. Liquidate short-term investments.

4. Delay other payables and expenditures.

5. Borrow.

6. Sell marginal assets. This is also likely to be difficult in a short time. (Of course, an ongoing program of liquidating unproductive assets is assumed to be in progress. See Chapter 8.)

7. Sell equity.

8. Sell productive assets; i.e. partial liquidation of the company. (Typically, a company will rarely go beyond option 5 and hopefully never beyond 7.)

Step 4: Build cushion, using the same options. (Note that this represents partial fulfillment of Goal #2, maintaining sufficient reserves.)

The need to build cushion diminishes as the speed and magnitude in which emergency funds can be obtained increases. Thus, if the company has a standby line of credit that can be activated by a phone call or has money in a highly liquid short-term investment such as a money market fund with wire withdrawal, there may be no need to build cushion in the actual bank balance. The creation of these near-cash reserves should be a permanent tactical goal of the cash manager.

Step 5: Disburse excess surpluses.

In determining the excess in WK. 4 in the instant case, knowledge of WK. 1 in the following month is important to determine the size of the excess. Knowledge of the outlook beyond that week is needed to gauge how quickly, if at all, the excess may need to be reconverted to cash.

Subject to reconversion, examine the options in order of highest return, which will probably reflect this pattern:

1. Buy back equity.

2. Pay off longer-term debt.

3. Pay off shorter-term debt.
4. Longer-term investment.
5. Shorter-term investment.

Of course, expenditures that cannot be reconverted to cash (such as dividends, salary bonuses, increased expenses) can also be considered if circumstances and company plans merit.

Thus, the completed budget at the beginning of the month looks like this after making the changes and additions of Steps 2 through 4:

	WK. 1	WK. 2	WK. 3	WK. 4	TOTAL
RECEIPTS:					
Cash Sales	1,000	1,000	1,000	2,000	5,000
Receivables Cllctd.	25,000	29,000	1,000	31,000	106,000
Maturing Investments	-0-	-0-	-0-	25,000	25,000
Total Receipts	26,000	30,000	22,000	58,000	136,000
DISBURSEMENTS:					
Cash Purchases	500	300	200	1,000	2,000
Payroll (Net)	12,000	-0-	12,000	-0-	24,000
Tax Deposits	2,500	-0-	2,500	-0-	5,000
Payoff Payables	14,000	14,000	16,000	17,000	61,000
Mortgage Payments	-0-	8,000	-0-	-0-	8,000
Note Payments	1,000	-0-	4,000	-0-	5,000
Total Disbursements	30,000	22,300	34,700	18,000	105,000
Net Cash Flow	(4,000)	7,700	(12,700)	40,000	31,000
Opening Balance	6,500	2,500	20,200	7,500	6,500
Oper. Surplus (Short)	2,500	10,200	7,500	47,500	37,500
Remedies:					
Liquidate Investments	-0-	10,000	-0-	-0-	10,000
Borrowings	-0-	-0-	-0-	-0-	-0-
Asset Sales	-0-	-0-	-0-	-0-	-0-
Equity Sales	-0-	-0-	-0-	-0-	-0-
Debt Payoff	-0-	-0-	-0-	20,000	20,000
New Investments	-0-	-0-	-0-	15,000	15,000
Equity Redemption	-0-	-0-	-0-	-0-	-0-
Net Remedies	-0-	10,000	-0-	(35,000)	(25,000)
Closing Balance	2,500	20,200	7,500	12,500	12,500

Note that the Receipts and Disbursements figures do not precisely match those in Step 1 (the first cut) as collections have been accelerated (to the point of bringing in an extra $1,000 this month) and some cash purchases and payables have been deferred until WK. 4. Note also in constructing the budget that an off-sheet interim operating surplus (shortfall) has to be calculated to determine what amount of remedies are needed. Then those remedies are selected and plugged in and week-by-week calculations completed.

> **Point of Interest:** *Sometimes it may be useful to "cross remedies" producing no net effect on the bottom line. For example, if interest rates float on company debt and had been lower than those on a fixed investment, but are now expected to rise above the fixed investment rate, the company might liquidate the investment and use the funds to immediately pay off the debt to pick up the rate spread. Thus, the Rolling Cash Budget also has a role to play in fulfilling Goal #3.*

In the coming weeks, each day's performance and each week's will be matched to the budget prompting revisions, especially in the "remedies" section, if substantial variances develop. It is this short-term fine-tuning that permits extrapolation to the larger strategic plan.

At the same time, the cash management function plays a pivotal role in the firm's fortunes. The cash manager has to act as an early-warning signalman who must be sure that his communications reach a broad range of managers responsible for a host of activities, to maintain solvency at minimum and achieve the profit plan in the final analysis. The cash manager, in our example, will not achieve the collections speedup, nor will he be delaying cash purchases and payables. Someone else is responsible for enforcing those measures. Therefore, the finishing touch to the Rolling Cash Budget has to be the institution of reporting relationships and lines of communication that are open, effective and responsive, so that the cash manager's critical observations are translated into gainful actions.

Chapter 3

Controlling
Pitfalls in Credit Extension

Credit is a sales tool. The more lenient a company's credit terms, the greater the attractiveness of its products and services. Credit availability can expand a market in terms of increasing the pool of buyers. Without readily available credit, the auto market, as one example, would be significantly smaller.

Credit availability can also help position a seller to increase its share of the existing market, especially if buyers perceive little other significant difference among competitive products. In other words, credit can be a product differentiator. The company that offers no credit or very restrictive credit may differentiate itself negatively.

But greater sales do not necessarily guarantee greater profit, especially when some of the sales are not paid for. Therein lies the essential conflict of credit management:

Maximize sales with minimum credit losses.

The conflict is tougher to manage when a third element is included:

Manage credit at least cost.

That simply reduces the resources brought to bear on the problem. The whole credit question is largely a matter of judgment calls. Thus, it's rather easy to justify great cuts or additions to the budget for credit analysis and control. This chapter focuses on ways to pinpoint credit extension activities within a framework of a credit extension strategy. Once those activities are clearly delineated, the money and manpower requirements fall into place for a given quantity of credit applicants.

THE SUBJECT

Credit extension is divisible into two parts:

1. The Macro-Questions:
   a. Is it credit?
   b. Should credit be extended at all?
   c. How much credit can the company safely extend?

2. The Micro-Questions:
   a. To whom should credit be extended?
   b. What is the maximum amount of credit that should be extended to each credit-worthy customer?

Obviously if Macro-Question "b" is answered negatively, no consideration need be given to the Micro-Questions.

The aspects of collecting an extended credit will be considered in the following chapter.

IS IT CREDIT?

To be precise, extension of credit is any assumption of financial risk that payment will be delayed or not be received for products or services rendered. In addition to the obvious situations of "we'll bill you" there are a few other arrangements that might not normally be thought of as credit extension, but are in fact assumptions of the credit risk.

1. *Accepting checks.* A check is nothing more than a promise to pay until the bank on which it is drawn pays out on it. A check returned NSF or on which payment is stopped puts the seller in the same position—waiting for payment—as if credit had been directly extended. If immediate credit is not granted when checks are deposited with the bank (see Chapter 9 on Banking), the good checks are no different as far as cash position is concerned, from direct credit. (From the accounting standpoint, however, checks are typically credited as cash when received with adjusting entries made for bad checks.)

2. *Recourse credit.* When a company arranges third party financing for its buyers and the seller accepts the position of guarantor on the debt, the risk of loss to the seller continues as long as the buyer's debt is outstanding. Arrangements of this sort are rarely found outside the durable goods and capital goods industries. Sometimes, the guarantee will take the form of a promise by the seller to repurchase its product from a repossessing creditor at a price equal to the remaining indebtedness, without regard to the market value of the product. While the seller will usually recover part of its costs from resale after repurchase, it usually will be with the absorption of some loss.

3. *Consignment selling.* Under a consignment arrangement, a seller places his wares in the hands of a distributor whose responsibility is limited to paying only for those goods that are not returned to the seller. While the seller waits for sales to be made and for money to be paid or goods returned, his costs, as represented by the goods, are at risk. The credit he is dependent upon is that of the distributor-consignee.

4. *Short-term rentals.* Any situation in which a renter takes possession of an asset in exchange for payment (or promise of payment) of a rental charge less than the cost of the asset or its value leaves the seller-renter with risk of loss.

These situations do not leave the seller without legal recourse, just as the seller would have in any other credit extension situation. The point is that in each of the above circumstances (and there are undoubtedly some others) the seller must still concern itself with the creditworthiness of its customers and should therefore establish at least some rudimentary credit control operations.

CREDIT — YES OR NO?

To a great extent, the question of extending credit is more a marketing one than a financial one—but financial input to the decision is absolutely vital. The techniques of marketing analysis and strategy development are beyond the scope of this book, but the financial input to appropriately moderating the marketing analysis is threefold:

1. Determining what the company can afford to do;
2. Offering direct credit alternatives;
3. Analyzing alternative credit cost-effectiveness and profitability.

Any company prepared to extend credit must first consider its own sources of funds. The sales projections of the marketing force should also include a projection of realistic credit sales. For example, assume the pristine situation of a new company with a new product and the following alternative projections from the sales department:

	Without Credit		With Credit	
	Per Unit	Total	Per Unit	Total
Annual Unit Sales		10,000		12,000
Dollar Sales	$100	$1,000,000	$100	$1,200,000
Cost of Goods	$ 80	$ 800,000	$ 75	$ 900,000
Gross Margin	$ 20	$ 200,000	$ 25	$ 300,000
Gross Margin %	20%	20%	25%	25%

Cost per unit is lower and the gross margin percentage higher in this example with credit because higher capacity utilization produces greater efficiency. This question is itself one that should be addressed, for in some companies, particularly where production is already near capacity, the opposite effect may be observed.

Enter the finance man. He adjusts this analysis with answers to the following questions:

1. What is the average amount of receivables expected?
2. What is the average expected age of receivables?
3. What is the expected amount of bad debts?
4. What is the expected cost of credit administration?

Unfortunately, the customers who take advantage of credit availability will not be limited to the incremental sales. Chances are that most customers will take advantage of credit if it is offered. Only in the retail field is there likely to be very much less than near universal customer usage of credit. Determining the number of customers who will use it is again a market/sales question. Assume, in our example that the estimate comes in at 90% of sales. Sales are also estimated to be smooth—i.e., equal amounts month-to-month of $100,000.

Thus, average monthly credit sales look like they will be $90,000.

Estimating average expected receivables age is a joint function of sales and finance. Estimates may be based on a variety of factors:

1. Industry averages for the seller's industry
2. Averages of pay times in the markets sold to
3. Analysis of the credit strength of the customer base
4. National or regional statistics, that may suggest improvement or deterioration in aggregate economic conditions

In this case, the estimate is 45 days or 1½ months. From here the average outstanding receivables are calculable:

$$(\$90,000/\text{month sales}) \, (1\tfrac{1}{2} \text{ months}) = \$135,000$$

These figures suggest that the company has to set aside funds to cover the cost of these receivables:

$$(\$135,000) \, (75\% \text{ cost of goods}) = \$101,250$$

Those funds must be paid for at the company's marginal cost of capital, assumed to be 12%, or 1% per month. Over the course of a year, this generates additional costs of:

$$(12\%) \, (\$101,250) = \$12,150$$

Bad debts are expected to equal 2% of sales, based on analyis of largely the same factors that went into the aging estimates. The loss:

$$(2\%) \, (\$1,200,000) = \$24,000$$

Last, the cost of credit administration over one year includes:

Personnel Time	$20,000
Personnel Support (20%)	4,000
Legal & Collection Expense	3,000
Total	$27,000

Note that legal costs include not only the costs of suing, but necessarily the costs of keeping abreast of the burgeoning regulation of credit. This expense seems to be particularly burdensome in the consumer field.

Recapping the sales and profit estimates, we find:

	Without Credit	With Credit
Gross Margin	$200,000	$300,000
Cost of Funds	-0-	−12,150
Cost of Bad Debts	-0-	−24,000
Cost of Administration	-0-	−27,000
Adjusted Gross Margin	$200,000	$236,850

Without the $60,000 saving through increased efficiency in production due to increased sales, the "without credit" scenario would be the more profitable.

The analysis should be further refined if the company has competing uses for the funds. The investment of $101,250 in receivables produces a $36,850 return or 36.4%. This return should be ranked against competing uses.

HOW MUCH CREDIT?

In examining this question, we are really looking at a cash and funds flow problem. The real question is not how much, but how much can be allowed as outstanding at any one time. If all credit were extended (and paid for) on a strictly overnight basis, the limit on how much would be allowable would be equal to the next day's Net Cash Availability. Net Cash Availability is the total funds available from all sources at any one point in time less all needs for cash at that same point in time, exclusive of the funding for accounts receivable.

Unfortunately, credit is rarely extended on an overnight basis (excluding the banking industry's overnight loans). The logical limit on receivables is then Net Cash Availability during the average age period.

This Net Cash Availability concept harkens back to Chapter 1 and considerations of funds availability at an acceptable cost. As receivables climb, the demand to fund those receivables (an Operations Demand) rises, and in so doing can increase the cost of funds. There will come a point when credit to fund receivables is no longer available or where the cost of those funds exceeds the rate of return the extension of credit will produce.

The aggregate credit extendable should be reduced from estimated Net Cash Availability to provide a cushion as two risks increase:

1. Creditworthiness Risk: The less credit-worthy the customer base or the heavier the concentration of poor credits in receivables, the greater the risk that cash flow from receivables will be constricted by bad debts and lengthened payoff times.

2. Forecasting Risk: The less reliable the forecasts on which credit planning is based, the greater the chance the company will be overextended before it realizes the condition it finds itself in.

WHO GETS CREDIT?

Before concentrating on individual accounts, minimum credit standards can be established by reference to Account Groups Analysis. Accounts of compable creditworthiness are grouped together and risks assigned based on market and credit research. The groups are ranked in order of declining creditworthiness. The lowest ranked group that will be permitted to receive credit will be the last one likely to deliver a profit on its sales.

Here's an example:

For a particular company, market research has determined who potential customers are, what is their relative credit standing and the sales each is likely to generate over the next year. Each account has been assigned to one of eight Account Groups, as there are, in this case, eight significant points of credit differentiation (such as industry, statistics and others — see further on in this chapter about non-financial and financial attributes).

Group	I	II	III	IV	V	VI	VII	VIII
Expected Sales	90,000	100,000	60,000	80,000	120,000	100,000	50,000	120,000
% Cost Sales	70%	70%	72%	74%	75%	75%	80%	80%
Cost of Sales	63,000	70,000	43,200	59,200	90,000	75,000	40,000	96,000
Max Gross Margin	27,000	30,000	16,800	20,800	30,000	25,000	10,000	24,000
% Bad Debts	1%	4%	8%	10%	12%	18%	25%	40%
Amount Bad Debts	900	4,000	4,800	8,000	14,400	18,000	12,500	48,000
Profit (Pre-Capital Costs)	26,100	26,000	12,000	12,800	15,600	7,000	(2,500)	(24,000)

In this example, credit will not be extended to members of or below Group VII. Note these points:

1. Gross sales by Group need not be uniform, though they may be. As sales are estimated according to comparable creditworthiness, there can be no assurance that equal buying power will show up in each Group.

2. Here it is assumed that each lower-rated Group represents incremental sales. Gross Margin tends to decline as less efficient production capacity is utilized. In some companies (as in our previous example) Gross Margin will tend to increase as economies of scale are encountered. Contributing here to the decline are the higher costs of collection and slower payoff of receivables that come with poorer credits.

3. A quick mathematical computation will reveal that the appropriate cutoff Group can be found without reference to estimated sales, so long as the percentages are known:

$$(1.00 - BD)\,(GM) \geq (BD)\,(1.00 - GM)$$

Where

BD = percentage of Group Sales expected to be uncollected (expressed as a decimal); and

GM = Gross Margin percentage applicable to the Group Sales (as a decimal).

Going one step further, it appears cutoff should occur when Bad Debts exceed Gross Margin. In fact, an earlier cutoff is appropriate to compensate for risk and to provide a minimum acceptable return on capital. If the left side of the inequality is higher, the Group is acceptable; if the right, unacceptable. Using the figures from Groups VI and VII for comparison:

Group VI

$$(1.00 - .18)\,(.25) \geq (.18)\,(1.00 - .25)$$
$$.21 \qquad\qquad .14$$

Acceptable

Group VII

$$(1.00 - .25)\,(.20) \geq (.25)\,(1.00 - .20)$$
$$.15 \qquad\qquad .20$$

Unacceptable

Carrying the mathematics a little further, the increase (or decrease) in profits on a given amount of sales will be equal to the differences in percentages from each side of the equation times that amount of sales. For example:

Group VI
$$[(.21)-(.14)] [\$100,000] = \$7,000$$

Group VII
$$[(.15)-(.20)] [\$50,000] = -\$2,500$$

These figures correspond to those in the table.

Despite all of the careful consideration that may be given to Macro-Questions, the key issue is that Groups of customers do not fail to pay bills, lone customers do. The inescapable conclusion and the primordial fact of life of credit is that good credit performance depends on the accuracy of analysis on each account.

INFORMATION COLLECTION

The credit department's basic function is the processing of information. Collection of that data is the first obstacle to be overcome. Any credit manager knows what data is needed to build a file on each potential customer, but for the record, a brief review:

Commercial Customers	Consumers
Balance Sheet	Personal Financial Statement
Income Statement	Credit Bureau Report
Bank References	Bank References
Trade References	Credit References
D & B Rating	

Of course, the primary source of data is the customer. However, the manner of approach should be designed to

1. Facilitate verification,

2. Facilitate analysis,

3. Minimize time and cost input.

A central issue of the approach is who collects the data: Sales or Finance? Neither choice is absolutely the only way. Industry, personnel, product, customers and method of sale all influence the decision and may lead to different conclusions under differing circumstances. Remember: The goal of credit is sales promotion. Credit activity that turns off sales is counterproductive.

These comparisons can be drawn:

	Finance	Sales
Advantages	1. Expertise	1. Established customer relationships
	2. Saves sales staff time	2. Keeps sales staff aware of credit developments and importance
	3. No fragmentation of focus on credit	3. Speeds credit data transmission
	4. Provides internal control	4. Encourages sales concentration on qualifying accounts

	Finance	Sales
		5. Skilled in dealing with customers
		6. Saves total personnel time
Disadvantages	1. May lack customer sensitivity	1. May lack credit expertise
	2. Generates overhead	2. Inhibits sales presentations
		3. Reduces sales time
		4. No check on commissioned sales people

Wherever the decision rests, and in most cases some sharing of responsibility occurs, sources of data and verification include:

Salesmen: Even if not directly responsible for developing specific credit data, their knowledge of and relationships with customers provide an invaluable source of information.

> **Warning:** *Salesman, if commissioned on gross sales, have a vested interest in painting the best possible picture of the prospect.*

References: The usual trade and bank references provided by a prospect are, of course, a primary source of experiential data with the prospect.

> **Warning:** *A prospect will usually try to provide the most favorable references.*

Public documents: One of the most effective ways to check on small businesses and individuals is examination of small claims courts records in the jurisdiction where the account is located. A series of suits indicates an unreliable prospect.

Credit Reporting Agencies: Always a logical option, although the cost can be high.

> **Warning:** *Their data may be obsolete.*

Trade Associations: Find out from the customer if he belongs to a trade association. Data on the standing therewith is itself significant. However, figures available from many associations may be useful in rating the prospect against his industry peers.

Prior History: Past and recent dealings with a customer by the company itself may mean the most.

NON-FINANCIAL ATTRIBUTES — SPECIFIC ACCOUNT TREATMENT

Most credit analysis quite rightly concentrates on the financial data obtained about a prospect. However, just as the internal accounting data of one's own company can be misleading and easily misinterpreted (see Chapter 1) the risk is doubly great with credit applicants because:

1. There is unfamiliarity with the applicant's accounting methods and conventions;

2. Many applicants consciously put their best foot forward by distributing the rosiest data they can legitimately develop;

3. Data released to creditors is usually several months older than the latest data on hand (which itself is usually somewhat behind the times) and virtually never includes forecasts.

4. The volume of credit applicants will usually preclude substantial investigation and confirmation of data.

Recalling once again that the purpose of credit extension is sales promotion, it would be pretty foolish if credit operations hindered sales. Yet, a frequent problem is delay in deciding whether or not a particular prospect is acceptable. The delay may well alienate a good customer and diminish the seller's reputation for fast and reliable service. The ideal credit review system, then, will not only accurately assess credit prospects, but will do so as quickly as possible.

There are certain constraints in each applicant's activities (such as type of business for commercial accounts or occupation for consumers) that are not really susceptible to pure numerical analysis (except, perhaps, through the use of subjective weighing systems) but these constraints are still a key ingredient in determining acceptability. After all, would you rather have a buggy whip manfacturer or a laser manufacturer as the next applicant? A corporate executive or unemployed day laborer?

These extreme examples show that these "non-financial attributes" can tell much. The best way to confirm and refine their meaning is to look at the company's data base of past and present customers and ask these questions:

1. What similarities exist among failed (i.e., bad debt) accounts?

2. What differences consistently emerge between failed and good accounts?

3. What similarities consistently appear among good accounts?

The following checklist of non-financial attributes is a useful one, because most of the attributes are generally found in a standard rating service report:

CHECK LIST
NON-FINANCIAL ATTRIBUTES

Commercial Applicants	Consumer Applicants	All Applicants
Industry (SIC)	Age*	Salesman Making Sale
Company Age	Marital Status*	Competitive Product Availability
No. Employees	No. Dependents	Product Line
No. Salesmen	Citizenship*	Initial Order Size
No. Branches	Time at Residence	Rating Service Rating
Type of Purchaser	Location of Residence*	Credit Reference Indications
Location	Time in Present Job	Special Factors
Public v. Private	No. of Jobs Held	
Domestic v. Foreign	Education Level	

*Extension or denial of credit on the basis of these factors may constitute discrimination and result in exposure to lawsuit and/or liability. Confer with legal counsel.

A few words of explanation are in order about some of these items:

Type of Purchaser: The customer buying a critical raw material from you is likely to be far more careful in maintaining a good credit record than the occasional buyer. The same reasoning can be applied to sale of services, as the customer who buys a repetitive and important service (e.g., vehicle fleet maintenance) will be more careful than the "one-shot" buyer (e.g., parking lot striping). The less critical the seller is to the buyer, the more stringent the credit requirements should be. Note however, that lower importance to the buyer may also make the sale harder to close and put more pressure on the salesman to go easy with credit.

Salesman Making Call: Some sales personnel may be found to consistently take the path of least resistance, which may well mean marginal credits. His name on the ticket may be an alert. Obviously, should such a situation be found, retraining, closer supervision or even dismissal has to be considered. But those steps are not within the financial analyst's control, so, until the situation is clearly remedied, this non-financial factor bears close scrutiny.

Product Line: Some products may be found to attract less credit-worthy customers. In addition to the closer watch on that line's customers, the product itself may deserve some attention as it might be failing and causing disputes or may be a line the company is better off without.

Competitive availability: The company without any competitors is likely to be more critical to its customers than one that is readily replaceable. Accordingly, somewhat less stringent requirements may be in order.

Special Factors: Included may be items such as other relationships (affiliated companies, suppliers, personal relationships, employees), social considerations (e.g. minority enterprise, charitable, educational or religious institutions) quality of management and similar credit-influencing factors.

The non-financial attributes are a simple and effective parameter for splitting customers into account groups and for isolating potential problems. Once meaningful groups are established, differing financial standards can be appropriately applied to each.

As the randomness of customer attributes presents too great a risk in pinning a definition on an account group based on a single attribute, various combinations of attributes are used for precise demarcations. The primary data base is the company's history with its accounts, which are analyzed for probabilistic occurrence of failure. Here's a simplified example:

A company has 10,000 commercial customer accounts for its equipment sales. These accounts show the following data breakdowns:

TYPE OF ACCOUNT

FACTOR	ATTRIBUTE		ATTRIBUTE		ATTRIBUTE		ATTRIBUTE	
	#	%	#	%	#	%	#	%
Type Purchaser	Distributor		Direct User		NA		NA	
	1,000	10	9,000	90				
Public vs. Private Ownership	Public		Private		NA		NA	
	1,500	15	8,500	85				
Rating Service Assessment	Class I (Best)		Class II		Class III		Class IV (Worst)	
	2,000	20	4,000	40	3,000	30	1,000	10
No. Employees	1 to 10		11 to 50		51 to 100		Over 100	
	4,000	40	4,500	45	1,000	10	500	5
Company Age	Less than 1 yr		1 to 5 yrs		More than 5 yrs		NA	
	1,000	10	3,000	30	6,000	60		

FAILURE BY TYPE

FACTOR	ATTRIBUTE		ATTRIBUTE		ATTRIBUTE		ATTRIBUTE	
	#	%	#	%	#	%	#	%
Type Purchaser	Distributor		Direct User		NA		NA	
	20	2.0	480	5.3				
Public vs. Private Ownership	Public		Private		NA		NA	
	70	4.7	430	5.1				
Rating Service Assessment	Class I (Best)		Class II		Class III		Class IV (Worst)	
	50	2.5	120	3.0	190	6.3	140	14.0
No. Employees	1 to 10		11 to 50		51 to 100		Over 100	
	200	5.0	220	4.9	50	5.0	30	6.0
Company Age	Less than 1 yr		1 to 5 yrs		More than 5 yrs		NA	
	170	17.0	170	5.7	160	2.7		

Please note that the percentages in the top chart are a percentage of the total universe of accounts. For example, 1,000 Distributors represent 10% of the total accounts of 10,000. The percentages in the lower chart represent percentages of the top chart classification that failed. For example, 20 distributors failed, meaning that 2.0% of the 1,000 distributors were failed accounts.

On the basis of these figures, the public vs. private distinction and the number of employees do not appear to have a material correlation to failure. In other words, these distinctions seem to show up randomly among failed accounts exhibiting all manner of other characteristics. The remaining three factors do seem to make a difference. A new table is constructed evaluating the 24 possibilities (Product of the attributes: 2 × 3 × 4 = 24) in terms of failure probability:

ATTRIBUTES			FAILURE DATA		
Distributor/Direct Distributor	Company Age Less Than 1 year	Rating Svc. Assess Class I	.# Type 0	.# Fail 0	% Fail 0
		II	0	0	0
		III	0	0	0
		IV	0	0	0
	1 to 5 Years	Class I	30	1	3.3
		II	60	3	5.0
		III	130	6	4.6
		IV	0	0	0
	Over 5 Years	Class I	300	2	0.7
		II	280	3	1.1
		III	150	2	1.3
		IV	50	3	6.0
Direct User	Less Than 1 Year	Class I	140*	24*	17.1
		II	360*	43*	11.9
		III	300*	57*	19.0
		IV	200*	46*	23.0
	1 to 5 Years	Class I	200	13	6.5
		II	1,780	44	2.5
		III	550	44	8.0
		IV	250*	59*	23.6
	Over 5 Years	Class I	1,330	10	0.8
		II	1,520	27	1.8
		III	1,870	81	4.3
		IV	500	32	6.4
TOTALS			10,000	500	5.0

*Indicates serious risk grouping.

Ranking these by % Failure, it is apparent that customers less than 1 year old present a very serious risk as do companies 1 to 5 years old rated as Class IV by the rating service. What would happen if an absolute prohibition on such accounts was entertained? Assume the average sale is 2 machines for $1,000, with an average cost of goods sold of $600. (This sort of sales analysis by customer grouping is itself an ingredient that should not be overlooked, but is more properly a function of the sales department, which should make the data available to credit.)

Of the 10,000 accounts, 1,250 would be eliminated, of which 229 were failures. (The asterisked rows are the eliminated accounts.) Here's the P & L on those sales:

Collected Sales: [(1,250 − 229) × $1,000]		$1,021,000
Cost of Goods: (1,250) × ($600)		750,000
Gross Margin Profit Contribution		$ 271,000

Thus, it appears that these sales will make money for the company. (Note that this result could have also been reached by determining the average Bad Debts for the Group and comparing to Gross Margin.) The next step is to segregate out the individual groupings and see if any of those are money-losers by themselves:

Group	Direct/ LT1/I	Direct/ LT1/II	Direct/ LT1/III	Direct/ LT1/IV	Direct/ 1-5/IV
Collected Sales Cost of Goods	$116,000 84,000	$317,000 216,000	$243,000 180,000	$154,000 120,000	$191,000 150,000
Gross Margin	$ 32,000	$101,000	$ 63,000	$ 34,000	$ 41,000

All happen to be profitable, but if analysis of average sales and cost of sales by these subgroupings yielded different averages, some of these categories might be found too troublesome to deal with. As it is, the gross margin percentage for the last three subgroups is just above 20%, which itself may make these undesirable, particularly if the reductions in sales allowed a drop in overhead costs (not reflected in this pure Gross Margin analysis) or reduced capacity pressures or relieved the company of some other burden. As it is, this analysis warns the credit group (and hopefully the sales group as well) to be on the alert when dealing with customers fitting this profile.

RELIABILITY

This technique is really a form of statistical sampling, wherein the analyzed customer base is theoretically a sample of all the world (an infinite population). Therefore, the extent of its reliability may be very limited if too small a sample is obtainable.

Proper sample size can be computed. For example, is the 250 sample size of the subgroup Direct/1 to 5/IV large enough to rely on?

We know that the break-even failure rate is equal to the Gross Margin, which is 40%. We therefore want to be sure that the margin of error in the sample does not allow us to realize a failure rate in excess of 40% if the company concludes from this analysis that it wants to continue selling to the group.

The statistical formula employed is: *

$$N = [(z^2) (P) (1-P)]/[(R-P)^2]$$

where: N = Sample Size Minimum

z = Confidence Coefficient (see below)

P = Observed Failure Rate

R = Maximum Acceptable Failure Rate

The table for some commonly used confidence coefficients is as follows: *

Confidence Level:	99.73%	99.00%	98.00%	96.00%	95.00%	90.00%	80.00%	50.00%
z	3.00	2.58	2.33	2.05	2.00	1.96	1.28	0.6745

* Formula derived from and table taken from Spiegel, M. R., Ph.D., *Schaum's Outline of Theory and Problems of Statistics*, p. 157–8, McGraw-Hill Book Co. (New York, 1961).

Confidence levels mean that by employing the confidence coefficient, the user can expect that x samples out of 100 samples will yield results like those observed in the instant sample. (Use of a 99% confidence level will mean 99 of 100 samples will be within the expected range.)

In this example, the proper sample size for the highest confidence level (99.73%) is determined by:

$$[(z^2)\,(P)\,(1-P)\,]\,/\,[\,(R-P)^2\,] = N$$
$$[(3.00)^2(.236)(1-.236)]\,/\,[(.40-.236)^2] = 60.334, \text{ rounded up to } 61$$

As our sample size is 250, it can apparently be relied upon with a good degree of confidence. (Note that unless the entire universe is sampled, 100% confidence is not mathematically achievable.)

However, there is always the risk that a particular company sample will be inaccurate. (It may be inaccurately good or bad.) That risk can be exaggerated if the company has followed policies that tend to skew the data base by attracting and accepting or repelling and rejecting an inordinate number of failing quality accounts. The best defense against that risk on an aggregate basis is to repeat the analysis over a period of time, say at least once a year, to be sure no extraordinary results are occurring. If they are, more detailed analysis is necessary.

That detailed analysis is going to be needed anyway, because it is still individual accounts that fail, not groups. The individual accounts need to be examined on the basis of financial attributes, too.

Before proceeding, a quick review of what's been accomplished with non-financial data:

1. It has established that certain accounts exhibiting specified characteristics require special handling — i.e., credit and sales are alerted to specially screen these applicants.

2. Various markets have been ranked by credit desirability for the Sales Department to consider in developing its marketing and sales plans.

3. It has determined where credit operations can provide the biggest return; i.e., gauged what kinds of accounts demand a higher input of resources that is likely to pay off with a higher output of safe accounts.

FINANCIAL ATTRIBUTES — SPECIFIC ACCOUNT TREATMENT

Financial analysis for credit purposes focuses on just the issues of:

1. Can Pay?
2. Timely Pay?
3. How Much Credit?

It is therefore less extensive than investment analysis or other financial analysis that may deal with return on investment, decision theories or other more esoteric methods. It is arguably less demanding as well.

This section will discuss a simple analytical tool that can shortcut some of the more complicated analysis and, together with data derived from the non-financial attributes study, provide a flexible method that can be changed with changes in circumstances. It is also a method readily amenable to computer adaptation, which offers the important benefit of quick turnaround on credit decisions. This can be an advantage in the marketplace, as well as in maintaining sales force morale and reducing friction with the credit department.

Can Pay

For the "Can Pay" question, two discreet financial tests are employed:

1. A Cash Test; and
2. A Condition Test.

A prospect must pass both tests to qualify for credit. It works like this:
Consider a four-quadrant graph set up with these axes:

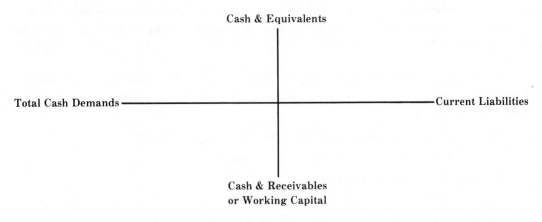

Each quadrant discloses a ratio as described:

	Cash Ratio
Average Days Cash	
Average Days of Working Capital	Acid Test Ratio

The values for all of the axes come directly from the financial statements. Total Cash Demands can be defined two ways:

1. Cash Outflow; or
2. Total Expenses Plus Inventory Change.

Cash Outflow can be pulled from a Cash Flow Statement if one is available. However, the typical credit report and many sets of statements received from applicants excludes such a statement. Total Expenses and Inventory Change are derivable from the Profit & Loss Statement. Depreciation and other non-cash expenses should *not* be deducted on the theory that they may fairly reflect cash demand for capital replacement and/or debt service. If the analyst knows more precisely what that demand is, then, of course, that knowledge should be used instead. Inventory Change is defined as Closing Inventory less Opening Inventory, which should be found in the Cost of Goods Sold calculation. A conservative approach would be to ignore inventory declines, on the theory that there is always pressure for growth, even if the particular cutoff point for financial statements happens to show a temporary decline. Other refinements can be introduced to the calculations, such as consideration of whether the statements are developed on the cash or accrual or some other accounting method.

To provide extra perspective to this test, the axis for Cash Demand uses a scale different from the other three axes. This scale is calculated at the ratio of 360 days to the applicant's collection period. Thus, if the applicant's collection period is 30 days, the scale will be 1/12 of the other three scales. As both of the ratios involving cash demand look at days supply, the logic is to reward the applicant that efficiently collects its own receivables, as those collections fund its payoff of our receivables. In the absence of those collections, the creditor is relying strictly on cash on hand. (Note: When dealing with individuals, the scales will not be adjusted.)

The figures for the applicant are plotted on the graph and the points connected to form a rectangle. Assume these numbers for an example (Definitions in parentheses refer to individuals as applicants):

Working Capital (Cash & Securities) $300,000

Cash & Equivalents (Cash & Securities) $60,000

Current Liabilities (Current Liabilities) $140,000

Sales (Salary and other income) $1,400,000

Total Expenses (Total Expenditures) $1,320,000

Opening Inventory (NA) $100,000

Closing Inventory (NA) $100,000

If the rectangle's length is greater than its width, the applicant, on this test, passes. Why?

Mathematically, cash and equivalents are being double counted, as they comprise a part of current assets. Subtracting current liabilities from current assets gives a surplus available for future commitments, of which our sale will assumedly be a part. If that surplus (giving extra weight to actual cash) is sufficient to cover needs through the next receivables cycle, the applicant will be capable of paying. That surplus is represented by length less width.

Here's how our example looks:

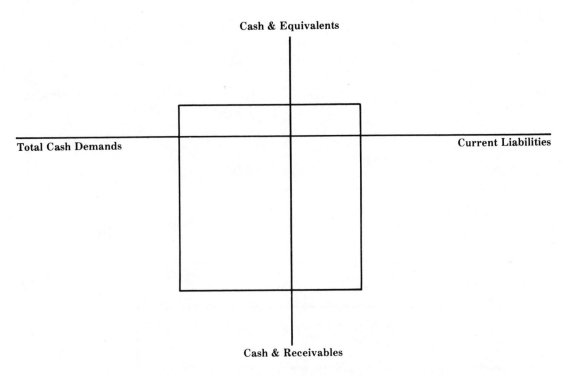

The Condition Test is similar. The labels for this graph's axes and the meanings of the quadrants are:

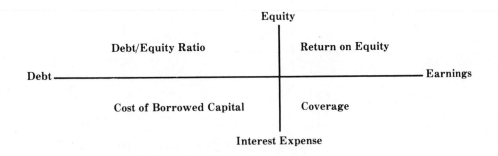

The Earnings and Interest axes are scaled at ten times the Equity and Debt axes, to provide symmetry in presentation. By so scaling, the analysis is implicitly focusing on 10% as a critical relationship of earnings to capital (not an unusual minimum acceptable return)

and on 10% as a critical relationship of interest to debt (not an unusual caution point). Different proportions can be used if market conditions indicate the need.

The passing applicant will have more area in the rectangular segment to the right of the lines connecting Debt/Equity to 0 and 0 to Coverage, than to the left of those lines. Why?

The areas of the sub-rectangles in the Debt/Equity and Coverage quadrants are bisected. What's really being compared is profitability in the Return on Equity Quadrant to capital servicing requirements in the Capital Cost Quadrant. Merely comparing earnings to interest without regard to capitalization would ignore a critical condition factor. Hence, the area test.

Here's an example:

Equity (Net Worth)	$600,000
Debt (Debt)	$500,000
Interest (Interest)	$ 40,000
Earnings (Annual Savings Buildup)	$100,000

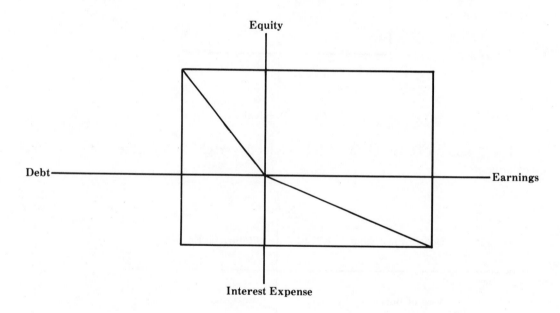

Timely Pay

The Timely Pay test is a simple analysis of the age of the applicant's payables calculated as:

$$[(Current\ liabilities)/(Cash\ Demands)]\ [360\ days]$$

or as:

$$[Trade\ payables/purchases]\ [360\ days]$$

If data are available, the latter formula is preferred, as it eliminates liabilities such as accrued taxes or accrued wages, which may distort the treatment that may normally be expected by trade creditors.

The resulting age is compared to the creditor's terms, to the creditor's average receivables age or to just a maximum acceptable time for payment, which will rarely be over 60 days. If the payables age is low enough, the applicant passes. Why? Because the applicant is apparently in the habit of paying his bills within a time frame acceptable to us.

The figures for this example come from the Can Pay test:

$$[\$140,000/\$1,320,00] \ [360 \text{ days}] = 38.18 \text{ days}$$

If we are using an average receivables age, and that age is 61 days, the applicant passes.

Having passed this test, and finding the applicant in an acceptable attributes group, the credit manager may still want to subject the applicant to some other scrutiny. However, the degree of need to do that may well be mitigated by the screening process and how well our applicant has come through it. Assuming we're now satisfied of creditworthiness, how much credit do we allow?

LINE OF CREDIT

It's a judgment call. Certainly, credit should not exceed the net worth of the applicant, and if the applicant is or has recently been losing money, that net worth figure should be adjusted downward to allow for losses. That's still a high maximum, because it is assuming that assets can be converted to cash at book value and used to pay us.

Practically speaking, the ability of the applicant to pay in the short run, for which initial credit is granted, will be a function of current position. Accordingly, a safe limit is the sum of the excess of current assets over all current liabilities, plus after-tax earnings during the receivable period, which will assumedly be reflected in the future through growth in the excess of assets over liabilities.

Somewhere between the high and the safe lies a good policy. The key to credit management in this area, however, is more properly found in the continual monitoring of these accounts, which will be covered in the next chapter. These two benchmarks of net worth and current excess plus earnings are more useful as triggers for account monitoring and reevaluation. Decisions on more credit can and should logically follow those reviews.

MODIFICATIONS

Quick review of these tests will reveal that a company showing losses will never qualify, as it will fail the condition test. This approach would therefore cut off a potentially significant market and be impossible to accept for companies selling primarily to cyclical industries or depressed areas.

Hence, a modification must be adopted. The simplest, and often the most effective, is the use of average results over three or five years, or throughout an identifiable economic cycle.

A second modification includes calculation of cash requirements generated by continuing losses compared against apparent lines of bank and investor credit. An applicant losing money while living with a high debt/equity ratio should not qualify, while a loser with great credit line reserves shouldn't be ignored.

As all of this process is judgmental in one respect or another, exceptions can be made on the basis of non-financial attributes (such as management quality) or on other grounds (affiliates). The point to be made is that these should be exceptions, not the rules. The company with loads of receivables from losing companies is obviously courting trouble.

Chapter 4

Action Techniques for Managing Accounts Receivable

The sale is ours. We've got the customer. He's got the product. Now we just want to get paid.

Having made the investment in receivables, this chapter tells how that investment is to be managed and sets the stage for dealing with and minimizing those aberrant receivables investments that demand special collection efforts.

Here, we'll examine the pre-collection process, breaking it down into these components:

1. Billing
2. Cash Discounts Policy
3. Accounts Receivable Monitoring

BILLING DESIGN

An invoice has not one, but five purposes:

1. Tell the customer how much he owes.
2. Remind him why he owes that amount.
3. Perpetuate a strong and attractive image of your company in the customer's mind.
4. Motivate the customer to pay promptly, preferably without a moment's delay.
5. Make it as easy as possible for the customer to succumb to the motivation to pay.

In designing the invoice to accomplish these objectives, these cardinal rules apply:

1. *Simplicity.* Keep the invoice as uncluttered as possible. Eliminate unnecessary material. Minimize data that has little or no meaning to the customer. (E.g., credit rating

codes. If you feel it makes sense to put them on an invoice, and it often does, let it show up only on the in-house copy.) Keep code numbers short. If you ask for an invoice or other reference number on the payor's check, don't confuse him with many to choose from. An easy way to reduce the number of figures is to use letters (you've got 26, instead of 10 to choose from) as part of the coding. When assigning account numbers, it's also often helpful to use part of the customer's name in the account code, as it facilitates identification.

2. *Completeness*. Don't go too far overboard in your attempts at simplification. Make sure that all of the material you wish to communicate to the customer is included:

A. Who is the invoice from?
B. Why is the money owed?
  i.   What was bought?
  ii. When was it bought?
  iii. What does it cost?
  iv. When was it delivered?
  v.   Any sales tax?
C. How much is owed in total?
D. How much time may elapse before you should be paid?
E. Where should payment be sent?
F. What will be charged if payment is late?
G. How much will be saved if payment is made early?
H. What should be sent back with payment (e.g., invoice copies)?
I. Who should be contacted if there's a problem?

A part of the completeness concept is the idea of "full disclosure" in the billing description, so that the customer is helped to feel full value is received for the money expended. Compare these two samples:

Bill I

1 Washing Machine, Complete	$400.00
Sales Tax	20.00
Total	$420.00

Bill II

1 GG Deluxe Washing Machine with automatic feed, Spin Cycle, clutch control, computerized settings, including delivery, installation and 1 year limited parts warranty	$400.00
5% South Carolina Sales Tax	20.00
Total Due	$420.00

Besides being good public/customer relations, the completeness is also likely to cut down on questions that may delay payment. For those dealing with businesses, the approach may also help a purchasing agent justify the expense of buying from you.

3. *Clarity*. Make the information clearly understandable. Avoid these three most common mistakes:

A. Incompleteness, e.g.,
   "Net 30 days"
   Does the seller mean 30 days from the date of shipment, receipt of merchandise, date of billing or receipt of the bill?

B. Abbreviations. You know what they mean, but will the customer? Be especially careful with product descriptions and information. Troubles frequently occur with computerized systems with limited "field" (i.e., number of characters that can be devoted to memory and/or print space) sizes. When confronted with an entrenched system that will cost a lot to modify, one solution is to print an abbreviations glossary on the back of the invoice. Don't put it on the front; your invoice will look cluttered.

C. Avoid trade jargon. Most industries and even many companies have their own particularized language, which may be confusing to outsiders. For example, a manufacturer of liquid products may bill a customer for:

   "1 case   Liquid Grease $18.00"

While the case contains six one-gallon containers, for which the price is $3.00 per gallon, if the customer's trade deals generally in products packed four to a case, the customer may think the price is an uncompetitive $4.50 per gallon. Or, being positive the price is only $3.00/gallon, he may remit only $12.00. Or, he may waste precious time disputing the invoice.

4. *Courtesy*. A seemingly obvious point, but somehow one that is still missed by too many. One example:
   "Please pay this amount" is certainly preferable to
   "Pay this amount."
Putting a thank you at the bottom of an invoice can't hurt. Get the customer's name right, especially when dealing with individuals. Include titles (e.g., Dr.) when they're appropriate. Including job titles can also help avoid questions about who ordered what in a company setting. There may well be more than one J. Johnson.

Most important (and most difficult to deal with in a computerized system), respond to customer requests regarding the bill. For example, if a customer asks:
   "Please include our Purchase Order Number on your invoice"
failing to do so is not only poor public relations, but will also probably slow the customer's processing of your invoice.

5. *Positiveness*. Make the invoice attractive and distinctive. If you have a logo, use it. Brightly colored paper, legible print, clearly defined columns and an uncluttered appear-

ance (simplicity) will make the invoice that much easier and appealing to process. Remember, several people will probably be involved in the customer's payment process. Even in a household, there's a husband and wife. You want to appeal to all those individuals.

6. *Ease*. Simplify the customer's work. Minimize the writing, calculating and reviewing he has to do. People will tend to do the easier job first. Problems may be laid aside for higher authority to deal with (perhaps when the boss returns from vacation). Provide enough copies. Include a self-addressed envelope. Make the bill fit smoothly with the proper fold into a standard window envelope. Remittance copies can even be turned into return envelopes.

Having designed the invoice, it's time to put it to use. If the job has been done right, we've got a collection tool and a selling tool that's going to help generate repeat business.

THE BILLING PROCESS

Speed is the watchword. Bill fast and payment will arrive that much sooner. To achieve maximum speed, billing cannot be viewed as something that "just happens." It only happens when the right information reaches the billing station (whether a clerk at a typewriter or a computer connected optical scanner) and is processed into hard copy that goes ASAP to the customer. Everybody knows that.

Aside from jiggling the office arrangement or installing a higher speed printer, where can a company compress the time frame in the billing process? Perhaps in two places—with the customer and with delivery of the bill.

Prebilling

In many service businesses, particularly those that deal with monthly contracts, a typical payment cycle looks like this:

Begin Work	Day 1
Complete Month	Day 30
Start Next Month's Work	Day 31
Bill	Day 32
Bill Received	Day 35
Customer Processes Payment	Day 59
End Second Month's Work	Day 60
Start Third Month	Day 61
Payment Sent Out, Bill 2nd Mo.	Day 62
Payment Received for Month 1	Day 65

Thus, by the time the first payment is received, the account has required 65 days of cash investment, and possibly more if the payment is not promptly deposited with *and* credited by the bank. Particularly in a service industry where the primary expense is labor, translated into frequent payrolls, the cost is immediate and real.

Assume for example, a contract of $1,000 per month with $700 per month in cash flow out and a start-up cost of $1,000 in the first month of the contract, and the above timetable.

Even with a reasonably healthy 30% per month cash margin, the account will not reach break-even payback on a cash basis until *after* the eighth month:

$$\frac{\text{1st Mo. Capital} + 65 \text{ days expense}}{\text{Revenue/Mo.} - \text{Expense/Mo.}} = \frac{1,000 + (65)(700/30)}{1,000 - 700} = 8.39 \text{ months}$$

In fact, the real time is longer when the cost of money is factored in. If the company is on an accrual basis for tax purposes, recognizing income upon billing and not when payment is received, the cost is potentially higher, as cash may be paid out in taxes before it is actually collected.

All that eats up cash and credit lines. It can put a lid on growth based on cash availability instead of operational capacity, thus devaluing that capacity and reducing the benefits of operating leverage. How can some of that be saved?

Prebill the customer on the very first day of each month with terms of Net 40 or so. This way the customer still owes nothing until the work is completed and he's had a chance to inspect and reap its benefits.

Meanwhile, several advantages accrue to the seller. First, terms of Net 40 seem rather generous even though the customer is really getting only Net 10 compared to the old system; but the psychology is compelling. Second, and even more important, the bill is likely to get into the customer's payment processing system 30 days faster. The psychological impact of an invoice sitting around for 30 days is meaningful, particularly when dealing with a minimally computerized customer. For those who may pay bills once a week or once a month, this method is likely to generate a few saved days. For larger payors, the advantage of getting a bill into the system or onto their computer also has real meaning.

Prebilling requires some selling and good customer relations, but if it is made a part of normal company policy and treated as such, with Sales Department cooperation customer resistance should be minimal. The key is providing that time for the customer review before payment. That way he can feel he's not paying for service sight unseen. Even if terms are expanded to Net 60, it's still worthwhile. Who knows, once in a while, payment may even be sent before the month is out.

Two other important points on prebilling:

1. Until the work is completed and the right to receive the money attaches from a legal standpoint, the income generally need not be recognized for tax purposes under the accrual method. The mere fact of billing will usually not cause income to be recognized. (See IRS Regulation 1.451-1 as reported in *Prentice-Hall Federal Taxes* Par. 20,131 et seq.) For cash basis taxpayers, the point is moot as no income is recognized until the payment is received.

2. Be sure when monitoring receivables to *not* factor in these prebilled accounts before they come due. Treating them as overdue can upset an on-time customer. Aging should also be adjusted to avoid distorting calculations and reporting. Without such adjustments, comparability to companies and industries not using prebilling will be compromised.

Mailing and Delivery

Difficulties with the U.S. Postal System and that of other countries coupled with the rising cost of mailing has led many companies to explore alternate methods for delivering all kinds of mail and to reevaluate mailing operations. Before considering alternatives, make sure that all is being done that can be done to facilitate mail delivery. Try out this checklist on your mailroom and billing operation:

1. Are addresses complete and legible?
2. Are zip codes included?
3. Is mail batched by zip code?
4. Do all envelopes carry the right postage? (Some mailing machines automatically weigh and stamp each piece.)
5. Does the mailroom know the deadlines for getting mail to the post office and are schedules synchronized to those deadlines?
6. Is the company careful to use envelopes of a size easily handled by the post office? Check with your local postmaster if there's a question.
7. If using a postage meter, is remaining postage carefully monitored to assure it doesn't run out at a critical time? If using stamps, is the supply similarly monitored?
8. Are envelopes properly sealed?

Also, to hold down postage, can these steps be taken?

9. Can lighter weight envelopes or paper be used?
10. Can smaller documents be used to save weight?
11. Can the backs of documents be used to reduce paper?

These last three steps will probably save printing costs, too.

O.K., all that's done and the results are still less than satisfactory. Look into private delivery services. High volumes within relatively small geographic areas can make such an alternative attractive.

In some circumstances, the bill can be enclosed with the merchandise to accomplish time and cost savings.

> **Beware this Pitfall:** *Be sure the customer receiving department can and will pass the bill along to the payment department. In most such cases it's a good idea to follow up with statements.*

> **Avoid this:** *Giving bills to salesmen can create a negative impact. The salesman has enough on his mind anyway and may forget to drop the bill off. It's a good way to demoralize your sales force and create internal friction.*

CASH DISCOUNT POLICY

To a large extent, the use of a cash discount seems a straightforward cost-benefit problem. Is the income foregone outweighed by the savings in interest costs and conservation of credit lines?

But the simple equation is complicated by a number of other questions:

1. What is the impact on sales? Does the competition offer it? How does the customer view it? Perhaps the discount is more effectively used as a price reduction to attract more sales?

2. What's the cost of chasing down unearned discounts? And the cost of monitoring them?

3. What's the real amount of time saved? Is it the difference between say 1/10 and Net 30? Or might the discounter have waited 45 days before paying?

4. Customers who do not take advantage of the discount are often those most prone to delinquency, as the rate of return for the payor is usually fairly high and accordingly not to be passed up lightly. (E.g., 1/10 Net 30 is a 1% cost for an extra 20 days use of money, equaling 365/20 or 18¼% annually.) Hence, the discount can help to monitor and evaluate credit customers. The discount may thereby reduce bad debts by alerting the credit department. That savings should be factored into the positive side of discount evaluation.

5. Educating customers about changes in discount policy also has a cost. It is not an item that can be changed too frequently, as you'll want the customer to pay as a matter of course. Confusion in policy can slow up payment. This insusceptibility to change also makes investigation difficult, as data collection through experimentation is inhibited.

Therefore, the decision will necessarily involve a good deal of judgment. Sharing that decision with sales management is often a wise and prudent course to follow.

> **Tax Tip:** *For accrual basis taxpayers who do offer a discount, receivables still eligible to take the discount can be reported as income without including the amount of the discount, lowering taxes. (See earlier reference to* Prentice-Hall Federal Taxes.)

Should a discount be offered, the handling of unearned discounts improperly taken must also be dealt with. Essentially, there are four alternatives to use in solving this problem:

1. Do nothing. This makes the discount equivalent to an outright price reduction. In some circumstances this is a valid alternative, not only because going after the discount may cause customer unrest, but because the administrative cost may outweigh the additional revenue.

2. Raise the price to abusive accounts to cover the lost revenue. Such a price rise might also trigger unrest. One may also question why, if prices can be raised to cover this contingency in a particular market environment, they are not at the maximum economically efficient level anyway?

3. Bill for the unearned discount. This task is fairly impractical without a computerized system. Where bills are being sent regularly anyway, it is recommended. There are two variations which make it more palatable for manual systems (and have an appeal for computers, too, because of the cost of forms, postage, etc.). Add the discount to the next bill, whenever it comes up, or accumulate the unearned discount and rebill for them once a year or when they hit a certain level.

4. Eliminate the discount. Again, this is potentially a bone of contention with customers, but perhaps superior to a price rise or to accepting the loss. Administrative savings are worth considering in evaluating this option. If administrative systems make it unfeasible to eliminate the discount on only selected accounts, elimination on a blanket basis has to be considered in light of all accounts, not just the offenders.

No discussion of cash discounts is complete without also considering the reverse discounts: interest and penalties. All the competitive considerations influencing discount policy apply here, too.

Without either interest or penalties for late payment, terms lack teeth. Loss of opportunity to take a discount may, in a sense, be a penalty for late payment, but once the time has passed for taking the discount, there's no incentive to stop delaying payment.

To be on the firmest legal grounds for collecting interest, obtain a signed blanket credit agreement from your customers. Ideally, it will be included as a part of the credit application. Typical language:

"Customer understands and agrees that if payment is not received by seller within thirty days from the date of billing, Customer will be assessed and Customer agrees to pay interest (or late charge) of _____ per cent per _____ on the unpaid balance until paid (or $ _____ for each _____ days the bill remains unpaid)."

If circumstances render that approach impractical, the next best thing to do is to send an acknowledgement of the order in which the terms are stated. Or, the customer may be induced to use your order form which includes similar language. At the very least, be sure to include the data on invoices. The goal is to motivate payment. If the customer is unaware of the motivation, the policy fails.

> **Warning:** *Especially if you deal with consumers, you should be aware of the requirements of the Fair Credit Practices Reporting Act (popularly referred to as truth-in-lending) and related regulations. A large number of states also have requirements about disclosure. The cost of compliance has thus become a deterrent to charging interest or penalties in some cases.*

The rate of interest or size of penalty is not of small import. It is a question of your preference provoking early payment or earning extra money on the account. The higher the rate, the more likely payment is received earlier. If there's a desire to use financing of customer receivables as an income source, rate setting should be viewed as a market problem. The rate should be above the cost of capital (including the cost of administration), but low enough to attract some takers. Rarely, however, is the finance business attractive for companies who do it as a sideline. In most cases, the better course is to set the rate as high as possible given competitive limitations.

> **Warning:** *Some jurisdictions still have usury laws. If you plan to charge interest or late charges (penalties may be construed as interest, regardless of nomenclature) be sure the effective rate is not in violation of any such laws.*

If you offer cash discounts and/or charge for late payment, be sure your accounting reflects the impact of those policies. Not only is segregation of the data important for evaluating the policies, themselves, but it can affect pricing strategies, market research and sales efficiency evaluations.

> **Keep This in Mind:** *Cash discounts, interest and penalties can present a frustrating and irritating problem. Abuses are just about inevitable. But their use or avoidance form a part of overall credit policy, which is a sales-directed issue. Don't lose sight of that critical relationship to sales.*

ACCOUNT MONITORING

Part of the receivables strategy focuses on early identification of problem accounts. As a byproduct of the monitoring system, information useful in evaluating receivables performance and in broader corporate planning is made available.

The principal monitoring tools are:

1. Aging Schedule(s)
2. Payment Schedule(s)
3. Credit Limit Positions.

Each is designed to focus on one kind of situation and elicit a particular kind of credit management response. First, a look at how they're developed.

Aging Schedules

The classic aging schedule groups accounts within 30-day periods. When terms are different from 30 days, the groupings ought to be based on the applicable terms. For example, if terms are 1/10, Net 30, with a 1½% penalty after each 30 days, the schedule should be broken into:

Discountable	Current	Penalty 1	Penalty 2	Penalty Over 2
Under 10 Days	11-30	31-60	61-90	91 and Up

This breakdown provides a quick reference for determining net amounts due, which will be useful in cash flow forecasting.

Effective aging is substantially facilitated by a computer, which permits complete cross-referencing. Aging schedules segmented by various parameters add a dimension to analysis that can lead to more rapid trouble control. The following list provides a number of categories for consideration:

Ordered Oldest to Newest

Alphabetical by Customer

Ordered by Account Size

Ordered by Invoice Size

Divided by Salesman

Divided by Sales Center (e.g. Branch)

Divided by Product/Product Line

Divided by Geographic Area

Divided by Customer Industry

Divided by Credit Analyst

In addition to pinpointing overdue accounts for dunning, the information suggests areas where extension of new credit may be a problem. For example, higher delinquencies in a particular geographic area might warn not only of impending credit trouble, but may also imply a coming dip in sales in that area. All of this type of data should be fed to top management in summarized form for strategic planning.

For each account grouping, four ages can be calculated according to this matrix:

	Simple	Weighted
Complete	Complete/Simple	Complete/Weighted
Oldest	Oldest/Simple	Oldest/Weighted

Take the following schedule as an example:

Account	Invoice #	Date	Amount	Age	(Not Appearing) Extension
Able Co.	5250	1/20	100	100	10,000
	5354	1/28	450	92	41,400
	5408	2/18	600	71	42,600
Subtot.	-3-		1,150		
Baker Co.	6040	4/20	600	10	6,000
Charlie Co.	6020	4/20	300	10	3,000
	6104	4/28	385	2	770
Subtot.	-2-		685		
Delta Co.	5280	1/24	40	96	3,840
	6080	4/22	320	8	2,560
	6099	4/22	1,500	8	12,000
Subtot.	-3-		1,860		
Group Total	-1-		4,295		

COMPLETE SIMPLE: Total of ages of each invoice divided by number of invoices . . .
$$397/9 = 44.1 \text{ Days}$$
OLDEST SIMPLE: Total of ages of oldest invoice for each account divided by number of accounts . . .
$$216/4 = 54.0 \text{ Days}$$
COMPLETE WEIGHTED: Amount of each invoice multiplied by age of each invoice (see extension column) divided by sum of the amounts . . .
$$122,170/4,295 = 28.44 \text{ Days}$$
OLDEST WEIGHTED: Amount of oldest invoice for each account multiplied by age of the oldest invoice for each account, divided by sum of the amounts of those invoices . . .
$$22,840/1,040 = 21.96 \text{ Days}$$

Here's what this information does:

TYPE OF AVERAGE AGE	TELLS	POOR RESULTS MEAN	ACTION TO TAKE
Complete Simple	How old, on average, all of the receivables are.	Widespread slow payment.	Concentrate collection efforts immediately on the slowest accounts and upgrade. Clamp down on credit extension, especially to delinquents.
Oldest Simple	How quickly, on average, all of the accounts are paying.	Poor customer credit base.	Review overall credit and collection policy. Revise sales efforts to attract better class of credit-worthy customers.
Complete Weighted	How long the average receivable dollar has remained uncollected.	Larger accounts are paying more slowly.	Concentrate on biggest accounts for collection. Review their credit limits. Concentrate new sales on better credits that may presently be buying in small quantities.
Oldest Weighted	How quickly, on average, the average dollar is being collected.	Serious delinquencies probably concentrated in larger accounts.	Weed out slowest accounts.

One other aspect of this particular example bears some additional discussion. Our mythical Delta Corporation has a small invoice seriously delinquent, probably due to a dispute or error. These kinds of niggling little problems can create false impressions and should be dealt with swiftly. If for some reason they cannot be cleared up and do not qualify for writeoff, a solution to use in purifying the aging schedules is to transfer disputed items to a receivables subaccount labeled "Receivables Suspense."

By segregating these receivables they command high attention and also identify themselves as serious candidates for writeoff. Management, particularly in the smaller company or division, is less likely to be sidetracked by these problems. One individual should be assigned to investigate these disputes and be responsible for their resolution through payoff, settlement, lawsuit or writeoff.

A suspense account also requires careful attention and control so that it is not used by anyone as a dumping ground for artificial cleanup of the receivables picture to cover up poor performance. The control on suspensing decisions can be based around and be as tough as those decision systems used on writeoff and credits.

Average ages should be scheduled at least monthly and preferably charted over a year or two. Trends are frequently more important than point-in-time status. Results compared to industry averages (often obtainable from Dun & Bradstreet and/or industry and trade associations) yield a reasonable basis for evaluating credit performance. Internal competition among divisions or regions in the larger organization also provide comparability.

Once developed, the aging schedules provide the prime tool for planning collection activity. More on that is coming up.

Payment Schedules

Payment schedules show time elapsed by account from billing to payment. An increase in payment times for an account may signal a deteriorating financial position and serve as an early warning system on coming collection problems. A frequent response is an adjustment of credit limit.

Note, however, that "one swallow does not a summer make" with these schedules. Occasional errant payments may stem from reasons ranging from post office foul-up to bookkeepers on vacation or simple oversight. It is the consistent drop from one level of payment time to successively longer times that causes alarm. Similarly, an appreciable improvement may indicate an opportunity for increased sales with a particular account.

Mathematically, the best control is a moving average of about the last half-dozen payments:

Account: Echo Company

Payment #	1	2	3	4	5	6	7	8	9	10	11	12	13
Days Elapse	20	28	26	29	30	34	34	33	36	37	40	38	43
6-Order Moving Avg.						27.8	30.2	31.0	32.7	34.0	35.7	36.3	37.8

The trend in this example is easily discernible from the time elapsed segment itself. Comparisons of the moving average show marked deterioration as well. However, to avoid printing all of this information each time, another calculation can be added which will give the same information without requiring the examiner to look at the entire history. By calculating a variance between the present payment and the moving average, *and then calculating another moving average on the variances themselves*, the latest data will tell the account trend accurately without risk of dramatizing the effect of a single errant payment.

Payment #	1	2	3	4	5	6	7	8	9	10	11	12	13
Days Elapse	20	28	26	29	30	34	34	33	36	37	40	38	43
6-Order Moving Avg.						27.8	30.2	31.0	32.7	34.0	35.7	36.3	37.8
Variance							6.2	2.8	5.0	4.3	6.0	2.3	6.7
6-Order Var. Moving Avg.												4.4	4.5

The variance is calculated by subtracting the PRIOR Moving Average from the present days elapsed. For example, the variance of Payment #11 is calculated:

Present Days Elapsed #11 − Moving Average #10:

40.0   −   34.0   =   6.0

In this example, the data in column 13 would constitute the payment schedule report on Echo Company as of Payment 13:

Payment #	13
Days Elapse	43
6 Mov. Avg.	37.8
Variance	6.7
Var. M. A.	4.5

Interpretation: This 13th payment was received 43 days after billing, nearly seven days later than the payments had been running on average. Payments have been falling behind established routine by 4½ days at a time on average. This indicates a rapidly deteriorating account.

When one payment is received for several invoices, the data should be segmented by invoice and the six latest invoices averaged. Six is not a magic number. However, too few magnify the effect of an errant payment, while too many will disguise latest results. For businesses with frequent billings and payments, higher order-moving averages can be used.

Again we encounter the danger of oddities distorting the data, such as disputed bills arriving late. Imagine the impact on our old friend Delta Corporation's record if that 96-day item is received and the last six items look like:

#	1	2	3	4	5	6	7
Time	28	30	26	29	28	27	96
Mov. Avg.	28.0	28.3	28.0	28.2	28.2	28.0	39.3
Variance	0.0	2.0	−2.3	1.0	−0.2	−1.1	68.0
Var. M. Avg.	0.0	0.3	−0.1	0.1	0.1	−0.1	11.2

Getting #7's data on a report would almost certainly prompt further action that in retrospect appears unnecessary. Handling through a receivables suspense account would strain out these oddities.

Payment schedules constitute the prime tool for precautionary credit control activity. This subject will be discussed later.

Credit Limit Positions

This report is a two-edged sword. Defensively, it serves as an alternate warning system. Offensively, it can help to guide the sales force to more effective selling.

Consider the customer whose payments are on time and whose record has been good. Suddenly, he's pushing his credit limit. Is it because his payments have slowed down or because he's ordering in larger quantities and/or with greater frequency?

There's only one way to find out and that's investigate. If the news is bad, the triggering device has worked and corrective action can be initiated. Perhaps the problem would have surfaced in the aging or payment schedules analysis, but the sooner it's found, the better. That's the defensive attribute.

But, if investigation shows the customer to be healthier than ever, perhaps it's time to reevaluate the account. Does it rate a higher credit limit? Should it receive more sales attention? Is a major customer opportunity developing? Is some new sales strategy paying off? With the exception of the credit limit query these are not topics belonging to the finance area. But they highlight this point:

Among your own personnel, don't be overly secretive with credit data. Sharing information with other company departments can help spawn greater productivity and profitability.

The credit limit report is relatively simple in format:

Customer	Date Began	Credit Limit	Current Balance	Credit Unused	% Used
Able	1/78	12,000	4,000	8,000	33.3
Baker	1/76	4,600	4,400	200	95.7
Charlie	2/76	8,000	7,100	900	88.8
Delta	4/78	15,200	27,500	−12,300	180.9
TOTALS		39,800	43,000	− 3,200	108.0

In this case, until the report is adjusted for Delta's extraordinary situation, the totals appear to be misleading. Once corrected, however, they tell how much farther receivables might be expected to grow with the current customer base. There will usually be some correlation between receivables levels overall and credit limit usage, if the credit limits are set with care. Examining that historical correlation may foreshadow fluctuations in sales. Additionally, if there is cyclicality to the correlation, the readings on levels may also help in planning cash needs to cover investment in receivables. These correlations lose their value for these purposes, to some extent, if the credit limits are substantially below the customer's demand for our products.

Total Report

Rather than three separate reports, all of the information can be pulled together in a single report. Moreover, it can well include some related information of potential use to the sales teams, to produce a "Customer Schematic."

Such a report deserves broad internal distribution, but its confidentiality as to the outside world should be closely guarded. Copies are to be numbered and accounted for. Additional copies will be prohibited from being made without special approval. Dated issues would be shredded or burned. Few documents could be as useful to competition. Few will also be as productive internally if properly composed and utilized.

```
                        CUSTOMER SCHEMATIC


  Company:              Address:
  Account #:            Sales Contact:          Phone #:
  Bank Reference:       Credit Contact:         Phone #:
  Branch Sold by:       Salesman:               Credit Analyst:


  SALES DATA
  Year-to-date Sales    Year-ago-to-date Sales    Difference    % Difference
  Projected Annual Sales:            % Projection Achieved to date:

  REMARKS:

  AGING DATA
  Total Owed:
  Suspense Items:       Invoice #       Date:      Amount:        Reason Suspense:
  Total Owed Subject to Aging:
  Invoice #      Date       Discountable      11-30 days      31-60 days      Over 60 days

  REMARKS:

  CREDIT LIMIT DATA
  Date Established      Credit Limit      Current Balance      Credit Unused      % Used

  REMARKS:

  PAYMENT DATA
  Last Pay Date:
  Time Elapsed:
  Moving Average:
  Variance:
  Variance Moving Average:
```

Having devoted one page to each customer, a final page is used to summarize the data, showing totals, averages, percentages and the four moving averages. In some cases, additional subtotal pages may be used to summarize customers in a particular category, e.g., by Branch servicing the account.

Additionally, an "Exceptions Index" is issued which details exceptions for follow-up action. These indices may be lists of companies selected according to single or multiple criteria, or they may be printouts of a portion or all of the schematic for each exceptional company. They are arranged alphabetically or by account number or by magnitude of the problem (e.g., highest receivable total). A potential list of criteria and indicated responses includes:

ITEM	RESPONSE
Year-to-Date Sales Lags Year Ago (Optional: By X%)	Intensify sales efforts. Review sales actions affecting account (e.g., Pricing, change in salesman, etc.)
Year-to-Date Sales Exceed Year Ago By X% or more	Analyze reasons for improvement. Duplicate causes elsewhere if possible.
Sales Below Projection Levels (Optional: By X%)	Seek causes. Revise projections?
Sales above Projections By X% or more	Seek causes, try to duplicate. Revise Projections?
High Number of Suspense Items	Intensify Purification activities.
Accounts Hitting 31 days for first time	Initiate investigation as to credit status changes. Perhaps start collection efforts.
Accounts over 60 days	Begin or intensify collection. Consider credit cutoff.
Accounts at Credit Limit (Or over X% Usage)	Investigate and determine if limit revision, credit problems or sales opportunity.
Payment Variance Moving Average Lengthening	Investigate for credit problems. Revise credit limits? Initiate collection? Cut off credit?

Exception reports, especially those emphasizing Problems, should also indicate the length of time the subject company has been appearing on that exception report, the frequency of appearance and some remarks about actions taken, person assigned the responsibility and status of the progress being made.

These reports allow managers to focus on the problems that managers want to review. Too many separate reports risk duplication and may overwhelm a manager with informational detail. Therefore, the input of recipients into system design and report distribution is useful. It makes little sense for the responsible credit analyst to receive a report showing companies above projected sales. Some reports may be superfluous either because the same conclusions can be derived from other reports or the benefits are outweighed by the costs of producing and distributing the report.

Ideally, other exceptions may be added or can be requested from the data base as the company involves itself in different planning, budgeting and control activities. To achieve this ideal, most companies will need a well-tuned computer. As practical constraints limit data manipulation, the manager cuts back on optional features. Changing needs and circumstances require monitoring of the usage of the system on a periodic basis. At least semiannually, the management should be asked to evaluate the information they are receiving and determine if some reports can be eliminated or if new reports are needed. Changes in format, combining of reports and deletions of segments of reports also deserve consideration.

Once the monitoring and control system is working and problems become readily identifiable, receivables information can be melded into overall strategic planning. At the same time, the tactics of dealing with those accounts that are problematical can get underway with maximum efficiency.

Chapter 5

20 Ways to Streamline Accounts Receivable Collection

Once problem accounts are identified, they are split into two basic groups:

1. Those still worth courting,
2. Those where collection is the overriding concern.

The treatment of Group 2 will be more severe and may mean the termination of the business relationship. While this is rarely desirable, it is sometimes unavoidable as more pressure for payment is brought to bear.

Group 2 customers will almost always have been Group 1 customers whose credit standing has deteriorated still further. The exception to this rule involves customers who are suddenly discovered to be in serious jeopardy, such as those who file for bankruptcy.

A flow chart of the progression and handling of a problem account follows on page 102.

This chapter will follow this flow chart, analyzing the nature of the different steps and determination of route.

COLLECTION PERSONNEL

The preliminary requirement to embarkation on the flow chart route is the establishment of responsibility for covering that route. Because of the overhead status attributed by many to credit operations, many companies have a tendency to minimize personnel qualifications in this area. That is frequently an erroneous attitude, as a very high return can often be achieved on the incremental investment in higher caliber personnel.

For example, a typical collections representative may cost $12,000 per year, whereas $15,000 will attract a much stronger candidate. If the average sale is $1,000 on credit and the stronger candidate saves just one extra sale each month, the return on investment is:

$$(12) (\$1,000)/(\$15,000 - \$12,000) = 400\% \text{ !!!}$$

COLLECTIONS

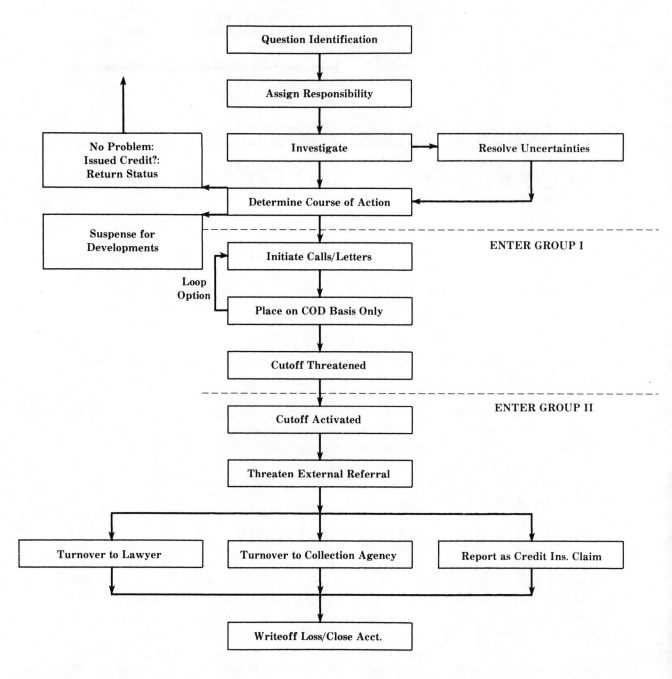

N.B. At any point in the chart, if payment is received, status may be returned to normal, although credit limit may be lowered. Additionally, partial restoration (moving partway back up the chart) is acceptable as the delinquent balance is reduced.

Practically speaking, these attributes make the ideal candidate:

1. *Negotiating Skill*. Much, if not all of the collector's customer contact will involve negotiation in one form or another. An ability to think on one's feet, respond quickly, understand the customer's needs, fears and goals, and possession of that intuitive feel for how far to push and where to settle, are all vital to good performance.

2. *Analytical ability*. The collector should be able to understand the customer's position in order to assess the urgency of a situation, the likelihood of payment and the customer's ability to meet commitments. Coupling that with negotiating ability will yield the tactical strengths that produce collection.

3. *Communications Skill*. The collector has to be able to get his points across and make the customer believe both promises and threats.

4. *Attitude*. Because of the ever-present risk of alienating customers (even slow payors have their profit value as we've seen earlier) the collector who can remain sensitive to salesmanship and can retain a customer's goodwill while still obtaining earliest payment is prized above all others.

5. *Efficiency*. As much of collection activity is related to speeding up customer payment as it is to preventing ultimate failure. The time value of money concept translates directly from the collector's use of his own time and allocation of resources. The more frequently a customer is contacted, the greater the chance of payment under most conditions. Therefore, a measurable kind of productivity exists, which an employer should indeed gauge and seek to improve. In making those measurements, however, the employer is forced to also impute a certain subjectivity in terms of the collector's ability to retain customer goodwill and minimize unnecessary additional contact by making each contact an effective one.

The right person is also going to require training in handling customers and in understanding the company's own operations. Knowing about his own organization, policies and procedures will help the collector deal effectively with these typical ploys:

1. *Postulation of phony disputes*. While the collector searches to check out the customer's allegation of poor performance, the credit has obtained a delay. The good collector will be familiar with all the parameters of the sale. He'll also know the sales value of different kinds of poor performance, and can ask the customer to pay everything except the disputed part until that's resolved. That way, at least part of the money's coming in and the veracity of the customer's claim can be tested.

2. *Questioned receipt or incomplete data*. The good collector will have all the documents on hand at the time of contact and will know how they relate and what they prove. He can make his point effectively and avoid delay occasioned by the credit's own inefficiency.

3. *Responsible person unavailable*. If the collector's own records are properly established, he'll have the information on the customer's chain of command and will know how to bypass the unavailable straw man or will know how to reach him.

4. *Provocations and "legal" arguments*. The good collector will be familiar with what the law provides and what company actions might invalidate or compromise the claim.

He'll be able to recognize the "bait" that would bring about just such a mistake on his part. He'll know whom to contact in the event serious trouble arises.

5. *Out of money, go ahead and sue me.* The collector will know the customer's financial condition and know whether or not suit is justified. He'll know what to look for as security for the debt, if the customer's cash is in fact depleted.

The creativity of bad credits is legend. Only with equally creative collectors can they be countered. If your company is using top people to obtain sales, it doesn't make sense to let their efforts go to waste by hiring marginal people to make those sales pay off.

INTERNAL COLLECTION ACTIVITIES — PRELIMINARIES

Before initiating contact activity with credits, these steps are taken:

1. Identify questionable accounts (see last chapter).

2. Assign the account to one responsible individual, who will control all collection activity with that customer. A fragmentation of authority and contact is almost always counterproductive, as the customer can play one off against the other and the lack of coordination may well mean that the company personnel are working at cross-purposes.

3. Investigate to verify data and determine the nature of the problem. Recall, for example, the material in the previous chapter showing how impurities in the data base can distort the credit performance of a single customer. Additionally, simple errors (missed postings, erroneous billings, etc.) can occur, even in the most highly computerized setting. Dunning a good customer can cause lost sales and wastes collection time that could be devoted to the real problem accounts.

4. Involve the salesman. Be sure that he understands the nature of the problem. He may throw some extra light on the situation. Equally important, if he's not informed he could inadvertently end up in the position of threatening the collection strategy. He may even be able to help with the collection effort. Finally, there's no sense in his devoting a lot of attention to an account that may not pay.

5. Before going full speed ahead on collection activity, particularly when the receivables report is yielding the first signs of trouble in an account, it may be a good idea to contact the customer for a credit data update. If the results are unsettling, collection activity might be accelerated. On the other hand, if the problems look temporary, a timely offer of assistance, perhaps in the form of a deferred payment plan, slowdown of deliveries under a fixed contract, technical assistance or even a direct loan (get it on a secured basis, with your inventory as the number one security) can produce an intensely loyal customer. And, one never knows when the shoe might be on the other foot.

Keep This in Mind: *Struggling debtors can often be a source of acquisitions well worth mining. (See the chapter on assets and expansion.)*

INTERNAL COLLECTION ACTIVITIES — TACTICS

All internal collection activity boils down to two types of communication:
Writings and Personal Contact.

While writings may often spur a customer to pay, their main focus should be on providing documentation for:

1. Follow-up. The various documents act as a "log" showing what's already been done.

2. Data for future study and planning. See the two immediately preceding chapters on Credit Extension and Management of Accounts Receivable.

3. Evidence in a lawsuit to compel payment.

Real success in collection work requires personal contact. That contact is designed to motivate payment, even if it means that the customer deprives another credit of payment in order to bring your account up to date. The most commonly relied on motivation is fear. Fears the customer may have that can be mobilized on your behalf are:

1. *Injury to reputation*. Whether an individual or a company, those who prize their creditworthiness will often be highly concerned about this item.

2. *Injury to image*. Very similar to reputation, but it differs for a company in that a tarnished image may cut into its own sales as people worry about its ability to retain quality in the face of cost pressures.

3. *Injury to credit rating*. When the tarnishing of reputation and image can be directly related to a line of credit, the fear becomes stronger.

4. *Loss of service/product*. When the customer believes he needs you more than you need him (as when you supply the raw materials) the threat of a cutoff in credit can carry tremendous weight, as the threat is aimed at his very lifeline of business.

5. *Collection "nuisance"*. While outright harassment is both prohibited by law and unbecoming to any adherent, the continuing disruption of calls, letters and the eventual lawsuit will often prompt payment. The threat takes on added potency if a collection agency may be brought into the picture. Very frequently, especially with perennially poor credits, the "squeaky wheel gets the grease."

6. *Loss of reciprocal sales*. In those cases where the customer is both customer and creditor, the leverage of lost sales can be a compelling factor prompting payment. However, where such relationships exist, it is often easier to continue buying and offset the debt owed to you with invoices from the customer.

> **Beware This Pitfall**: *Some contracts (e.g., leases) may prohibit offsets. While perhaps technically unenforceable, they may create embarrassment and reduce the leverage of your position. Check with your counsel who will probably arrange to obtain a written consent to offset.*

7. *Additional costs*. These may include interest, penalties, court costs, attorney fees, higher prices, cost of finding alternative sources of supply, etc. The more danger of

escalating expense to the debtor, the greater the chance of forcing payment. A sample letter that one creditor has used effectively looks like this:

Just a note to let you know we are looking forward to early payment and to let you see the costs that will result if our earlier requests for prompt updating of your account go unanswered:

10% Late charge	$ 100.00	
Court Costs	75.00	
20% Attorney Fee	220.00	
Your lost time	250.00	
Higher priced competitor	500.00	(over the next year)
Your present balance	1,000.00	
Total	2,145.00	
Present balance	−1,000.00	
Extra cost	$1,145.00	
% increase	114.5%	
For 6 months delay	19.08% per month!!!	

Why not just borrow the money and pay us? It will be so much less expensive and save us both a good deal of trouble.

Obviously, such a letter went out rather late in the collection process to what had become a Group 2 account.

8. *Lawsuit*: The ultimate weapon, it can also be the most costly to the user.

There is another side to the coin, that of positive motivation. A few examples:

1. "If you want our business . . . "
2. "If you'll pay now, we'll discount the bill . . . "
3. "If you'll pay now, we can let you in on our special price deal . . . "

   Warning: *On both of these last two, use with extreme caution, taking care to avoid providing an incentive to pay late in the future. At the very least, your good credits should be treated no worse than the poor ones.*

4. "If you want the order shipped . . . "
5. "It would really help (me) (us) (our company) (my boss) (etc.) if you'll pay now."

Whatever approach is used, the key to results is negotiating leverage of one sort of another. Empty threats, vacant promises, inconsequential pleas or a disorganized campaign will rarely modify the target's payment plans.

CONCRETE PROTECTIVE TACTICS

To make collection efforts work, they've got to have teeth. The following steps can be taken to strengthen your position and improve your chances of ultimate value receipt on the investment in the account.

1. A signed credit agreement has already been discussed. (See the chapter on Credit Extension.)

2. When selling tangible goods, obtain a signed financing statement, which can be filed in accord with the Uniform Commercial Code (not enacted in Louisiana) to obtain a lien on the sold property.

3. Where practical, do not deliver title until full payment is made, but merely permit the buyer use and possession pending full payment.

4. Obtain other security if services or non-lienable tangibles are involved, or if the tangibles will deteriorate rapidly in resale/repossession value.

5. Obtain a confession of judgment in extreme cases, such as very marginal creditors.

6. Have the customer sign a note, permitting you to recover interest and costs of enforcement. Such a note will, if properly drawn, facilitate suit and undermine counterclaims and defenses based on poor performance.

7. Charging of interest and penalties has also been previously suggested. Where permissible, structuring these in an accelerating fashion (e.g., 1% for the first thirty days, 2% for the next thirty, 3% for the following thirty and so on) can cause more pressure to build and will also tend to compensate for the increasing costs of delay and pursuit.

8. Sell on a prepaid, deposit, COD or reciprocal payment basis, where no new credit will be allowed until an old invoice of an equal or greater amount is paid off. This last approach is tantamount to a reduction in credit limit.

9. Cut off credit entirely. The assumption is that the customer really needs to keep buying from you. Otherwise the gesture is an empty one. When should credit be cut off? At the point that ultimate payment becomes doubtful, or when the costs of collection, including the interest cost of subsidizing the receivable, bring the sale's value below minimum acceptable profit levels.

Once the process for many of these approaches is established and becomes familiar to company personnel as standard operating procedure, the incremental costs of collection will decline along the learning curve. Nevertheless, despite best efforts, and recognizing that all of the above list is not universally applicable, sooner or later outside help has to be considered.

EXTERNAL COLLECTION — ALTERNATIVES

Three* alternatives (or supplements) to internal collection efforts are available:

1. Collection Agencies

2. Attorneys

3. Credit Insurance

Once a company decides to offer credit, its use of one or more of these alternatives should be lined up to handle the problems beyond the abilities of internal staff, to avoid expending additional time choosing the alternative and the specific agent when the problems surface.

---

*A fourth alternative, that of "selling" the receivables, is considered in the chapters ahead on Banking and alternatives to Bank Debt.

The major question to be answered is how deeply into the collection process a company should go before turning over the account to outside help.

That decision should be made on the basis of cost-benefit analysis, looking at these factors:

1. Availability of personnel to handle the account.
2. Incremental costs of handling the account.
3. Opportunity costs of handling the account, particularly as it applies to personnel.
4. The extra time saved or expended in turning over the account.
5. The increase or decrease in risk resulting from turnover.

Collection Agencies

Collection agencies may offer two significant advantages over in-house collection:

1. Greater level of skill; and
2. Lower ultimate cost.

Greater skill translates into greater efficiency. That efficiency may show up as faster payments, saved accounts or as a smoother relationship and prevention of customer alienation. A corollary of the skill advantage is the psychological value of introduction of a third party into the collection process. Companies that can afford to pay, but are intentionally slowing down as a part of cash management, will often be jolted to immediate payout by such intervention.

Many collection agencies work strictly on a performance basis, taking their fees out of the moneys they collect and basing their fees solely on those accounts collected. That arrangement may be superior to the continued overhead of a collections operation. However, those fees are not low. In making a comparison of costs, the analyst will want to look at the reductions in internal cost that will result from turnover of some accounts, not at the entire cost of the credit unit, as a part of that cost need be retained to evaluate new customers and coordinate activity with the collection agency.

The largest cost savings are likely to accrue when the customer is geographically distant and the collection agency operates in that region.

> **Try This:** *Use an agency for out-of-area collections only. Keep local collections in-house. The overall cost will probably be lower than using either method exclusively.*

When choosing a collection agency, look for these things:

1. *A sound reputation.* Any outfit that is known for strongarming credits can do you great harm. If you actually appoint one as your agent, you're liable for its actions.
2. *Sufficient staff.*
3. *Sufficient geographic coverage.* This does not require that you deal only with national firms, even if you're a national company. The use of several regional agencies may be a superior tactic, as it gives a basis for performance comparison and allows you to take advantage of any special facilities each may have by virtue of its regional familiarity. But,

within the area you assign to an agency, you want to be sure they can adequately (if not superiorly) cover it.

4. *Systematic reporting*. You'll want to be kept abreast of developments with minimum initiation of follow-up on your part.

5. *Bonding*. If they collect for you (as opposed to prompting payment to you, which may complicate administration of the collection) you'll need security as they then control a portion of your assets.

6. *Confidentiality*. Your customer lists and credit problems can be very useful to competitors. Additionally, disclosure of customer problems in some situations can expose you to liability.

7. *Payout*. When they get your money they should remit it promptly.

8. *Acceptable cost*.

> **Keep This in Mind:** *In recent years, several types of collection agencies have entered the marketplace, offering unbundled services, such as letter writing, calling, monitoring. Many are computerized. By calculating your costs on an unbundled basis, you may find use of such services more advantageous than using a full service concern.*

Having a collection agency under contract does not entirely release management from the burden of credit control. It must still evaluate the agency's performance. And it must develop an effective procedure for tagging an account for agency referral. Because ths cost associated with an agency is fairly high, the tendency to dump all problem accounts into its lap must be avoided. It's another judgment call. Using a time factor (e.g., anything not paid in 90 days goes to outside collection) is *not* recommended, because you may easily end up having done all the spadework and turning the account over just as it pays off. Some agencies allow a grace period (e.g., ten days) within which no charge or a lower charge is made if collection occurs. If your favored agency has no such policy, try to negotiate one. In any event, the most effective method for determination on individual accounts is through an individual decision maker, assigned to the account, who clears his decision with a superior.

One other trend in collection agency usage is to establish a subsidiary or affiliate agency. Frequently, the company's own credit unit is adaptable to such an arrangement. From the credit standpoint, the ability to get that third-party psychological advantage is still obtainable, particularly if the trade name of the organization does not reflect the affiliation, which itself is not widely publicized. There may be certain other organizational, tax, accounting and legal advantages, but their repercussions and ramifications are far too broad to consider here. Suffice it to say, that where a large in-place credit operation exists, the situation may be ripe for spinoff.

Attorneys

The consideration of attorneys does not vary dramatically from dealings with collection agencies. The major disadvantage accruing to the use of attorneys is that they must be localized in operation. Thus, a company operating over a broad area may have to maintain a "stable" of attorneys, which can add to the collection administrative burden. For this reason, attorneys are often resorted to through collection agencies, which may be more able to evaluate attorneys and be more familiar with the details of their practice.

Frequently, the operations of attorneys are also not geared to give the degree of reporting that many managers may require.

If you are going to use an attorney, you can substantially improve the attorney's effectiveness and cut collection time by providing this important information in full:

1. Legal name of the customer.
2. Headquarters, home address and registered office address.
3. Telephone numbers, with area codes.
4. Business form. (Corporation, individual, sole proprietorship, partnership, joint venture, trust, association, et al.)
5. Names of principals, partners and officers.
6. Location of branches, especially within your jurisdiction.
7. Bank and account number.
8. Precise description of goods delivered or services rendered, including dates.
9. Clear statement of amount owed, including interest, late charges and attorney's fee. Be sure you have the right to claim these, which can be done if included in the contract (oral or written) between you and the customer, if not limited by law.
10. Complete copies of documentation, such as invoices, purchase orders, delivery tickets, bills of lading and correspondence. Also available should be all the documentation on prior dealings with the account (including of course, the credit application) as the previously established pattern of trade between you can be a determining factor in adjudication of your claim.

The advantage found in direct referral to a lawyer is that he represents access to ultimate collection power. Accordingly, that power may prompt payment, just by being brandished. A collection agency cannot muster that kind of power, except by resorting to its own attorney.

Most attorneys handling collections will also be compensated in the same way as collection agencies, taking a percentage of collections. To reduce these collection costs, an attorney might accept a straight hourly or retainer fee, rather than commissions.

Carrying this logic a little further, most companies will probably find that an hourly rate will save costs in some cases, but the percentage will cost less in others. If the cheaper cost can be determined in advance with some certainty, a combination of both methods might be considered. Accounts likely to require relatively little time might be assigned to one attorney on an hourly basis, whereas those expected to be more difficult and time-consuming can be given to a different attorney on a percentage basis.

Credit Insurance

Credit insurance is an approach that deserves more consideration than it usually receives. While it is *insurance* against a particular set of risks, it also has special merit as a credit/collection tool. It works like this:

The creditor buys a policy from the insuror guaranteeing payment on all receivables above a certain amount of loss. That amount is in the nature of a deductible, here called the "Primary Loss." Hence, credit insurance does not guarantee that every dollar of receivables will be paid. It does not obviate the need for a credit department or credit vigilance.

Once the Primary Loss is absorbed by the creditor, additional losses are taken by the insuror, who is subrogated to the creditor's rights upon paying off the loss. Many policies are written with a 10% or 20% co-insurance clause, reimbursing the creditor for only 90% or 80% of the sale value. Logically, co-insurance reduces the creditor's premium. In some cases, the insurance will be written by the insuror only if co-insurance is included.

The claim under credit insurance is typically made after 90 days have elapsed from the date payment was due. However, if the debtor is insolvent (e.g., in bankruptcy) the claim can be turned in immediately upon the creditor's receipt of notice of insolvency.

The Primary Loss is essentially set by the insuror based on the characteristics and expected characteristics of the creditor's receivables. The individual corporation's receivables' characteristics are usually examined within the context of the creditor's industry. Premiums and deductibles are expressed as a percentage of sales.

Those are the basics. The principal insurance characteristic is that the creditor is protected against extraordinary bad debt losses.

Is it financially rewarding to use credit insurance? The cost-benefit analysis looks like this for a policy without co-insurance:

	Without Insurance	With Insurance
Total Credit Sales	$10,000,000	$10,000,000
Total Bad Debts	250,000	250,000
Primary Loss (2% Sales)	-0-	200,000
Reimbursed Losses	-0-	50,000
Bad Debt Losses	250,000	200,000
Premium (0.3% Sales)	-0-	30,000
Net Cost	$ 250,000	$ 230,000

On a formula basis, break-even on the policy occurs when:

$$\text{Premium} = \text{Bad debts} - \text{Primary Loss}$$

or, if co=insurance is involved:

$$\text{Premium} = (\text{Bad Debts} - \text{Primary Loss}) - (\text{Bad Debts} - \text{Primary Loss}) \times (\text{Co-insurance \%})$$

or:

$$\text{Premium} = (100\% - \text{Co-Insurance \%})(\text{Bad Debts} - \text{Primary Losses})$$

More positively, if the left-hand side of the equation exceeds the right, (i.e., if break-even or better is not achieved), the cost has been the price of buying the risk protection and these other subjective benefits:

1. High-caliber assistance in credit analysis and control. In providing that help, the insuror hopes to cut losses to or below the Primary Loss amount, so it is to the insuror's benefit to keep the creditor's risk and losses as low as possible.

2. Improved creditworthiness of customer base. As assistance and stronger credit operations pay off, the customer base itself improves, freeing resources and time from credit work.

3. Collection assistance. Once a loss is reported, the insuror will attempt to collect the debt, usually through its subsidiary collection agency. Use of credit insurance thereby brings external collection efforts into play. After an initial cost-free period (usually the ten days after the first contact between the insuror's collection agency and the debtor) the creditor is charged a collection fee on payments received by the insuror. These charges are sometimes less and very rarely more than the typical collection agency will charge. Nonetheless, the insuror's expertise in collection can be helpful and may bring in more dollars than the creditor can obtain alone. The cost-free period is also the time when the psychological intervention is likely to pay off, providing an edge over the ordinary collection agency.

4. Insured receivables will usually carry greater collateral value when borrowing.

5. Credit insurance stabilizes cash flow and facilitates confident forward planning.

6. Reduction in credit and collection administration expenses may result.

The one situation in which credit insurance is almost a necessity is an international transaction. International credit insurance policies are slightly different and can include "political" coverage, protecting the insured against social upheaval in the customer's country. Insurance can be generally obtained on individual transactions or on a blanket basis under a so-called "Master Policy." The economic choice between the two alternative policy forms is usually a function of volume and destination.

Credit insurance is not practical for every company, or, in fact, even available to everyone. Companies with unusually poor credit customers may find premiums prohibitive until the customer base is upgraded. Credit insurance is probably marginal for companies with a very broad customer base, where no single customer, or, better yet, no small group of customers represents such a large portion of receivables, cash flow and profits that their failure will be catastrophic. For such companies, the pure insurance utility of the policies is limited. Similarly, companies selling to a highly varied customer base, where it is improbable that events, such as an economic recession, will cause simultaneous multiple failures, may find this concept marginal. Companies with a low proportion of credit sales (i.e., heavy cash sales) probably don't need credit insurance. The same is true for companies whose volume is heavily laced with federal government sales. (Some may argue similarly for companies with primarily blue chip clients, but after the experiences of recent years involving Penn Central, W.T. Grant and Franklin National Bank, those kinds of companies are precisely the ones who may most need credit insurance as the failure of one such primary client might drag them down too far to recover.) Companies selling on a secured basis may not need credit insurance if their security is sufficiently strong. Last, credit insurance is not offered to certain industries, such as retailing.

Even if your receivables performance is excellent, the exercise of considering credit insurance may be useful in and of itself. The insuror's review of your credit operations and its rate quotation process will help highlight the weaknesses and strengths of those credit operations and help you to determine their real efficiency with a good degree of confidence.

CREDITS

Sometimes your company will be in error. Whether the fault is a clerical mistake or a failure of product, an adjustment is in order.

The most important fact about issuing credits is that they are money. Yet, a surprisingly large number of companies do not control them nearly as carefully as they control cash. Four kinds of credits control are:

1. *Countervailing authority*: No single individual has the authority to issue credits. Ideally, managers from separate departments (e.g., sales and credit) must approve credits before issuance to customers. Obviously, one of the managers should not have the authority, direct or indirect, over the other.

2. *Documentation*: Back-up documentation for issuing credits is mandatory to facilitate audit. A Credit Request form ought to look something like this:

```
┌─────────────────────────────────────────────────────────────────────┐
│                         CREDIT REQUEST                                │
│  Date of Request:                         Date of Sale:               │
│  Invoice # Affected:                      Invoice Total Amount:        │
│  Customer Name:                                                       │
│  Customer Address:                                                    │
│  Salesman:                                Amount of Credit Requested: │
│  Reason:                                                              │
│               Request Initiated By: _____ │
│                                            Signature                  │
│             Approved  Disapproved              Approved  Disapproved   │
│  Sales Mgr. [      ] [       ]    Credit Mgr. [      ] [      ]        │
│                Initials                          Initials             │
│  Credit Amount Issued:          Credit #:      Issued By:             │
└─────────────────────────────────────────────────────────────────────┘
```

3. *Audit*: A periodic examination of credits issued would look for collusion or other malfeasance by looking for large numbers or amounts of credits issued to:

A. Particular account

B. Particular address

C. One salesman's accounts

D. One individual

Such an audit can also be useful from an operational standpoint in uncovering poor performance by checking for credit issuance frequency of:

A. Reason for issuance

B. Product or product line

C. One location (e.g., parts manufactured by one plant or supplier)

D. Salesman

E. Serviceman or team

F. Delivery means (e.g., high frequency of breakage through one carrier or in-house driver.)

4. *Physical security:* Prenumber credit forms. Keep them under lock and key. If processed by optical scanner or other electronic means, use a code or printing key that will foil forgeries if attempted.

Despite these security measures, credits, when justified, should be issued quickly as a customer/public relations gesture. Furthermore, given the established utility of maintaining a well-purified receivables system, quick execution of identified credit cases will yield the benefits previously described regarding that maintenance. Usually, the trick to getting rapid response and flexibility into a security oriented process is to minimize the number of levels through which the authority must be phased and establishing a daily routine for credit request examination. However, as in other internal control circumstances, too much familiarity among the participants can lead to opportunities for collusion. To help guard against that possibility, more frequent audits and the periodic (say monthly) publication of credit reports to higher management can be employed.

BAD DEBTS POLICY

A certain number of bad debts is a cost of doing business. Prompt decision-making regarding bad debts, when the accounts do, in fact, turn bad, offers these advantages:

1. Reduction in administrative burden.

2. Realism. Receivables aging, receivables turnover, profits and net sales are all affected by write-off *and* by failure to write off.

3. Taxes. Bad debts expense for accrual basis taxpayers is a legitimate deduction. (For cash basis taxpayers, who have not recognized the revenue, the cost of the bad debt is already reflected in their cash-out expenses. If a cash basis taxpayer actually loans money, the deduction can be taken, so long as the other requirements for deduction, discussed below, are met.) Under the tax code, a standard allowance for bad debts can be expensed, even though the specific failed accounts may not be identified at the time the expense is booked. However, the size of the allowance must be reasonable, a quality which is primarily determined with reference to the company's own history. Whether writing off accounts under an allowance or on a specific identification method, the creditor has to essentially establish that the account is totally worthless, not just that collection is unlikely.

Despite these advantages, the decision to write off should not be made in haste, as it often means an end to collection efforts. The decision should be handled in the same way that credits are. Control should be as tight. If the debtor is still solvent, and the debt is written off, no income tax deduction will be allowed.

Note This: *When credits are issued or accounts written off, be sure that the salesman's commissions are reduced accordingly. Ideally, commissions should be based on sales paid and collected.*

CREDIT AND COLLECTIONS SUMMARY

In these last three chapters we've looked at credit and collections from both a macro and micro standpoint. We've seen that effective micro control is most efficiently achieved from a coherent macro policy and set of well-defined procedures. Those hidden dollars in credit operations can be a source of both funds and profits:

1. Credit as a selling tool;
2. Credit extension planning and control;
3. Credit alternatives;
4. Credit monitoring for improving operational efficiency;
5. Expedited collection to speed funds flow;
6. Collection loss minimization.

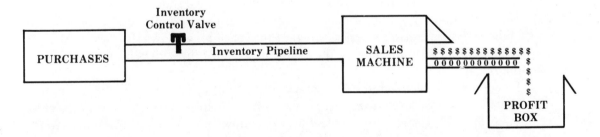

Chapter 6

Seven Ways to Winning Inventory Management

Of all the places a company might look to find funds savings, inventory is always a prime candidate, because it is virtually impossible to run it perfectly. Conversely, it is often a principal cause of business failure, and a very cruel kind of failure at that, because it frequently negates business ideas that are fundamentally well-conceived and needed in the marketplace. The insidious cause of failure through inventory mismanagement occurs when funds are converted into inventory via purchase (or production) in anticipation of sales, but the inventory is not converted back into funds quickly enough.

Picture a "Sales Machine" fueled by inventory:

Too little inventory in the pipeline and the sales machine slows down its dollar output being collected in the profit box. Too much inventory will cause the pipeline to burst, shutting down the machine altogether.

Thus, the inventory question becomes one of how tightly the control valve is manipulated to control the rate of inventory flow. It boils down to a question of timing. The manager has to time his inventory decisions to match the rate of flow to the capacity of the sales machine and, to a lesser extent, the ability of the pipeline to pass along that inventory.

To complicate this question of timing, a consistent conflict exists. On the one hand, there is always the incentive to increase inventory flow to spur growth. On the other hand, many are tempted to clamp down on the control valve to conserve funds.

Few concepts in business management are, in pure theory, easier to grasp, more logical and direct than those in inventory management. And few are as readily distorted by the facts of application.

This chapter leads the manager through:

a. The theory of inventory/funds relationships;

b. The relationship of inventory control to corporate objectives;

c. The pressures created by these relationships; and

d. Principals of practice that permit resolution of the problems created by the pressures and the application of the theory.

THE CONFLICTS

We begin here, because the setting of inventory management often dictates the direction of decisions. As so much of inventory theory and management will be found to embrace forecasting and prognostications (always an uncertain science) the manager who understands the pressures beforehand and remains conscious of them in the decision-making process will be the one most likely to deal objectively and successfully.

Different segments of the corporate population have different goals for inventory:

Sales desires an unlimited inventory, so that it can immediately deliver on every order received. In some cases, the ability to deliver quickly (or just more quickly than the competition) will clinch the sale. Put differently, too long a delay on delivery and the sale is lost. Like credit, then, inventory is a sales tool.

Production desires an unlimited raw materials and supplies inventory, so that its job of production will not be hampered. In many businesses, shortage of a raw material will be costly in production downtime. Production also desires to maintain the flow of finished goods into inventory at a steady pace, whether that pace may be too slow or too fast, as Production would like to minimize adjustments in its scheduling, thereby achieving peak output efficiency.

Procurement is inclined to buy as much as it can at one time to get the maximum discount, the best price and the greatest savings in time, delivery and other costs subject to economies of scale. Hence, Procurement also puts upward pressure on inventory levels. Procurement will also want to avoid the heat that will be generated if sales are lost or production held up because of shortages.

Arrayed against these powerful pressures is the Finance unit, which wants to keep the investment in inventory as low as possible to keep funds free and minimize carrying costs.

POLICY

With these inherent conflicts (exaggerated here, perhaps, but nonetheless real) borne of honest adherence to each unit's mission, the development of inventory policy should not be the exclusive domain of any one unit.

Accordingly, top management has to take a hand as arbiter in policy development and disputes. Naturally, top management should not be biased. To reduce conflict, try these steps:

1. Establish an inventory policy committee comprised of coequal representatives from each affected unit.

2. Have all inventory policies codified in writing and signed off on by affected department heads.

3. Be sure that overall corporate objectives as they relate to inventory are clearly communicated to each department head.

4. To the extent permissible under security guidelines, transmit these objectives and data to lower level personnel, so that they are in concert with the policy and do not unwittingly create pressures for uneconomic change.

5. Review the policies on a regular basis.

6. Allow for a decision path that can override policy in the face of emergency (e.g., the possible loss of a major customer).

7. Avoid dealing in too great detail or developing a cumbersome set of rules and regulations. Keep it general, but meaningful. For example, do not set out a requirement that physical inventories be taken quarterly, but rather that each inventory will be subject to physical count on a scheduled basis, the schedules for which will be determined by finance and inventory control units.

Exclusivity in policy development is often, however, not the first, but the second or third biggest problem of inventory policy. The major problem is that many companies simply fail to articulate any policy at all. As a result, each involved unit will tend to interpret inventory policy to its advantage. If there is no predominantly strong department that can provide at least a consistent direction (even if the direction is not the optimum) the "policy" will tend to change with each new crisis.

A lost sale or two will likely prompt a huge purchase of the stocked-out item so "We'll never run out of *that* again!" Perhaps the same thing happens with production. The finance people, seeing this sudden surge in inventory and concomitant drop in cash reserves, puts on the pressure to hold down spending for inventory — until the next crisis erupts. In a very real sense, the results of this non-policy are random. The stocked-out item may be one that is really critical, or merely peripheral. As varying crises coalesce around different inventory items* the likelihood of a very uneven inventory is high, with some items grossly overstocked and others terribly thin.

POLICY AND FINANCIAL RESPONSIBILITY

In developing a policy, even when using a committee structure, certain phases deserve more input from certain units than at other times. For example, the input of the sales

---

*Throughout this chapter, the term "item" refers to the generic components of stock. The term "inventory unit" will refer to one single piece of inventory from that generic stock. Example: Electric Motors are an item. An electric motor is an inventory unit (or sometimes "unit").

department to policy regarding the taking of physical count should generally be limited to assuring that the counting procedure will not unduly interrupt or hinder sales activities.

Policy development can be divided into these six phases:

1. Budgeting — Cash investment in inventory
2. Content — What is bought for stock
3. Quantity — How much is kept in inventory at a time
4. Order Control — When and how much is ordered at a time
5. Physical Control — Receiving, storage and disbursement
6. Valuation & Reporting — Tracking and measuring inventory, including the interpretation of performance in the other five phases.

The role of the Finance Function in each phase is:

1. *Budgeting*. Finance should be the leader in the macroscopic determination of investment in inventory, as it has the essential role of coordinating inventory funding with the funding of all other operations. The microscopic aspects of budgeting among various items should be determined largely by the priorities for items established by the sales group for resale inventories or by the user group for internal inventories.

2. *Content*. Finance audits inventory content to maintain procurement/production/sales accountability. Write-off and write-down decisions are made primarily by Finance.

3. *Quantity*. Once the budget is set, Finance's principal input as to content will be systemic, in terms of helping to refine inventory management procedures.

4. *Order Control*. Same as Quantity.

5. *Physical Control*. Audit for internal control, security and efficient operation. Systemic input is generally on an ad hoc basis.

6. *Valuation and Reporting*. This is primarily (if not entirely) a Finance responsibility.

The development of the six phases will vary with the *kind* of inventory under consideration. Given the different purposes and circumstances of different inventories, there is no reason that one policy must be universally applicable throughout a company.

For example, valuation and reporting of the shop supplies inventory under parameters established for finished goods is almost sure to be an inefficient use of time, especially when the materiality of the former is likely to be so much smaller than the latter.

Each inventory needs its own policy. That is not to say that the identical policy may not be suitable for more than one, or even all inventories, only that a universal policy not be assumed as mandatory. Furthermore, there may well be cases where one inventory, for policy purposes, ought to be conceptually subdivided into separate inventories in order to accomplish certain objectives. Consider the following illustration.

Consider a distributor of small sailboats. Each year the manufacturer introduces new models, much like the auto industry. Also like the auto industry, these boats are available in a wide variety of colors and with a wide range of optional accessories. Consequently, the distributor wants to carefully control sailboat inventory, so as to fill all potential orders, while avoiding oversupply of a product with a short full-value life cycle.

Our distributor also sells trailers as a complementary product. The trailers can be used on any model-year and style boat. Trailers are almost never sold by themselves, and the great majority of sailboat sales include the purchase of a trailer. Hence, stockouts on trailers can have a disastrous effect on overall sales, as a buyer won't wait for the accessory item if the buyer (who seeks to maximize boating time) can get the object product (the boat) in immediately usable condition elsewhere. The same buyer, however, may be willing to place a particular style boat on order and await delivery.

The priority of *objectives*, and, hence, the policies on the two inventory items, will be different, even though the cost, pricing, margin, physical storage and carrying costs are similar for the two items. The primary sailboat objective is control. The primary trailer objective is sales support.

INVENTORY BUDGETING

Setting limits on inventory is based on three constraints:

1. *Cash*. A company cannot tie up more than a certain amount of cash in inventory without crimping its overall operations.

2. *Physical storage capacity*. Included in this constraint are all aspects of physical handling. The inventory labor force, inventory movement capabilities, warehousing and security systems all have finite limits, which, if exceeded, expose the inventory and/or operations to loss.

3. *Demand (Sales or Usage) Potential*. There is no sense obtaining inventory that cannot be used.

In the short run, the constraint mandating the lowest level of inventory will be the determining constraint.

Assuming a price and market that will yield profits if sales (or other efficient usage) potential is reached, an inventory determined by cash limits or physical shortcomings is not an ideal inventory, as the lower level forces the company to give up profits that could be made. (If the price and market will *not* yield a profit, there is a more fundamental problem at hand than inventory management.)

Thus, in the long run, demand potential should be the determining factor. Cash and physical necessities should be modified to accommodate demand. Inventory budgeting is the process of planning those modifications *and* planning for a level of inventory that will allow the most profitable fulfillment of demand.

Complicating that planning task are these characteristics of the typical inventory:

1. Diversity of content. There is usually more than one item to deal with, and not all items within a given inventory deserve the same priority of stocking.

2. Uncertainty of demand. Planning is a forecasting process that by definition is uncertain, both aggregately and finitely, by item.

3. Diversity of demand. Different end users draw differing items and quantities of items.

4. Diversity of Source. Different items are frequently obtained from different suppliers.

5. Short demand lead time. Rarely will an order be placed that says "Fill at your convenience."

6. Uneven Demand. Peaks and valleys, the appearance of which are generally unpredictable with precision, put varying stress on inventory servicing and investment.

By isolating the constraints and keeping these complicating factors in mind certain policy implications are derivable.

Cash Flow

Once a total budget is determined for inventory (the mechanics of that are coming up later in the chapter) commitments to individual items need be worked out. Rarely, if ever, will all needs be satisfied. By borrowing, it may be possible to stretch to accommodate a larger portion of inventory needs, but the cash limitation remains a real one. What policy implications will help a company more easily tolerate those limits?

To answer that question, first draw the crucial distinction between inventory held for sale and inventory held for use. The use inventory does not generate funds (at least not in a direct sense), whereas the sales inventory is self-renewing as to cash. Thus, increase in demand for a use inventory does not imply the ability to raise the cash constraint as greater sales would imply in the consideration of a sales inventory.

Hence, for a use inventory, funding and budgeting should tend to be more inflexible and restrictive. Every dollar committed to a use inventory is ultimately a dollar out of profit. (Note that inflexibility and restriction are spoken of as a *tendency*. Absolutes carry the danger of obsolescence and unresponsiveness, missing the requirements of changing circumstances and emergencies.)

The real budget cost for a sales inventory, however, is measured by time from expenditure until collection on the sale. (Arguably, the end-point for measurement is to the time of sale, with the costs between sale point and collection a responsibility of credit. From the standpoint of departmental performance measurement and goal determination, such a distinction may have merit. But from the standpoint of strategic planning it does not.) Period to period, then, the budget for a sales inventory will be concentrating on funding growth (or reaping the cash benefit of shrinkage). Therefore, the cash flow constraint is measured by investment in inventory, not expenditure for inventory.

This somewhat subtle point looms large in policy development, for usage inventories are tightly aimed at cost control in most situations. Carrying costs of usage inventories compound the expense effect, creating a more than dollar-for-dollar impact on profitability. The exceptions to those situations should generally be where the inventory items do not require a materially large tie-up of capital but do have a critical role in operations. For example, if a stockout of $2 drive belts will shut down an assembly line, or even one machine, drive belt inventory deserves special treatment. The same could not be said for paper clips in the office supplies inventory.

Sales inventories can be less constrictively managed, as the carrying costs are the only expense. (Write-offs and write-downs for breakage and obsolescence are considered as carrying costs.) Overstocking has a less than dollar-for-dollar effect. Unfortunately, given the relative size of most sales inventories, mistakes will tend to drive a company to insolvency with far more speed than the same mistake made with regard to a usage inventory.

From these facts, it can be further stated that item to item, a company will be inclined to err on the side of overstocking sales inventories, so long as the total investment is within cash limit acceptability. Conversely, it will seek to understock usage inventories to limit costs. Moreover, when considering inventory support, such as the purchase of storage space or equipment, sales inventories deserve priority. Last, when a company is looking for ways to cut costs and conserve funds, it should first look at usage inventories. A surprising number of companies do not even consider the control of such inventories until a crisis surfaces.

Physical Storage

While facilities management and manpower assignments are generally not within the purview of financial officers, an eye should be kept on physical constraints whenever inventory problems arise. Overcrowding, underutilization, shortages of resources may play a role, even a leading one in keeping inventory levels high. A frequently encountered example is that of decentralized inventories serving remote sites with the same items. A centralized inventory will always mean a lower aggregate inventory. Where analysis is needed is in the costs of providing better distribution to eliminate the duplication. In such circumstances, the savings will extend not only to the inventory level, but to the storage facilities and perhaps labor and handling equipment as well. Accomplishing such centralization will usually require a thorough understanding of the operational ends of the affected portion of the business, but the rewards can be mighty. A frequent fallout benefit is better information on inventory levels and conditions, which facilitates distribution accuracy.

Demand Potential

At last we reach the desired determinant, recognizing that the greater the demand for a particular product, the greater the inventory will tend to be. Inventory control is concerned with satisfying that demand through inventory by reference to three essentials:

1. Reorder Points — determination of when to stock;
2. Order Quantities — determination of how much to add to stock;
3. Stocking limits — Maxima and minima for the items.

REORDER POINTS

The typical mathematical model for reorder point for a single item looks like this:

Reorder Point = (Usage/Day) (Receipt Time)

Verbally, the reorder point for any one item equals the daily usage for the number of days between the time the order is placed and received. Most systems will adjust this model by adding some "safety stock" to allow for variance in the rate of usage or reorder time, so the formula becomes:

$$\text{Reorder Point} = (\text{Usage/Day}) (\text{Receipt Time}) + \text{Safety Stock}$$

This system is in general use, but it frequently breaks down because one of the variables is not correctly estimated. Interestingly, most inventory managers will define a breakdown as a stockout. That, however, is only one form of breakdown, and, in the aggregate, not always the most serious one. Overstocking, tying up too much cash and increasing carrying costs, is often a less visible problem, until the total inventory has ballooned to an unacceptable level, which itself is generally defined as the point where cash has run short, because inventory is too high. If half of inventory items are overstocked by a factor of 2 to 1, the total inventory reported to management will be right on target, if the other half of inventory is stocked out! Such a fallacy again highlights the concept of segmented inventory reporting and control.

Returning to our reorder point formula, the inventory variables tend to fail because they are not adjusted with sufficient frequency. As sales programs shift, as prices change, as technology shapes demand, usage will vary. Seasons, the financial condition of suppliers, equipment wear and replacement can all affect the components of the formula. Judgments and perceptions of adequate safety stock size will be colored by circumstances and temporal pressures.

Ideally, the demand will be well forecasted. In the cases of in-house demand, very good forecasting can frequently be achieved. However, even plans of that sort can and do change. When forecasts contain too much uncertainty, or when a method for confirming forecasts is desired, the best way to construct the system is to make it *self-adjusting*

1. Usage is determined in the formula by taking a moving average over some time period. Each time an order is entered (or each day) the average is recomputed.

2. Reorder time is best determined by a daily appraisal of delivery status time, based on contact with suppliers and carriers. The cost of daily communication may, however, be too high. Alternatively then, a moving average of delivery times may be used, or the last delivery time may be included in the formula. Upon each delivery, the new reorder time standard is input into the formula. Intelligent monitoring of the system is required, however, to be sure that an inappropriate time, such as the receipt of an item after unusual delay, does not become the standard.

3. The statistically appropriate safety stock will be the standard deviation of reorder points calculated from the changing usages and reorder times over the time period selected for the moving average calculation of daily usage.

Presenting a mathematical example, assume that daily contact for delivery time is maintained and that the appropriate time interval for calculating the moving average is ten days. These figures are available for the last twenty days, including the resulting calculations and formula output:

-1-	-2-	-3-	-4-	-5-	-6-
DAY	DAILY USAGE	MOVING AVERAGE ORDER 10 OF DAILY USAGE	SAFETY STOCK = STD. DEV. OF DAILY USG	DELIVERY TIME IN DAYS	REORDER POINT*
1	40				
2	51				
3	60				
4	38				
5	36				
6	53				
7	46				
8	49				
9	62				
10	30	46.5			
11	40	46.5			
12	38	45.2			
13	41	43.3			
14	41	43.6			
15	54	45.4			
16	60	46.1			
17	55	47.0			
18	38	45.9			
19	29	42.6	10.5	8	352
20	41	43.7	9.5	7	315

Column Explanations:
1. Self-Explanatory
2. Self-Explanatory
3. Sum of last ten usage figures from column 2 (inclusive) divided by 10.
4. Standard Deviation of last ten daily usage figures (inclusive).
5. Derived from daily contact as separate input figure.
6. Col. 3 Times Col. 5 plus Col. 4

*Always rounded up to next integer.

TIME PERIOD

Throughout the preceding discussion of reorder points "some period of time" was used as a benchmark for calculating the averages. Intuitively, the wrong period of time will yield incorrect results. If it is too short a period of time, the system is making decisions on an incomplete data base. If it is too long a period of time, the system becomes unresponsive, being mired in obsolete information.

Several possibilities for choice of time period include:

1. *Inventory Turnover Period*: Calculated as (Sales/Average Inventory) (365). The logic behind using this period is that it represents a complete inventory cycle. "Average Inventory" is generally the month-end figures summed and divided by twelve for the latest twelve months. If overall inventories tend to remain fairly constant, the latest inventory figure can be used. The disadvantage with this benchmark is that it may perpetuate a less than optional situation. One way to possibly avoid that pitfall is to use budgeted inventory rather than actual inventory in calculating turnover. Forecasted sales may also be used, but if sales diverge widely from the forecast, there is the risk of the entire system being severely compromised.

2. *Average Receivables Age*: Defined in an earlier chapter as (Sales/Receivables) (365). The logic here is that it represents a selling cycle.

3. *Manufacturing Cycle*: The time for a production run on a particular product. To be useful, this interval will generally apply to a raw material inventory item which is a component of a relatively complex finished product.

4. *Selling Cycle*: The time in which a sales force is expected to cover its entire territory, the theory being that all customers' orders will be represented in the calculations, thereby giving an accurate picture of overall demand.

5. *Sales Program Cycle*: The time in which a sales program (e.g., an advertising campaign, sales special, etc.) will run, assuming that such programs are regularly timed and tend to have relatively predictable results and are a major determinant of sales.

6. *Experience Tested Cycle*: From historical data, the interval that tends to give the best prediction of future demand (all viewed with hindsight) as determined by trial and error.

> **Keep This in Mind:** *It is not necessary that all inventory items be measured on the same time period or even using the same method for determining the time period.*

Seasonal and cyclical adjustments can be made by changing the safety stock calculations in anticipation of seasons and cycles.

BUILDING THE BUDGET

Having determined a demand-dictated reorder point inventory level for each item, it is easy to determine the minimum expectable investment in inventory, absent error in the system. That point will be the aggregate of the safety stocks, on the theory that if all the inventory items hit their reorder point in just such a way as to schedule simultaneous receipt for all of them, at precisely the right time; then immediately before that simultaneous receipt, all the items would be drawn down to their safety stocks.

Taking an even more scientific approach, one could refine the minimum investment by allowing a margin for error (e.g., 2%) and testing against some theoretical confidence level (e.g., 95%). In point of fact, few inventories comprised of any significant number of items will ever reach the minimum expectable level, as all of them are not going to be drawn against to the point of precision that yields only safety stocks on hand. Still, the minimum provides a critical starting point for building the budget.

Its corollary, the maximum expectable investment in inventory, is not hard to find either. Switching gears once again to an individual item, its maximum stock will be reached when the new purchase is received into inventory, if orders are standardized and received in full (i.e., no partial deliveries are accepted). If the overall system is right on target, that receipt will occur just when the safety stock level is reached. Therefore, the aggregate of safety stocks plus reorder quantities will equal the maximum expected inventory level.

And how are these standardized (by item) reorder quantities calculated? The typical ECONOMIC ORDER QUANTITY is well-known to most business school students and looks like this:

$$\frac{(2)\ (D)\ (E)}{(P)\ (C)}$$

where D = Demand, in units, for an entire period, usually a year, of which this order will satisfy a part
E = Expenses generated by each order placement (such as personnel time for placing the order, receiving costs, accounting, etc.)
P = Price per unit
C = Carrying charges expressed as a percentage for the entire period.*

The maximum is, like the minimum, a largely theoretical level that will not be reached. Having established these extremes, the actual inventory level, item by item, will fluctuate between these extremes. If sales rates remain constant, the inventory level for each item will develop a kind of harmonic motion pattern, typically referred to as a saw-tooth pattern:

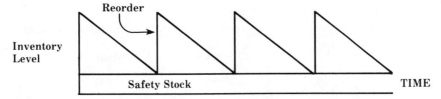

It is easy to assume that the inventory level will average out to the halfway point between the extremes for each item, and that the aggregate halfway point is a good figure for the inventory budget. As a rough approximation it's better than nothing, but a far more refined prediction can be prepared with important ramifications and applications.

The refined assumption considers a normal curve for the entire inventory. Students of the normal curve are aware that the area under the curve represents 100% probability and that the area under any segment of the curve represents a discreet probability. Further, the X-axis is expressed in "standard units" running from −3.9 to +3.9 as follows:

---

*See Johnson, R.W., *Financial Management*, 3d ed. Allyn & Bacon, Inc., 1966 at pp. 144-148 for derivation.

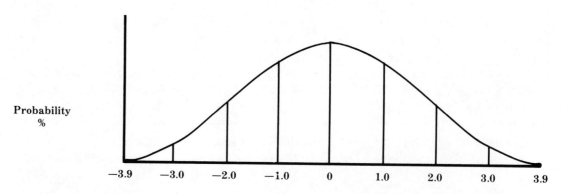

Thus, the areas bounded by the X-axis, the curve and each pair of like standard units comprise the following probabilities:

FROM	TO	REPRESENTS
−1	+1	68.26%
−2	+2	95.44%
−3	+3	99.74%

Working either side of the curve, these probabilities appear as one moves away from the 0 point:

Std. Unit =   0.0   0.5   1.0   1.5   2.0   2.5   3.0   3.5   3.9
% Prob. =   00.00 19.15 34.13 43.32 47.72 49.38 49.87 49.98 50.00

Hence, from −1 to +1 = 2(34.13) = 68.26%

Now, take the X-axis and superimpose the maximum and minimum inventory amounts, assuming the following parameters:

	Minimum	Maximum
$$$	20,000	100,000
UNITS	4,000	20,000

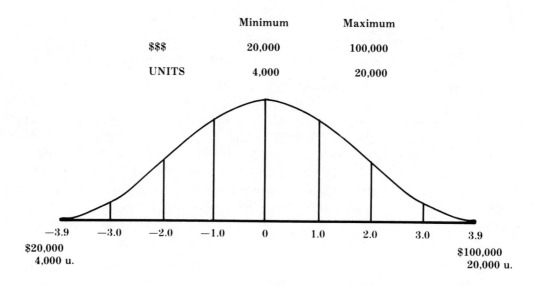

The inventory manager, building an inventory budget, is concerned with the probability of the largest amount of money that would be invested in inventory, tying up the largest amount of money and requiring the greatest handling and storage capabilities at any one time. Say, for example, that our manager in this case is satisfied to accept a 10% chance that the inventory level will exceed his budget, or, in other words, he plans maximum budget requirements at the 90% point on the normal curve.

50% of the 90% is covered on the left-hand (minimum) side of the curve. By moving rightward along the X-axis from the 0 midpoint, 40% of the additional area will be bounded at a point between 1.0 and 1.5 (see table above), from which we can interpolate:

$$43.32\% - 34.13\% = 9.19\%$$
$$40.00\% - 34.13\% = 5.87$$
$$1 + (5.87/9.19)\ (1.5-1.0) = \underline{\underline{1.32}}$$

Therefore, 1.32 is the 90% probability mark along the X-axis. The total distance from -3.9 to $+3.9$ in standard units equals 7.8, and from -3.9 to $+1.32$ equals 5.22, or 67% (5.22/7.8) of the total distance from the minimum to the maximum:

$$(67\%)\ (\$100,000 - \$20,000) + \$20,000 = \$73,600$$
$$(67\%)\ (20,000\ u - 4,000\ u) + 4,000\ u = 14,720\ u$$

Therefore, by budgeting a dollar investment of $73,600 and budgeting 14,720 units, the inventory manager is 90% certain not to exceed the budget while operating the inventory system without bumping against the cash or physical constraints.

> **Caution:** *This approach does not work on an item by item basis, but only for the total inventory, as different items cycle at different points. Each individual item will always fluctuate between its maximum and minimum, reaching both.*

Is the budget acceptable? Can the company afford to have $73,600 tied up in inventory? Can it store and handle 14,720 units of the different items?

If not, how much coverage will the company's capabilities give. For example, if the company can safely afford to tie up $65,000 and 14,000 u in inventory, we can work backwards from the earlier data:

$$\frac{\$\ 65,000 - \$20,000}{\$100,000 - \$20,000} = 56\%$$

$$(56\%)\ (7.8) = 4.4$$

$$4.4 - 3.9 = 0.5$$

0.5 shows 19.15% probability on the chart. Added to 50% (for the interval -3.9 to 0.0) gives coverage of 69.15% for the dollars. Unitwise:

$$\frac{14,000\ u - 4,000\ u}{20,000\ u - 4,000\ u} = 63\%$$

$$(63\%)\ (7.8) = 4.9$$

$$4.9 - 3.9 = 1.0$$

1.0 gives 34.13%, plus 50% equals 84.13%.

If the lower of these probability coverages is not acceptable, the company has two basic choices:

1. Reduce the inventory.
2. Take the necessary steps to expand the budget. If cash is the problem, either borrow, or reduce the budget in other areas in order to provide funds. If physical problems are the prime constraint, facilities need to be expanded.

   Bonus: *This technique has auxiliary benefits for intermediate and long-range planning, as it can highlight future capital and facilities requirements—or surpluses.*

INVENTORY ITEM PERFORMANCE REVIEW

Whether forced by circumstances to keep a lid on inventory, or merely exercising prudent control, every company needs to have a regular program to maintain funds in inventory at minimum levels.

Just as each employee has a performance review at least annually, each inventory item deserves the same scrutiny. The following checklist provides a working format for the item's performance review, with comparative references to:

1. Forecast/Budget
2. Prior Item History
3. Other Inventory Items

ITEM	REVIEW PERIOD'S DATA	STATISTICS
Units on Hand	At month-ends and latest	High and Low and Avg.
Value on Hand	At month-ends and latest	High and Low and Avg.
Cost Per Unit	Latest	Highest
Average Cost	Based on Month-ends	Based on end-points
Usage	Monthly, Yearly	Highs and Lows for Months, weeks and days
Safety Stocks	Month-ends and latest	High, Low and Avg.
Stockouts	Number and time length	Frequency
Deterioration	Yearly	Rate per month and per order
Source Investigation:		
Sources	Current evaluation	Paid to Source
Last Alternative	Results	Paid to Alternate

Ultimately, the review concentrates on inventory item profitability in terms of both percentage of profit and total profitability (i.e., profit per unit times total unit sales). All inventory items should be ranked according to these two measures. That ranking will be used as an indication of which items can be cut in funding, which are candidates for discontinuance and for other related inventory decisions. The ranking may also highlight where operating costs are being uneconomically expended in inventory handling. Performance against prior forecasts and historical data can be used to help confirm the rankings.

The sales department has to provide a good deal of the input to the inventory review. Their forecasts, evaluations of sales potentials and explanations of variances from earlier forecasts are critical to making most of the subjective inventory judgments necessary to an effective program.

Production and Procurement departments' input are equally important to be sure that new forecasts and cost profiles are reliable. Information on technological developments and their application, both substantively and timewise, may have an overwhelming impact on planning.

Every inventory item, at the time of review, is subject to "testing" for discontinuance on these points:

1. *Real Cost*. Total costs, including inventory carrying costs may make the item unprofitable, either on a per unit basis, or on an aggregate basis for the item if certain item-incurred fixed costs are not adequately covered. Of course, new product introductions should be analyzed against a less rigid standard, but a standard of maximum acceptable loss still ought to be applicable.

2. *Opportunity Cost*. An item ranking low in profitability and requiring a new or recurring commitment of funds may not deserve continuance, if the funds could be more profitably employed elsewhere.

3. *Risk Cost*. Uncertainties about a product (in terms of its reaching its sales potential, not exceeding its costs, meeting operating reliability standards, etc.) make the risk of loss outweigh the chances for reward. Under those conditions, the product would be discontinued. Product liability lawsuits have greatly increased the potential for discontinuance (or non-introduction) on this basis.

4. *Substitution Cost*. Lower margined products are "stealing" sales from higher margined ones at an uneconomical rate. For example:

	DELUXE WIDGET	ECONOMY WIDGET	TOTAL
Price/Unit	$10.00	$8.00	
Cost/Unit	7.50	6.50	
GP/Unit	$ 2.50	$1.50	
Sales-Both Sold	100 u.	100 u.	200 u.
$ Profit-Both	$250	$150	$400
Sales-A only Sold	180 u.	-0-	180 u.
$ Profit-A only	$450	-0-	$450
$ Saving Carry	−$50	$100	$ 50
Total A Only	$400	$100	$500

Thus, while unit sales are lower when B is cut out, total gross profit is 20% higher.

5. *Support Cost*. While the product alone may be profitable, it cannot be sold in sufficient quantity (i.e., profitably) without also selling and stocking other products that are not profitable enough, so that in the aggregate the product group falls below acceptable profit standards. Of course, if only part of the supported profitable

product's sales will be lost by phasing out unprofitable supporting products, it would be foolish to discontinue the whole product group. Therefore, each item is still entitled to its own performance review.

INVENTORY CONTAINMENT STRATEGIES

Short of outright discontinuance, there are a variety of less drastic measures that can be implemented to keep inventory levels down. They are best applied to those items that tend to have lower inventory performance rankings, and are used when the overall inventory is nearing or at a level exceeding cash or physical constraints. The advantage over total discontinuance is that these measures can usually be temporary and can be turned on and off with less strain than full discontinuance and restart.

1. **Cut Safety Stocks:** This action will result in more stockouts. Accordingly, deeper cuts should be made in the safety stocks of lower priority items, gradually decreasing the size in the cuts until high priority items are reached, where no cuts should be allowed. If this tool is adopted, care need be taken that stockouts do not become so frequent and widespread as to hurt the corporate image or customer relations on sales inventories or hurt employee morale by frustrating people from carrying out their responsibilities on internal use inventories.

2. **Seek Delivery Speedup:** This tactic can cut the reorder point, thereby allowing items to get by with lower minimums. The costs of such speedups (e.g., purchasing and procurement costs, acquisition of in-house vehicles for greater delivery control) have to be compared against overall savings. Sometimes, closer cooperation with suppliers and carriers can achieve the goal with little cost, as adherence to the supplier's or carrier's optimum operating procedure will give them both the incentive and leeway to expedite.

3. **Drop-Ship:** Rather than stock distributed items, have the manufacturer fill orders by delivering directly to customers. Be sure that the manufacturer and customer will not deal directly and cut you out of the picture thereafter. Similarly, where usage inventories are being received at one location and then internally redistributed, have the supplier ship to each individual location. Beware of suppliers who add extra charges for multiple shipments, although it may turn out that those charges are more than offset by internal redistribution cost and by the savings in inventory expense. Also be sure that the multiple recipients are prepared to check in the merchandise and vouch for the account payable.

4. **Sell on Consignment:** This tactic reduces cash investment, but will not solve a physical constraint problem when acting as consignee. Similarly, as consignor, the cash problem remains unsolved, but the physical storage problem is alleviated. Beware, when acting as consignor, of duplicate costs from returned items handling. Naturally, credit control as a consignor is a major concern.

5. **Stretch Payment Times:** Obviously better payment terms (whether negotiated or seized) reduce cash tied up in inventory.

6. **Priority Purchasing:** When cash is tight or inventory investment high, low ranked inventory items are not restocked on schedule.

7. **Standardize Items:** By making one item serve several needs, stocks can be cut. Engineers and users should be encouraged to eliminate overlapping items. Safety stock duplication is where the biggest saving will be found, as the same demand will generally

reflect itself in higher levels of the standardized stocks. Use this tactic with caution when dealing with sales inventories, as a cutback in the variety of customer options may hurt image and sales.

8. **Negotiate Blanket Purchases with Partial Releases:** By purchasing on a blanket order that allows the company to receive partial shipments, that stock which is being accepted for the purpose of realizing quantity discounts in ordering may be saved. Additionally, the overall price and terms of a contract may be more favorably affected if the supplier knows he is facing a larger and more stable demand. Of course, the other side of that coin is that the buyer need be sure he's not passing up better purchasing opportunities in the future that will be foreclosed by the blanket contracts.

9. **Raise Prices:** If low-ranking items cannot carry their own weight, they deserve to be discontinued. By raising prices, demand will probably decline, requiring a lower inventory level. Price rises may come in several forms, including extra delivery or other charges, minimum purchases, prepayment requirements or other demands on customers. While this is a decision that generally belongs to Sales, instigation by Finance or Inventory Control is an appropriate responsibility.

ACCOUNTING AND VALUATION

No new great theory of accounting for inventory will be propounded here. It is an incontrovertible fact that in the transition from inventory theory to inventory reality, many a soul has been lost in the recordkeeping jungle and the rapids of the information river.

The recordkeeping conundrum embraces both the dynamic side of inventory, which involves control, and the static side involving its valuation for reporting. Once again, we are faced with sometimes conflicting responsibilities and goals.

Accounting for inventory will seek to satisfy these many goals:

1. Control, which has been the primary focus of this chapter.
2. Taxation, which gives the incentive to keep inventory low, moving greater amounts into expense, cutting income taxes and keeping property taxes low.
3. Asset value, which gives the incentive to build up inventory as a component of assets representative of net worth, providing collateral and financial strength.
4. Pricing, which demands an accurate reflection of costs for determining acceptable margins and acceptable products.
5. Administration, which demands a system that is not unduly costly or burdensome to maintain.
6. Reflective of Reality, which means that the system tells what the company really owns, how much it's worth, where it is, what condition it's in and whether or not it's usable as intended.
7. Alerting the company if standards of performance are not met.

For aggregate reporting, the usual methods of CPAs — LIFO, FIFO, Cost or Market, Weighted Average, Percentage of Completion — all have their advantages and disadvantages. It should be the CPA's task to guide the company toward choosing (and, perhaps, occasionally switching) a method for reporting. In carrying through with that method, the company is, of course, dependent on its inventory control system to accomplish the task.

In the management accounting and reporting scheme of things, reflection of reality is the essential consideration. As data comes through the system, the task becomes to respond quickly and accurately. The overall inventory information system and budget that allow for cross checks and flexibility will be most amenable to the task.

EMPHASIZING THE DEMAND CONNECTION

One cannot emphasize enough the importance of demand as reflected in accurate and timely forecast and reporting. The greater the inaccuracies in sales forecasting and reporting, the greater the risk of inventory error.

Weekly, if not daily, review of demand is the first line of defense. As significant variances are detected, the inventory manager is wise to recognize that he controls but one half of the system. The customer who is exercising demand and the salespeople catering to it, control the other half. The inventory watcher therefore has the responsibility to raise possibilities outside the sphere of his direct control. Thus, if inventory is out of whack, it may be that the best way to bring it back in line is to affect demand.

When a salable inventory is having a hard time keeping up with demand, the company may be receiving a signal that price changes are in order. Slumping sales and overstocked inventory may indicate that prices are due for a cut (perhaps with a "sale," "rebate," "special" or other temporary reduction). Any such price change assumes a certain elasticity in demand, the determination of which is up to sales.

> **Avoid This Mistake:** *Refusal to support a price reduction because a loss will be incurred on a slow-moving item ignores the doctrine of sunk costs. What's spent cannot be undone. The appropriate course is to maximize the future, even if it means that an accounting loss is realized over the entire life of the item.*

Once an item becomes troublesome, the goal should be to convert it back into cash. That, in a nutshell, is the crux of inventory management. One seeks to manage the asset from its birth out of cash to its transition back into more cash with a minimum of cost and time. Hence, inventory precision and even the minimization of inventory size are not the real goals of inventory managers. The supreme goal is demand support at least cost. The manager who reaches that goal is the winner. The summary of steps for the winner to take reveals:

1. He watches demand trends.
2. He exchanges information on a regular basis with sales and user personnel.
3. He manages his inventory relative to demand.
4. He keeps the policies flexible, but not marshmallowy.
5. He keeps excellent records and keeps them up to date.
6. He uses these records to test both inventory and sales data and assumptions.
7. He is not consumed by his mistakes.

Chapter 7

Insurance : Essential
Profit Conservation Techniques

Insurance management has three goals relative to corporate financial management. First, insurance coverage must protect the company against a sudden catastrophic drain on funds resulting from a great casualty or liability. Second, insurance coverage should also economically protect against non-catastrophic loss that will crimp operations and decrease profts. Third, insurance management seeks to prompt a safer, more efficient operation that will be less prone to losses.

In considering this topic, recognize that insurance is not a profit producing activity, it is a profit conservation activity. Like most investment activity, varying the investment in insurance will vary the company's risk. As risk deals with uncertainty, the judgment of management as to the kinds and levels of uncertainty the company may safely accept will determine the "proper" amount of insurance coverage and expenditure. With hindsight, it is always possible to know precisely what insurance decisions would have been best. With foresight, no one can be sure. This chapter will relate the goals of insurance to operations, to funds flows and to profits, so that management may make its decisions about the insurance "comfort level" with confidence and without excessive cost.

WHAT INSURANCE COVERAGE?

As different risks surface, the company has to evaluate the threat each risk presents. Relative to that risk, the company must also evaluate the costs to avoid part or all of that risk. Such costs may include not only the insurance premium, but other risk aversion options which will be detailed later.

A logical sequence for evaluating these risks and costs is represented by a flow chart which follows on page 136.

Using the step numbers, we'll pace through a good portion of this chapter, concentrating on ways to cut insurance costs by applying the chart as the outline for a comprehensive review/planning program.

135

INSURANCE

RISK ACCEPTANCE FLOW CHART

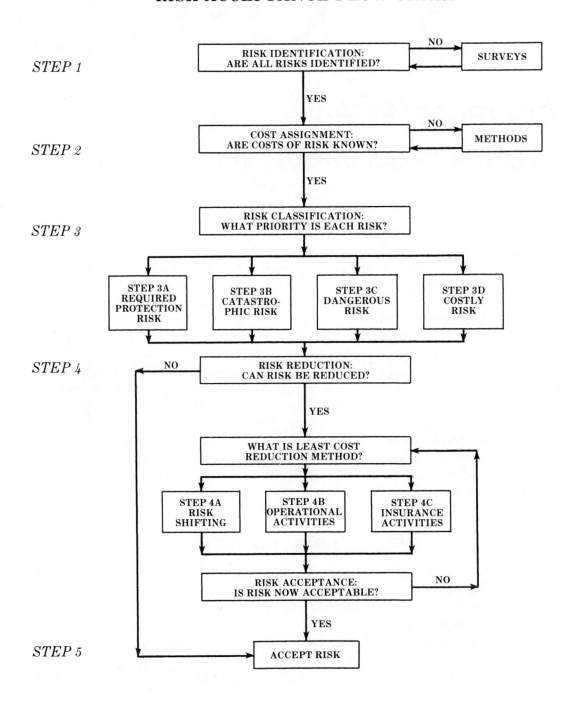

Step 1 — Risk Identification

There are really three reciprocal approaches to risk identification. First, given risks that have previously been identified, we ask "Are they still a threat?" An easy example is the risk of fire to a building which was owned by the company. If still owned, the risk is reidentified as demanding acceptability or control. If the building has been disposed of the risk has obviously terminated. Second, we ask "What risks exist that have been previously dismissed as not threatening, but may now deserve more attention?" For instance, as facilities grow older they may become more accident prone, so that the level of a particular risk demands a greater tolerance for acceptability or an initiative of control. Third, "What new risks have been discovered?" New employee tasks may mean a different level of risk to worker safety.

While conceptually easy, risk identification takes on potentially staggering practical dimensions. Every operation down to the most minute detail can be fraught with risk if the reviewer uses his imagination. For example, in the review of a purchase of land for a new plant site, one might ask "What is the risk that a form of dinosaur is actually hibernating just beneath the ground and may be awakened if construction begins?" Asking questions of that sort is clearly a waste of time and energy. Yet, twenty years ago, in the development of plans for nuclear power plants, should anyone have asked the question "What are the risks of construction delay due to vehement environmental protesters, and what are the costs associated with such delays?" How then does the insurance manager develop identification procedures?

Use a two-phase, five-part survey procedure:

PHASE I:

Part 1: Contact insurors for risk protection areas of recommendation.

Part 2: Review company records for past activities that have similar characteristics for risk similarities.

Part 3: Survey managers involved in the operation/project for their priority listing of identifiable risks.

Part 4: Survey a cross-sample of workers involved in the operation/project for a similar listing.

Part 5: Survey outsiders connected with an operation/project (e.g., consultants, sub-contractors, suppliers) for a similar listing.

PHASE II:

Part 1: Consolidate all the material received from all sources, noting data intercepts.

Part 2: Construct a new list composed of all the prior lists, prioritizing risks by frequency of mention.

Part 3: Resubmit the consolidated list to all original parties for comment.

Part 4: Reconstruct a composite list based on the comments, with appropriate editing.

Part 5: Proceed to Risk Classification. (Step 3.)

A few brief notes about this procedure. The surveys themselves can offer a couple of byproduct advantages:

They can give you a good idea of what insurance coverage is generally available.

They can give an idea of risk-shifting opportunities available through involved outsiders.

They can give an idea of worker concerns, which may be useful in the labor relations activities of the company.

They can make managers more aware of the need for risk control, stimulating care in management planning.

They can also produce these disadvantages:

They may inflame worker concerns.

They many inflame the concerns of outsiders. (N.B. Never undertake customer surveys on this subject without first obtaining the approval of sales and marketing units.

They may intimidate managers.

Therefore, survey planning and implementation cannot be undertaken in isolation. It is not essential to undertake all parts of the survey. The one survey that is critical is the manager survey, as the managers are the one group who will largely determine the success or failure of risk control apart from the activities of the insurance group.

Step 2 – Cost Assignment

Having recognized that a risk exists, what steps can be taken to manage it? These alternatives are available:

1. Reduce the exposure.
2. Insure the exposure.
3. Accept the risk.

In fact, some combination of alternatives will be used in nearly every case. There is a cost incurred in the pursuit of alternatives. Naturally, the risk manager is looking for the least costly and most cost-effective alternative. Reduction of the exposure will take one of these forms with its attendant costs:

a. Increased personnel costs. Example: Worker safety training time to reduce injury and downtime.
b. Incur expenses. Example: Purchase of protective gear for workers.
c. Capital expenditures. Example: Retrofitting machinery to decrease dangerous operation.
d. Foregone revenue. Example: Production line slowdown to decrease injury dangers.

The costs of insuring the exposure will include:

a. Premiums.
b. Management time for evaluation of coverage and insurors.
c. Contributions to self-insurance reserves.

The costs of accepting the risk will be zero if the peril does not occur. If the peril does occur, the costs will be composed of:

a. Uninsured portion.

b. Portion of the insured loss excluded from compensation.

An example: A building worth $100,000 is insured for only $81,000, with an 80% co-insurance clause and a $1,000 deductible. In a fire that destroys the whole building, the first $1,000 is excluded by the deductible. Of the next $80,000, 20% or $16,000 is excluded under the co-insurance clause. The remaining $19,000 is uninsured. Total cost = $46,000 or 36%.

The management question begins to crystallize. What combination of approaches will produce the least cost? The uncertainty is compounded because the cost may prove totally unproductive. Many perils carry a low likelihood of occurrence and if the favored odds turn up, the expenditures are arguably wasted. Most other management decisions involve uncertainty about the *extent* of productivity, rather than the complete absence or presence thereof.

Before the risk can be accepted, the cost of doing so must be compared with the cost of other alternatives, requiring some assignment of cost to the risk. There are several cost assignment methods. These will be illustrated with the following example:

RISK PROFILE

Type: DANGEROUS
Definition: Destruction of Key Parts Plant
Maximum Value Breakdown:
  Building + Contents + Revenue Loss + Management Time = Total
  $450,000 + $200,000 + $300,000   + $50,000   = $1,000,000

The easiest cost assignment method involves simple probability. If there is a subjective ½% chance of loss, then the loss assignment is:

$$(½\%)\,(\$1,000,000) = \$5,000$$

This simple method may be misleading, however, as lesser included risks receive no consideration. In this example, a less serious fire will still incur some costs and is a risk worth reducing by expenditure of some resources. Rather than consider each such risk separately, it would be more efficient to consider all the lesser included risks with the maximum risk.

Most perils carry less chance of the maximum risk than a lesser loss. A small fire is more likely than a bigger one. A fender bender is more common than a total wreck. A minor injury occurs more often than a death. If the loss size can be graphed against the relative risk, a continuum can be developed from which a cost assignment can be derived.

Experience indicates that most such continua are likely to take the mathematical form of an inverse power curve:

$$y = ax^b \qquad \text{or:}$$
$$\text{Risk \%} = (\text{Constant})\,(\text{Loss Size})^{\text{Exponent}}$$

In the ongoing example, assume that some empirical research develops an approximation of the curve for fire losses at the plant of major size, $100,000 to $1,000,000:

$$\text{Risk \%} = (5000)\,(\text{Loss Size})^{-1.00} \qquad \text{or, restated:}$$
$$\text{Risk \%} = (5000)/(\text{Loss Size})$$

The curve looks like this:

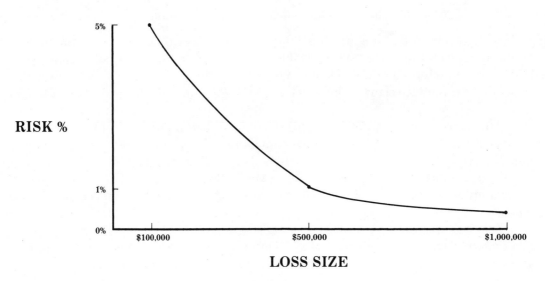

LOSS SIZE

This curve may be called the "Aggregate Risk Curve." If every loss point on the curve were multiplied by the percentage probability of occurrence, the total of the resulting expected values would equal the cost assignment. Theoretically, there are an infinite number of such loss points on the curve. To circumvent that problem, the following mathematical method can be applied:

1. Convert the Aggregate Risk Curve to a straight line using logarithms.
2. Calculate the length of the resulting Aggregate Logarithmic Risk Line by trigonometry.
3. Convert the length of the line segment back to an aggregate loss.
4. Calculate the average applicable percent of risk by end-point averaging of the logarithms and determination of the antilog.
5. Multiply the aggregate loss by the average percentage.

In this example, three points (two to draw a line and one to confirm its accuracy) are calculated by taking the logarithms of the coordinates:

LOSS = (x)	Log (x)	Risk = (y)	Log (y)*
100,000	5.000	5.0%	−1.301
500,000	5.699	1.0%	−2.00
1,000,000	6.000	0.05%	−2.301

(*Logarithm of percentages expressed as decimals.)

Graphing that data:

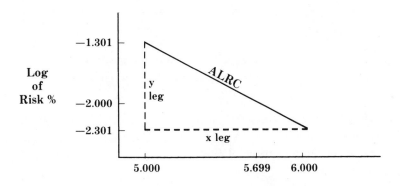

Log of Loss Size

To calculate the length of ALRC, imagine the graph forming a right triangle wherein the ALRC is the hypotenuse. The Pythagorean Theorem states that the length of the hypotenuse is equal to the square root of the sum of the squares of the lengths of the two legs of the triangle. We know, in this example, the length of the legs:

$$\text{“X” leg} = 6.0 - 5.0 = 1.0$$
$$\text{“Y” leg} = (-1.301) - (-2.301) = 1.0$$

Hence, ALRC:

$$\text{ALRC} = (1.0)^2 + (1.0)^2 = 2 = 1.4142$$

Therefore, the ratio of the hypotenuse to the X axis is 1.4142/1.0. This ratio holds for the ALRC itself, so the aggregate risk equals:

$$(1.4142) (\$1,000,000 - \$100,000) = \$1,272,792$$

The average risk is calculated from the average of the logarithmic Y axis endpoints:

$$\frac{(-2.301) + (-1.301)}{2} = -1.801$$

$$\text{Antilog of } -1.801 = 1.58\%$$

Hence, cost assignment based on ALRC is
$$(1.58\%) (\$1,272,792) = \$20,110$$

This cost assignment is complete for the interval \$100,000 to \$1,000,000. For losses under \$100,000, what result?

The interval from \$0 to \$100,000 may be approximated by one or more additional functional equations, each of which will be built on its own empirical data. The same ARC method is repeated and the sum of the cost assignments for all of the intervals yields the net cost assignment. In some circumstances, a single function may define the whole risk. In any event the net cost assignment will serve as the benchmark for resource allocation in defending the risks.

Step 3 – Risk Classification

Having developed an effective method to assess the magnitude of various risks, it will be helpful to classify them by magnitude to set priorities for attacking them. The recommended classification is as follows:

A. **Required Protection Risks** are the special class of risks for which some kind of protective program is mandated by outside forces, thereby requiring the setting aside of some fixed portion of the resources available to the company for risk reduction purposes.

B. **Catastrophic Risks** are those of such magnitude that they can destroy the company's capacity to survive if the full extent of the peril occurs.

C. **Dangerous Risks** are those that could seriously harm the company's financial position. While a single dangerous risk would not mean the collapse of the company, each dangerous risk in combination with one or more additional dangerous risks, could threaten the company's ability to survive.

D. **Costly Risks** are those whose costs will impair profits or assets, but, except in combination of great frequency, will not threaten survival.

Assigning risks to one of these classes is (except, perhaps, for the first) a largely subjective procedure, as is much of insurance management. Note that lesser risks are included in the maximum risk. All or only part of a building may be destroyed by fire. This is a factor that will receive more attention.

There is, by the way, no magic in four classifications. More or fewer may be used if the manager finds it helpful in budgeting resources to protective activities, However, the four classifications here have a logic revealed in Steps 3A through 3D.

Step 3A – Required Protection Risks

Certain insurance and other protective activities are mandatory. Statutes require some, such as workmen's compensation. Contractual obligations may require insurance or implementation of risk reduction procedures. Lenders, for example, may condition their loans on the insurance of collateral. Lessors may limit the area in which leased equipment may be used. Union contracts will lock in certain kinds of insurance coverages and mandate certain safety efforts. Franchises and licenses often include insurance and indemnification provisions.

If the risk under consideration does not fall into a required protection category, we may move on to the next step. However, note that in some cases *part* of a risk may fall into the required class. For example, a mortgagee may demand hazard insurance coverage to the extent of the mortgage, while the remainder of property value becomes, for all intents and purposes, a separate risk. This phenomenon of subdivided risk is to be welcomed, for the ability of management to compress a larger risk into successively smaller manageable segments is the ability to develop acceptable risks.

Step 3B — Catastrophic Risks

Catastrophic risks can put the company out of business in one fell swoop. They do so by wiping out the company's cash. Mathematically, a catastrophic risk is defined in terms of its peril (i.e., the fruition of the risk) as:

$$\text{Peril} > \text{Cash} + \text{Cash Equivalents} + \text{Available Credit}$$

Once identified, catastrophic risks undoubtedly deserve the greatest allocation of risk protection resources.

Of course, the data in the inequality will be constantly changing. What may technically be a catastrophic risk at one moment may be something less at another moment. To make a determination, begin with a one-year time frame. That period is not chosen arbitrarily. The typical insurance policy will either be written for or paid for on a year-to-year basis. Additionally, the year is also the standard forecasting and reporting period.

Searching through that prospective year, find the anticipated low point in the rightward sum of the inequality. That low point will be used as the benchmark, for if the peril occurs at the time when the rightward portion is at the low point, the company will be destroyed. The greater the difference between the sides of the inequality, the higher the priority that must be attached to reducing the risk.

The other difficulty in this inequality is obtaining a reliable denomination of the peril's greatest loss potential. (Within reasonable expectation, of course. Although it is possible that a company auto may be involved in an accident that could set off a chain of events and losses that will ultimately prove catastrophic, judgment must be used to avoid this permutation of the dinosaur syndrome.)

That difficulty is compounded in defining a time period for effective evaluation. For example, the loss of a plant by fire has a direct cost in terms of asset value. However, the cost in terms of impact on manufacturing, sales and opportunity cost may not be so readily measured. This particular example illustrates the important point that we are identifying discreet risks that can be made subject to management action, such as the purchase of insurance. Here, the losses represent two separate risks as far as insurability is concerned, but they spring from one risk as far as management is concerned. One insurable risk is the value of the physical plant, while the second is the business interruption stemming from the hazard.

The example also illustrates that the complete effect of losses has to be traced. The search for critical loss factors will refine risk management objectives. Critical loss factors are those factors of a peril that are responsible for a disproportionately large amount of loss. In this example, the destruction of certain parts of the plant, such as the reception area, will produce little, if any, consequential damage. The critical loss factors in this case revolve around the production line and especially those segments of the line where substitute output cannot be readily purchased or fabricated. Hence, a small fire strategically located may be nearly as deadly as the destruction of a whole plant. These critical loss factors, "risks within risks," deserve special loss prevention attention, beyond the basic goal of preventing any fire in the plant.

Steps 3C and 3D – Dangerous and Costly Risks

These risks receive respectively lower priorities. They are defined by altering the catastrophic inequality as follows:

$$\text{Dangerous Risks: Peril} > \text{Cash} + \text{Cash Equivalents}$$
$$\text{Costly Risks:} \quad \text{Peril} \leq \text{Cash} + \text{Cash Equivalents}$$

Verbally, dangerous risks would force the company to borrow to weather the peril's effects. Costly risks embrace all risks that do not fall into other classes and can individually be absorbed, although it may be cost-effective to combat them. All of the other logic and procedures detailed in the preceding section on catastrophic risks apply to these two classifications.

Step 4 – Risk Reduction

The term "risk reduction" does not necessarily mean the odds of the peril occurring are decreased, but that the risk of loss to be absorbed by the company is ultimately reduced. There are essentially three methods for achieving that reduction:

1. *Risk Shifting:* Placement of another party between the company and the risk.
2. *Operational Activity:* Introduction of operational and procedural methods designed to limit risk.
3. *Insurance:* Acquisition of a guarantee of indemnification in the event of a risk's fruition. (While arguably a form of risk shifting, insurance procedures deserve special focus.)

The order of examining these methods should proceed from the expectedly least expensive.

Step 4A – Risk Shifting

The basic way to shift risk is through contractual arrangement. Agreement that certain losses will be indemnified, in whole or in part, by suppliers, co-venturers and even customers, can be achieved either through negotiation or in a *de facto* way by inclusion of appropriate language in standard documents. In some cases, after-the-fact indemnification may be supplanted by insurance coverage obtained at the cost of the other party. Where such agreement is reached, demand certification of insurance with cancellation allowed only with adequate advance notice to you. The other side of risk shifting is the avoidance of assumption of risk through the same kind of contractual obligation.

The cost of risk assumption and the value of risk shifting should themselves be assessed to determine how high their priority in negotiation or what impact they may have on pricing and purchasing. The ARC method can be used to evaluate the risks. If risks are assumed or cannot be satisfied by shifting away, then those same risks become subjected to this same analysis format.

Step 4B – Operational Activities

The very fact of operations is most often the source of risk. It is the profitable operation of the business that the company seeks to protect against perils. The more cavalierly operations are planned, the more casually they are undertaken, the more likely that their long-run cost will be excessive and, in today's world of frequent litigation and excessive awards, even crippling or fatal.

The other side of the coin is that the cost of prevention should not exceed the danger of the disease. These programs, generally described here, are worth considering as risk reduction *options*, not mandatory undertakings:

1. *Asset Risk Analysis*. Risks are associated with different assets and the costs, as assigned by ARC and costs of reduction, are considered in capital budgeting. Products lacking warranties, safety features, guarantees and a healthy maintenance record will be lower rated. Procurement activities can, in part, control their market by detailing "specs" that include risk reduction features as an integral part of efficiency. (More about this subject in the chapter on Fixed Assets.)

2. *Supplier Risk Analysis*. The wherewithal and reputation of those from whom the company buys is another factor that can influence risk. Frequency and magnitude of supplier related losses have to be recorded and monitored to stay abreast of supplier capability. Keeping tabs on the *supplier's* credit is often a wise move as well, for the company in financial trouble may often be tempted to cut costs by cutting quality. (See the earlier chapter on Credit Extension for evaluation methods.)

3. *Customer Risk Analysis*. The same kind of customer classivication by attribute (industry, size, etc.) as was used in credit management (see earlier chapter) can be applied to loss reduction. Cooperation of credit and insurance departments in credit procedures can pay off here. An obvious application is the product liability area, but other risks associated with production and delivery may also be analyzed in this fashion. Where the customer can be identified as the cause of heightened risk, the extra risk may be compensated for or avoided by:

A. Price increase

B. Warranty reduction

C. Cost (e.g., insurance premium) reimbursement

D. Refusal of sale

E. Product modification

F. Customer indemnification guarantee

4. *Employee Risk Analysis*. Frequency and magnitude of loss again may determine company action. Incentives and raises tied to safety and loss control may be worthwhile. Some companies use bonuses for x number of accident-free work hours. Circumstances may suggest that a work-group's right to bonus be dependent on the performance of all members. Other companies include safety and quality control performance in raise and promotion evaluation. Training, awareness and motivation have to be provided to reduce losses.

5. *Locational Risk Analysis*. While not as readily subject to policy changes and quick-change decisions, greater frequency/magnitude losses associated with particular loca-

tions (e.g., crime areas, earthquake zones, weather loss areas) may influence later business patterns.

6. *Line-of-Business Analysis.* The obvious situation of subsidiary's risk performance or divisional performance will be embraced by this type of analysis. Other more subtle situations may also merit it. Natural disjunctions in operations may offer opportunity for line-of-business analysis: product lines, products and their repair services, manufacturing phases (e.g., production vs. packaging), transportation. Line-of-business analysis may actually encompass the other analyses. Product analysis is included by definition as a form of line-of-business analysis.

The point of all these analyses is to seek ways to cut losses by cutting risks. Consultants and insurors can often pinpoint ways of using these analyses in specific situations to cut losses profitably. Suppliers, customers, and employees can also be a source of the solutions if the problems are accurately identified.

Step 4C — Insurance Procurement

Try as a company might, there is no certainty that losses will not occur. Only so many operational adjustments can be made before a company hamstrings itself. Only so much risk can be shifted to others. Inevitably, some risk must be assumed. When all is said and done, some insurance will be purchased. The trick, as in any other procurement operation, is to get the most quality for the least cost.

Premiums for particular coverages can generally be cut by a number of stratagems. The advantages and disadvantages of these require a careful construction of each finally accepted insurance policy:

1. Higher deductibles mean lower premiums. The drawback to higher deductibles is that loss recovery is guaranteed to be lower. Companies looking at frequent small losses should tread carefully in raising the deductible too far.

2. The greater the percentage of co-insurance, the lesser the premium. Co-insurance and deductibles should be related to each other in arriving at the net potential loss that could be borne by the company. Refer to the building loss example earlier in the chapter.

3. Greater exclusions mean lower premiums. Most standard policies contain established exclusions, which are usually not subject to variation. Nonetheless, where exclusions are optional, there may be a cost opportunity. However, exclusions mean *no* coverage for the excluded risk, so that if the excluded peril occurs, the loss may be too much to bear. It may be that exclusions themselves can be insured for less if handled separately.

4. Insurance procurement alternatives may cut costs. These alternatives include:

A. Direct purchases. Direct contact with an insuror, as opposed to the use of agents and brokers may cut costs.

B. Conversely, the use of brokers and agents may save even more than they cost, especially since they are likely to have a broader grasp of the insurance market.

C. If agents are used, query more than one to be sure you are getting the best policy, not just the one with the best commission structure.

D. Captive Insuror. For large companies, the formation of a captive insuror can be a profitable move. The subsidiary, able to obtain its own financing, acts as primary insuror for the parent. As the bona fide insuror, the sub will have access to the reinsurance market, through which the parent can throw off some of the risk at a cost less than the parent could achieve directly. At the same time, the off-balance sheet (as to the parent) financing of the sub does not impinge directly on the parent's credit lines. Some capital goods companies also use their captives to insure customer purchases of the parent's products. The parent's specialized product knowledge and ready replacement put the captive in a unique intelligence position for underwriting the risk.

E. Captive Agencies. For the smaller companies unable to justify or afford the captive insuror, a relatively less expensive method of forming a captive agency offers some real benefits. The major advantage is the saving on policy costs achieved by retention of commissions by the captive. From a purely financial point of view, if the commissions savings exceed the cost of captive formation and operation (including a reasonable return on the investment) the captive makes sense. Some "soft" advantages, however, include:

   i. Greater clout with the insuror that an agency will generally carry in the event of dispute.
   ii. Ability to assist customers with insurance related to sales of the parent, thereby boosting sales. In addition to casualty insurance during ownership, delivery insurance, product liability insurance and performance bonds may be important areas for the parent's customers where the agency may be able to help out.
   iii. Specialized knowledge and control over insurance that a full time agency will offer.
   iv. Profit center accounting with complete cost and overhead data.
   v. Opportunity for incentive compensation based on savings.
   vi. The potential for diversification of business. The agency may well prove to have the capacity to attract outside business.

F. Syndicated Captives. If your company is too small or otherwise unable to benefit from its own captive agency or insuror, consider forming a syndicate of companies to develop a joint venture captive.

G. Association Insurance. Soaring insurance costs and, in some cases, unavailablity, have impelled many trade and professional associations to expand their insurance programs from the original group health and life into casualty and liability. Insurors enjoy selling through associations as the associations assume a good part of the marketing burden, cutting the cost of sale for the insuror, and the insuror also has the opportunity to obtain fairly dependable diversification in a homogeneous market. Consequently, the rates on such insurance (frequently handled through an agent appointed by the association) are often among the lowest available.

   Tip: *If your association lacks the kind of insurance you need, suggest they look into it. Chances are more than one member will be interested.*

H. Government Programs. The Small Business Association and other agencies offer certain types of casualty insurance (e.g., flood insurance, crime insurance for high-crime areas). Often these policies are the only ones available to cover high-risk situations that private insurors will not underwrite. Some programs do require company qualification. If your company is "small" (as defined by legislation or regulation), "minority owned," in a "disadvantaged area" (e.g., natural-disaster stricken, deteriorating urban environment), a government contractor or subcontractor or a borrower under a federal program or federally guaranteed program, there may be coverages and savings available. A few states also have programs.

I.   Lloyd's of London. Lloyd's is licensed in only the states of Illinois and Kentucky to sell standard insurance. Consequently, most of the business that Lloyd's writes in the U.S. (aside from reinsurance) is so-called "surplus line insurance," which is insurance that American underwriters do not want to take. Lloyd's brokers are paid by Lloyd's out of the premiums paid, so that there is no extra cost in investigating insurance with Lloyd's. Foreign exchange risks, service of suit in litigation against the insuror and financial stability are all guaranteed by the Lloyd's group, which is essentially one large syndicate in which all members stand behind each member to the full extent of personal liability. Lloyd's also maintains its premium account on U.S. business in the U.S., so that funds for claims are readily available. In addition to the advantage of being able to get insurance for unusual risks, Lloyd's offers the opportunity to insure risks that the businessman may not typically think of as insurable. Lloyd's prohibits its members from offering financial guarantees, but the line between insurance and guarantee is a gray one. For example, consider the case of a company that has developed a new technology in a rapidly changing field. The cost of investment in machinery to capitalize on the new technology may be insurable against obsolescence. While projected profits cannot be guaranteed, neutralization of huge losses and the recoupment of cash to reinvest to keep up with the market make innovative thinking a profitable pastime in this market. Multinationals are also likely to find Lloyd's very competitive in non-surplus insurance for risks outside the regulatory reach of the states. It is also worth noting that a Lloyd's-like operation is being launched in New York under the name of the New York Insurance Exchange. This expansion of the surplus line marketplace is likely to increase the activity in that marketplace as more and more companies discover risks and ways to classify risks that deserve insuring.

J.   Self-Insurance Program. In its simplest sense, self-insurance is the retention of risk and the concomitant absorption of losses. Deductibles, co-insurance and exclusions are forms of self-insurance. Simple failure to purchase insurance amounts to self-insurance by default. However, a self-insurance *program* is the retention of risk with a specific plan for funding losses. Losses are funded either in advance with the establishment of a self-insurance reserve into which payments are made, much in the nature of premiums, or losses are funded after-the-fact with payments made against moneys borrowed to cover the loss. The advantage to prefunding is that the money is still within the company's grasp. No commissions or other expenses are involved. However, under present law, no tax deductions are allowed for payments into a self-insurance fund.

Point to Remember: *Self-insurance makes no sense for a company with a few centralized risks. If a loss occurs, the blow may be too devastating before the company has a chance to build up a sufficient reserve.*

Step 5 — Risk Acceptance

If the level of risk still seems too great after these efforts, cycle through the flow chart again. Sooner or later, an acceptable level of risk will be achieved. In economic terms, that point will be where the marginal dollar for risk reduction cannot produce at least a one-for-one-plus savings in risk cost. In both initial and subsequent cycles, insurance agents, brokers and consultants may be able to offer suggestions that can further reduce exposure and costs.

After all is said and done, insurance and risk management is at best an uncertain science. If too many losses occur, if not enough insurance is obtained, if the wrong kind of insurance is purchased, the results can still be destructive. But at least a carefully thought out and balanced approach can minimize the risks, keeping them in perspective and thereby allowing the company to pursue its regular operations without either playing fast and loose or hamstringing profits with exorbitant risk prevention.

Chapter 8

Seven Ways to Systematize Fixed Assets

The principal involvement of the financial manager in fixed asset control is in acquisition and disposal. Accordingly, this chapter is built around a framework of an effective decision-making system on these points, including consideration and comparison of alternatives to outright purchase. Last, it explores effective monitoring and conservation methods to ensure the full realization of asset utility potential.

ACQUISITION FORMAT

A systematic approach to asset acquisition permits a reasonable comparison among asset choices, because all can be measured against the same standards. Outlining the steps in the system:

    I.   Determine Asset Objectives
   II.   Classify Assets
  III.   Collect Asset Costs
  IV.   Project Asset Benefits
   V.   Project Asset Operating Expenses
  VI.   Project Disposition Impacts
 VII.   Calculate Net Benefits

ASSET OBJECTIVES

Assets are normally acquired not for the sake of owning them, but for the utility they provide. The root motivation for owning a drill press is the holes it makes in this or that raw material. If the holes would materialize on their own, drill presses would be unnecessary.

151

To the extent that utility is quantifiable, the task of determining relative profitability among asset choices is that much easier. Implicitly, then, profitability on investment in assets is ordinarily the prime objective. The configuration of that profitability may make it difficult to identify, and, therefore, companies might be led (or even misled) toward skewing asset purchases to only those assets that produce "hard" (i.e., specifically measurable) benefits. For the experienced manager with a gut instinct for his operations, the identification difficulty can be not only frustrating, but also costly to his company in terms of lost opportunity. Hence, we will seek to develop a procedure for analyzing and comparing seemingly disparate investment choices.

ASSET CLASSIFICATION

For these purposes, we can identify three fundamental classes of assets:

A. *Productive Assets:* Defined as those amenable to strict input-output accounting. They throw off tangible, measurable benefits and have no meaningful intangible benefits apart from the tangible ones. The tangible benefits are stated in terms of dollars of marginal revenue attracted or marginal costs saved. The pristine example is a production line machine.

B. *Booster Assets:* Defined as those which throw off tangible, measurable benefits like their productive cousins, *but* which also yield recognizable intangible benefits. An example of a Booster Asset would be a corporate jet. A private plane obviously saves money that might otherwise be spent on transportation alternatives like commercial air travel. The savings may or may not be as great as the cost of operating the private airplane. That's the tangible benefit. The intangible benefit is the boost to efficient use of management time as demonstrated by greater scheduling flexibility, executive comfort, prestige, morale and privacy. Such intangible benefits almost certainly deserve some consideration in asset evaluation, but a decision based on thinking like "It'll make the boss happy" isn't evaluation, it's speculation.

C. *Convenience Assets:* These assets yield no material tangible benefits, but do provide strictly intangible benefits. A classic example is a conference room chair. No doubt, people can meet, think, talk and decide either standing up or sitting down, but a conference room without chairs is just plain unthinkable.

VALUE ASSIGNMENT

These classifications are useful for developing a management perspective on asset acquisition. In few cases will a corporate jet save more in airline fares than is spent in operating costs. But, if straight tangible benefits are to be the only benchmark for decisions, no one need spend time considering airplane acquisition.

Where the assets involved are Booster or Convenience Assets, tangible benefits should be the point of departure to valuation of intangible ones. These values necessarily involve some subjective reasoning, but subjectivity, if appropriately disciplined, makes them no less real. Let's examine three specific cases, one from each asset class for a mythical chemical manufacturing operation.

Our subject Productive Asset is a new mixing machine. By putting it to use with existing tanks and related equipment, the company can speed up production, adding two production runs per day to the present standard of eight per day, with no increase in labor, energy usage or other semi-variable expenses. If the average gross margin per run (among the various chemical products) is $500, the value of the machine's benefits is $1,000 per day, or $250,000 per year (assuming 250 work days per year). Hence, annual benefits (not *net* benefits) are just $250,000 as there are no intangible benefits available here.

The Booster Asset under consideration is a computer to be dedicated solely to management reporting. The company already has a medium-sized computer in place for payroll, accounting, inventory control and other basic operating applications. However, real time constraints prevent the computer from producing all of the desired management reports in a timely routine fashion. As a result, many of the reports are done by hand, while others are curtailed in scope or completely dispensed with. The new computer will replace two clerks, saving $25,000 in payroll and fringe costs annually. At the same time, a poll of the managers (one innovative way to evaluate assets subjectively) indicates that with all of the desired reports timely delivered, they anticipate a 5% increase in their own efficiency and a 2% savings in overhead costs on a gross basis; i.e., without regard to the costs engendered by the computer itself. These subjective observations are quantifiable. We'll assume that the mathematics show the value to be $181,000. Total benefits are therefore:

Tangible	$ 25,000
Intangible	181,000
	$206,000

Try This Refinement: *Get three estimates—"best case," "expected case" and "worst case"—and run three evaluations to get a wider view of the possibilities, the risks and the rewards.*

The Convenience Asset to be evaluated is an effluent control filter. No tangible benefits are derivable. It adds nothing to productivity. It is strictly a matter of social responsibility. Subjective benefits, in terms of image, morale and public relations are pegged at $150,000 on a one-shot basis. After the filter's in place and the fanfare has died down, it's likely to be forgotten. Determining these benefits might be accomplished using a comparative cost analysis, which would ask what amounts would have to be expended to obtain the same publicity (e.g., advertising expenses), produce the same employee morale (e.g., additional fringe benefits) and the same sense of responsibility (e.g., by charitable contributions). Some assistance may be needed from advertising, public relations and personnel departments to develop the data, but that development's subjectivity can itself be limited. For example, the number of people that will be reached by press releases and attendant publicity is translatable into advertising dollars. Personnel's experience may allow it to estimate with some precision the savings in turnover that might otherwise result among conscience-stricken employees.

We have now succeeded in assigning value to the benefits to be generated from each of the three proposed assets. Now, by calculating the costs associated with the generation and ranking the assets on a net basis, we can turn our subjective conundrum into an objective decision.

Before analyzing costs, two nuances of value assignment are worth discussing. One of these is the concept of avoidance value, the other is contingent value.

Suppose that in regard to the effluent control filter, corporate counsel advises that proposed environmental regulations would subject the company's officers to criminal prosecution if effluent is not filtered. The *avoidance* of that risk has a value. Elimination of a negative occurrence is just as includable in benefits as a direct cash inflow.

This example also demonstrated contingent value. If the proposed regulations are not adopted, then the avoidance value is zero, as the risk is preempted. How is that uncertainty to be handled? The issue is very much like an insurance problem: What's it worth to avoid the risk? That's contingent value and it may be evaluated subjectively or statistically. (See the chapter on Insurance.)

The sum of direct value, contingent value and avoidance value (any of which may be zero in a particular case) is the total value against which costs are to be compared. Parenthetically, if there is such a thing as negative benefit, it is probably more appropriately considered with costs.

> **Point to Remember:** *Too many projects justified on non-financial bases can lead to financial problems. Value assignments are worthy of the most vigorous scrutiny when choices are being made among a group of profitable investment alternatives. In any event, capital expenditures should always be made within the framework of cash and operating budgets.*

A checklist of utility benefits may be helpful as a means of initiating value assignment consideration:

Cash Flow	Product Differentiation
Morale	Productivity Improvement
Publicity	Share Price Improvement
Earnings	Appreciation Potential
Liquidity	Stockholder Relations
Public Relations	Regulatory Compliance
Advertising Value	Customer Relations
Capital Conservation	Political Clout
Safety	Employee Relations
Early Purchase v. Inflation	Legal Precedent
Image Enhancement	Market Development
Union Avoidance	Employee Development

COST ASSIGNMENT

Generally speaking, costs will be of four types:

A. *Acquisition Costs:* Defined as all those expenditures necessary to get the asset into operation. Frequently, some of these costs are overlooked in the prepurchase evaluation stage, so this short checklist is provided:

Ordering Costs	Receiving Costs
Purchase Price	Delivery Charges
Sales Tax	Preparation Costs
Licensing Fees	Interest on Deposits
Registration Fees	Operator Training
Installation Costs	Start-up Supplies Purchases

Operating Tip: *Evaluate acquisition costs of completed acquisitions from time to time and keep a list of the different kinds of expenses discovered for future purchase evaluation.*

B. *Carrying Costs:* Defined as those costs associated with retention of the asset, without regard to the costs of actually operating the asset. In other words, carrying costs are the fixed costs associated with possession and/or ownership of the asset. Examples include:

Interest on Debt/Lease	Storage Costs
Facilities Costs	Insurance
Property Taxes	Security Expenses
Depreciation (More on this particular item later)	

C. *Operating Costs:* Defined as the recurring input of costs to yield a productive output from the asset. These costs encompass such items as:

Supplies	Operator Labor
Maintenance	Repairs
Warranty Costs	Utilities (Electricity, etc.)
Inventory Input	Management Time

D. *Disposition Costs:* Defined as those costs incurred to divest an asset.

When assigning costs, follow these standards:

1. Document the assumptions underlying *each* cost. Nothing is so tragic as a beautiful analysis containing a flawed assumption, as a result of which the wrong result is precisely arrived at.

2. Consider the likely range of costs. Ideally, analyses can be performed by or at least supplemented by computer to simulate results throughout the combinations within the ranges of all costs. But even if only a simple "best estimate" is used, consideration of the limits of the costs in the assumptions stage of the analysis will likely sharpen the estimates.

3. Have several people make independent estimates. Pool and compare them to thrash out the best results.

   Warning: *It's best to have all of the participants at the same level in the organization, to guard against undue weight being given to the estimates of more highly-placed participants.*

4. Compare estimates to historical figures for similar projects undertaken in the past.

5. Make comparisons to a variety of projects, not just one that seems to be on point—in case it's not.

6. In the course of assigning costs, keep a sharp eye out for ways to reduce them.

ASSET EVALUATION

Once all of the costs and benefits are identified, several measures of productivity can be applied to rank and compare the assets. Which measure or measures deserve the most attention depends on the company's circumstances.

The departure point for these measures is differentiating between earnings and cash flow as the principal objective. Every company must be concerned with the cash flow ramifications of an investment, but earnings may be of secondary importance for a private company and probably not at all meaningful for the nonprofit institution. Furthermore, public companies with large amounts of stock outstanding may not be particularly concerned about earnings in relation to purchases and investments that are not large enough to have a material effect on per share earnings.

On either a cash flow or earnings basis, these standards can be calculated to rank differing investment options:

Payback: This method calculates the time to recover the capital expenditure. For example, a $9,000 machine that yields $2,000 per year has a payback time of

$$\$9,000/\$2,000 = 4.5 \text{ years}$$

If the $9,000 machine yielded this schedule of returns:

Year:	1	2	3	4	5
Return:	2,000	2,000	2,000	2,000	3,000

Payback is calculated by determining the year in which cost is fully recovered, prorating the return of the last year:

Cum Return	2,000	4,000	6,000	8,000	11,000
Unrecovered	7,000	5,000	3,000	1,000	NA

$$\text{Payback} = 4 \text{ years} + 1,000/3,000 = 4.33 \text{ years}$$

> **Point to Ponder:** As the purchase of an asset does not ordinarily result in an immediate charge against earnings, is Payback a meaningful earnings statistic? Probably, it is just useful as a cash flow measure.

The deficiency of Payback is that it tells nothing of final profitability. It only assures that the status quo can be more or less resumed. It is, however, a technique that is of great importance to companies that are operating under severe cash constraints and/or have very limited access to additional capital.

Lifetime Cumulative Return (LCR): Total return over the useful life of the asset is divided by the original cost of the asset. (Cost in this sense includes all costs of acquisition capitalized and not considered matched to revenues.) Take a $3,000 asset with this schedule of net returns over the asset's six-year life:

Year:	1	2	3	4	5	6
Return:	500	0	0	1,000	2,000	3,000
Cum Return:	500	500	500	1,500	3,500	6,500

LCR Index: Cum Return/Investment = 6500/3000 = 2.17

This index can be mathematically manipulated to also provide an LCR increment which shows the increase in assets resulting from the investment:

$$2.17 - 1.00 = 1.17$$

which carried further can be expressed as an average annual return on the initial investment:

$$1.17/6 \text{years} = .195 = 19.5\%$$

LCR is most useful for comparison among assets with similar lifespans, where the company is concerned primarily about its position at the end of the life span, without great interest in its circumstances during the interim. In other words, LCR considers overall profitability, but it lacks sensitivity to timing. For example, would anyone prefer a $3,000 machine that will produce $100,000 of return 100 years from purchase, but will produce nothing in the intervening 99 years, to another machine for the same price that will yield $6,500 in six years? Probably not, but given only an LCR Index they'd be hard pressed to discern the difference.

Present Value LCR: PVLCR utilizes essentially the same concept as LCR, with the added calculation of discounting the future returns using the classic present value formula:

$$\frac{X_n}{(1 + i)^n}$$

where: X = Return in Year n; and
      i = Discount Rate.

Look again at the same $3,000 machine with the six-year life span:

Year:	1	2	3	4	5	6
Return:	500	0	0	1,000	2,000	3,000
Pres. Val. @ 10% Discount	455	0	0	683	1,242	1,693
Cumulative Present Value	455	455	455	1,138	2,380	4,073

PVLCR Index: 4,073/3,000 = 1.36
PVLCR Increment: 1.36 − 1.00 = 0.36

The average annual return under PVLCR is calculated a little differently:

0.36/6 = 0.06 = 6% + Discount Rate = 6% + 10% = 16%

The discount rate is added back, because the total return in any year has been reduced in the calculations by the implicit cost of money, i.e., the discount rate. Therefore, to arrive at the total return for any one year, the discount rate must be added back in.

PVLCR intrinsically accounts for an estimated cost of the capital used in the acquisition of the asset. PVLCR also tends to be most useful when comparing assets of similar life spans or when seeking to determine the company's position at a particular time (e.g., 5 years from now) with different asset purchases.

The deficiency of PVLCR is that a particular discount rate has to be assumed. Guess wrong and the integrity of the analysis suffers. The last method corrects this deficiency by determining a maximum acceptable cost of capital.

Internal Rate of Return (IRR): The other substantial benefit of IRR is that it provides a basis for comparing any assets. Differing costs, differing lives, differing schedules of returns are all reduced to a least common denominator—which can accept the highest cost of capital, which is the obverse of saying productive of the highest rate of return. It is calculated using a variation of the Present Value Formula:

$$C = \frac{X_1}{(1 + i)^1} + \frac{X_2}{(1 + i)^2} + \ldots + \frac{X_n}{(1 + i)^n}$$

where: C = Original net capitalized cost of asset; and

X = Return in each year (but not necessarily a constant, or, for that matter, not necessarily even positive in each year); and

n = Last year; and

i = Internal Rate of Return,

and i is the variable solved for. Without a specialized calculator or computer, i is ordinarily calculated by trial and error.

Methods Summary: All four of these methods tend to have a bias for cash flow as the determinant of asset preference, because the calculations made using the capitalized asset cost versus earnings returns is arguably mixing apples and oranges. The vagaries of accounting for earnings do not necessarily reflect real productivity, which must ultimately be measured in terms of cash.

Nonetheless, it is worth noting that where the asset is a project involving a charge against earnings, these four methods are certainly applicable. For example, the costs of conducting a training seminar for factory line productivity is much like the purchase of the asset, while the savings or incremental earnings are very much in the nature of comparable returns.

ORGANIZING THE ANALYSIS

To allow management to see the whole picture and permit rankings on all four measures (if desired), all of these elements have to be considered:

Inflows (Cash Flow)   Taxable Profits
Outflows (Cash Flow)   Taxes
Revenues (Earnings)   Net Cash Flow
Expenses (Earnings)   Timing of Transactions

To accommodate all these factors a Time Matrix Statement is used calculating the incremental earnings, tax effects and cash flow resulting from the asset. The accuracy of the Statement is a function of accurate identification of the revenues, expenses, inflows and outflows that will result only because of the purchase of this asset and will not result if this asset is not acquired. The Statement is formatted like this:

```
                         TIME MATRIX STATEMENT FORMAT

Periods                             0    1    2    3 . . . . . . . . n   n Periods Totals
Earnings:
List Revenues: R1
               R2
Total Revenues:

List Expenses:
Acquisition Costs (excludes those capitalized)
Carrying Costs
Operating Costs
Disposition Costs
Total Expenses

Pretax Net Earnings
Income Taxes
After Tax Net Earnings
Cumulative After Tax Net Earnings

Cash Flow Adjustments:
List Cash Inflows: CI1
                   CI2
Total Cash Inflows

List Cash Outflows:
Acquisition Costs (includes those capitalized)
Carrying Costs
Operating Costs
Disposition Costs
Total Cash Outflows

Net Cash Flow Adjustments

Net Cash Flow
Cumulative Net Cash Flow
Present Value Net Cash Flow @ i%
Cumulative Present Value Net Cash Flow
Internal Rate of Return
```

The Statement's second half dealing with cash flow adjustments is not meant to repeat costs or revenues accounted for in the first half, but to reflect adjustments to the first half, even though the expense category nomenclature is repeated. For example, carrying costs might include property taxes, which would be recognized on an earnings basis when due and paid. However, on a cash flow basis, advance property taxes might be paid into an escrow account held by a secured lender, thereby giving a different cash flow result from the earnings result. Similarly, insurance premiums will ordinarily be capitalized and amortized, although all the cash goes out at one time.

The Statement can be recalculated to consider various levels of benefits. It can range from the most conservative evaluation that credits only tangible certain benefits, to the most generous evaluation that considers all benefits, tangible and intangible, contingent and non-contingent.

To demonstrate the use of the Statement, we'll look at the three assets discussed earlier, although a few of the assumptions will be changed to illustrate some finer points. The three examples will all consider all of the potential benefits, thereby exhibiting the most generous results.

MIXING MACHINE (000's) EXAMPLE #1

Periods:	0	1	2	3	4	5	6	7	8	9	10	Totals
Earnings:												
Revenues:												
Gross Profits		250	250	250	250	250	250	250	250	250	250	2,500
Salvage Sale											50	50
Total Revenues		250	250	250	250	250	250	250	250	250	300	2,550
Expenses:												
Acquisition Costs		15										15
Carrying Costs		100	91	82	72	63	53	43	34	25	15	578
Operating Costs		15	17	13	15	16	19	20	25	26	29	195
Disposition Costs										5	5	10
Total Expenses		130	108	95	87	79	72	63	59	56	49	798
Pretax Net Earnings		120	142	155	163	171	178	187	191	194	251	1,752
Income Taxes (55% Rate)		66	78	85	90	94	98	103	105	107	138	964
After Tax Net Earnings		54	64	70	73	77	80	84	86	87	113	788
Cum After Tax Net		54	118	188	261	338	418	502	588	675	788	
Cash Flow Adjustments:												
Inflows:												
Addback Depreciation		91	82	73	64	55	45	36	27	18	9	500
ITC Tax Savings*		50										50
Total Inflows Adjs.		141	82	73	64	55	45	36	27	18	9	550
Outflows:												
Acquisition Costs	500											
Net Cash Flow Adjs.	(500)	141	82	73	64	55	45	36	27	18	9	50
Net Cash Flow	(500)	195	146	143	137	132	125	120	113	105	122	838
Cumulative Net CF	(500)	(305)	(159)	(16)	121	253	378	498	611	716	838	
PV Net CF @ 12%	(500)	174	116	102	87	75	63	54	46	38	39	295
Cum PV Net CF @ 12%	(500)	(326)	(210)	(108)	(21)	54	118	172	218	256	295	
Internal Rate Return	Neg	Neg	Neg	Neg	Neg	9.9	16.6	20.7	23.2	24.9	26.0	26.9

*ITC = Investment Tax Credit

MANAGEMENT COMPUTER (000's) EXAMPLE #2

Periods:	0	1	2	3	4	5	Totals
Earnings:							
Revenues:							
Costs Savings		25	25	25	25	25	125
Salvage Sale						50	50
Intangibles		181	181	181	181	181	905
Total Revenues		206	206	206	206	256	1,080
Expenses:							
Acquisition Costs		45					45
Carrying Costs		234	154	105	87	86	666
Operating Costs		83	84	69	70	71	377
Disposition						50	50
Total Expenses		362	238	174	157	207	1,138
Pretax Net Earnings		(156)	(32)	32	49	49	(58)
Tax Savings (Costs)		86	18	(18)	(27)	(27)	(32)
After Tax Net		(70)	(14)	14	22	22	(26)
Cumulative A.T. Net		(70)	(84)	(70)	(48)	(48)	(26)
Cash Flow Adjustments:							
Inflows:							
Addback Depreciation		200	120	72	54	54	500
ITC Tax Savings		33					33
Total Inflows		233	120	72	54	54	533
Outflows:							
Acquisition Costs	500						500
Net Cash Flow Adjs.	(500)	233	120	72	54	54	33
Net Cash Flow	(500)	163	106	86	76	76	7
Cum Net CF	(500)	(337)	(231)	(145)	(69)	7	
PV Net @ 12%	(500)	146	85	61	48	43	(117)
Cum PV Net @ 12%	(500)	(354)	(269)	(208)	(160)	(117)	
Internal Rate Return	Neg	Neg	Neg	Neg	Neg	Neg	

EFFLUENT CONTROL FILTER (000's) EXAMPLE #3

Periods:	0	1	2	3	4	5	Totals
Earnings:							
Revenues:							
Tangibles							-0-
Intangibles Certain		150					150
Intangibles Contingent		100	100	100	100	100	500
Total Revenues		250	100	100	100	100	650
Expenses:							
Acquisition Costs							-0-
Carrying Costs		130	130	129	129	129	647
Operating Costs			2	2	2	2	8
Disposition Costs							-0-
Total Expenses		130	132	131	131	131	655
Pretax Net Earnings		120	(32)	(31)	(31)	(31)	(5)
Tax Savings (Cost) 55%		(66)	18	17	17	17	3
After Tax Net Earnings		54	(14)	(14)	(14)	(14)	(2)
Cum After Tax Net		54	40	26	12	(2)	
Cash Flow Adjustments:							
Inflows:							
Addback Depreciation		120	120	120	120	120	600
Outflows:							
Acquisition Costs	600						600
Net Cash Flow Adjs.	(600)	120	120	120	120	120	-0-
Net Cash Flow	(600)	174	106	106	106	106	(2)
Cum Net Cash Flow	(600)	(426)	(320)	(214)	(108)	(2)	
PV Net @ 12%	(600)	155	85	75	67	60	(158)
Cum PV Net @ 12%	(600)	(445)	(360)	(285)	(218)	(158)	
Internal Rate Return	Neg	Neg	Neg	Neg	Neg	Neg	

Refer to the examples as these points are covered:

1. The period number is also the exponent used in the present value calculations. Thus the purchase of the asset at time "0" is assumed to set the chain of events in motion.

2. In Example #1, the categorization of "Gross Profits" under revenues relates to the incremental gross profits derived from installation of the machine. Think of its treatment here as net revenue. Alternatively, the incremental sales and direct costs could have been listed (with the costs appearing under operating costs). It may simplify matters to work with the net figures where they are readily calculable.

3. Salvage Sales in Examples # 1 and #2 are treated as a revenue, because a corporation will treat the sale of fully depreciated salvage as ordinary income (according to present tax law), just like other revenues.

4. ITC stands for Investment Tax Credit, which is shown as an inflow, since it assumedly reduces taxes. Were the projects undertaken by a company without tax liability, or by one with liability sufficient to absorb only a part of the credit, the results would be shown in the years in which they were finally realized, if realized (and shown) at all. Hence, an overall idea of the company's operating picture must be available to make best use of the technique.

5. Depreciation is included among carrying costs in expenses and is later added back as a cash inflow adjustment, as well, to reflect the tax saving it produces. The same limitations relative to overall tax liability apply as with ITC above. In these examples, depreciation was calculated using "Sum of the Years Digits" in Example 1; "Double Declining Balance" in Example 2 (switched to Straight Line in Year 4); and "Straight Line" in Example 3.

6. The 55% tax rate is the sum of all rates—federal, state and local—as applicable. Where assets are taxed based on location, or the allocation of income for tax assessment purposes are based on location, the applicable tax rate may be adjusted for the anticipated placement of the asset. Additionally, if the rate is expected to change over time (e.g., the company anticipates moving into different brackets or expects changes in applicable rates or laws), the tax rate applied might not be a constant.

7. In these examples, it is assumed that tax benefits are realized during the transaction year, as quarterly estimated tax payments are affected by the asset's results. If the impact would not be realized until later (say, for example, via carry-forward of the ITC) the figures would show up in the column for the year in which the cash would be realized or net earnings impacted.

8. These examples have not listed all of the individual components of revenues, costs, inflows and outflows. Doing so may be desirable to aid the analysis and permit more attention to cost control. If not listed in the Statement they should be contained in detail in a back-up document.

9. The discount rate used to calculate present value has been held steady in these examples, although it is possible to vary it on a year-to-year basis if the applicable cost of money is expected to vary *and* can be reasonably estimated.

10. Present Value and IRR calculations are here made discounting the transactions in each entire year, as if they all occurred exactly one year from the date of asset acquisition. Of course, transactions will occur over the course of the year, and some analysts may therefore prefer to knock one-half off each exponent (by subtraction) in the formulae, so as to discount the transactions at the midpoint of each year, thereby "averaging" the influence of the transactions.

11. These analyses also consider each year discreetly, implying that acquisitions of assets occur only at the very beginning of the year. Of course, that's not practically true. Therefore, the transactions that occur in the remainder of the first year might be separated and discounted as a single period (with an exponent of x remaining months, e.g., 9, divided by 12 months per year an exponent of .75). Succeeding full years would then be discounted by integers plus the fractional exponent.

Example: Periods: 0   .75   1.75   2.75 . . . . . . .n .75

This refinement may be particularly important where effective tax rates are expected to change after the year of acquisition.

12. Internal Rate of Return calculations appear for every period, showing performance to date. They are indicative of, but not necessarily equal to, the results that would be achieved if the asset were prematurely disposed of, because proceeds of disposition might be received, recapture of tax benefits might be required and similar ramifications would probably have to be cranked into the calculations. A highly sophisticated analysis (read "computerized") would consider those possibilities and expand the format to reveal the results of those calculations.

13. LCR and PVLCR calculations could be included if the analyst were interested in making a decision on that basis. In these examples, it is assumed that the critical issue is rate of return and the mixing machine of Example #1 is clearly superior. If LCR and PVLCR calculations are included, they can also be shown for each year as IRR has been portrayed.

14. Payback has not been discreetly calculated, but is apparent in each case where cumulative figures change from negative to positive. However, in Example #3, note that there is no payback, as an initially positive status deteriorates to a negative one. Payback must be permanent to be real.

15. As stated, the mixing machine is clearly superior, but if we have limited capital in our mythical company and some of our officers may go to jail if we do not install an effluent control filter, can we really stand by and let that happen? Would we? Probably not, which raises the caveat that some subjective evaluations cannot be absolutely or blindly trusted just because they've been committed to paper or computer. The analyst and the manager must continue to exercise business judgment and common sense in the use of this tool as in the use of any other.

16. One asset or project may be subdivided into a number of alternatives, each of which deserves its own Statement, based on method of acquisition. Acquisition options include:

Purchase new asset

Purchase used asset

Rent (as distinguished from Leasing, which is a financing method)

Make (as opposed to buy)

Convert/Upgrade/Downgrade existing assets

Refurbish assets slated for retirement/replacement

Share cost of purchase with another user (Joint Venture)

Purchase service the asset would provide

Add personnel to provide service asset would provide

ASSET DEPRECIATION

A few words are in order about the various depreciation methods currently available under the tax code.

There are three basic methods of depreciation for non-realty assets:

Sum of the Years Digits (Accelerated Method) (abbreviated SYD)

Double Declining Balance (Accelerated Method) (abbreviated DDB)

Straight Line (Non-Accelerated Method) (abbreviated SL)

Ordinarily, an asset owner will prefer to maximize depreciation as soon as possible to defer the greatest amount of taxes. Thus, a choice must be made between SYD and DDB.

DDB is computed by doubling the reciprocal of the asset life and applying the resulting percentage against the depreciable asset value, often called the "base," which is progressively reduced by each year's depreciation. An asset with a depreciable base of $10,000 and a five-year life would be calculated as follows:

$$\text{Rate} = (2)(1/5) = 40\%$$

Yr.	Base	×	Rate	= Deprec.	Base	–	Deprec.	= New Base
1	10,000	×	40%	= 4,000	10,000	–	4,000	= 6,000
2	6,000	×	40%	= 2,400	6,000	–	2,400	= 3,600
3	3,600	×	40%	= 1,440	3,600	–	1,440	= 2,160
4	2,160	×	40%	= 864	2,160	–	864	= 1,296
5	1,296	×	40%	= 518	1,296	–	518	= 778

Note that DDB does not yield full depreciation, leaving 778 undepreciated in this case. Full depreciation can be accomplished by switching to Straight Line after the midpoint of the life, which would yield depreciation in years 4 and 5 of 1,080 each year, which is found by dividing the 2,160 remaining by 2. It can be mathematically shown that immediately after the midpoint is the logical place to switch where DDB is used.

SYD is computed by applying a changing ratio to the depreciable base. The denominator is the sum of the numbers 1 to n, where n = asset life. The numerator for each period will be these same numbers taken in declining order. Looking at the same $10,000 asset with 5-year life, SYD yields:

$$\text{Denominator} = (n/2)(n+1) = (5/2)(5+1) = 15$$

Yr.	Ratio	×	Base	=	Depreciation
1	5/15	×	10,000	=	3,300
2	4/15	×	10,000	=	2,700
3	3/15	×	10,000	=	2,000
4	2/15	×	10,000	=	1,300
5	1/15	×	10,000	=	700

Total Depreciation = 10,000

Because DDB gives higher first-year depreciation (and can be mathematically proven to always do so if the same life is used) many managers assume it is the preferable method. However, SYD will give higher depreciation in *every* year after the first. Which then is preferable?

The answer can be calculated by treating the depreciation foregone in year 1 using SYD as an investment, with the excess depreciation in subsequent years viewed as returns on that investment. Using the rate of return formula previously explained, an indifference point can be calculated for various lives, which point would be compared to the company's marginal rate of return, as the value of the future returns would have to exceed the present value of the depreciation foregone if SYD is to be preferred.

Making these calculations, one finds that if a company can be sure of depreciating for at least four years (whatever the life, as long as more than 4 years) SYD will just about always be preferable, as the breakpoint rate of return would have to generally exceed 28%. Where depreciation beyond 3 years is questionable (i.e., because the asset may be disposed of) the following rates apply, with the rule being that if the company's marginal rate of return exceeds the breakpoint rate, DDB is preferable:

Life in Years: 50   45   40   35   30   25   20   15   10   7   5
Breakpoint
   ROR %:   1.95 2.15 2.41 2.74 3.16 3.76 4.63 6.00 8.49 11.18 13.81

As the company's marginal rate of return is likely to be above most of these breakpoints, with the possible exception of 7- and 5-year assets, the general rule of thumb might be applied that any asset to be depreciated more than four years should be handled by SYD if permissible under the tax code.

Note that marginal rate of return is that rate of return that the company normally expects to achieve on its next dollar invested. Alternatively, the average rate of return for all company assets could be substituted.

ASSET MONITORING

Once the assets are obtained, a new set of responsibilities is assumed:

1. Conservation: Security and value retention.
2. Full Utilization: Most profitable use at all times.
3. Performance Appraisal: Measured against the objectives and expectation from the purchase evaluation.

The starting point for asset monitoring is the establishment of and maintenance of an asset inventory record, which should include information about:

Cost	Maintenance
Basis	Breakdowns
Purchase Date	Installation Date
Supplier	Location
Warranty Data	Insurance Data
Depreciation	Responsible Personnel

This record will be the source and repository of the critical information needed to fulfill these responsibilities, which can be implemented as follows:

Conservation

A. Assign one person the ultimate responsibility for each asset—typewriter to secretary, production machine to operator, calculator to financial analyst. If part of an employee's responsibilities and job evaluation include the condition and performance of particular assets, those assets are likely to be more carefully protected.

B. Take a physical inventory of all assets at least once each year. Confirm their location and condition in writing in the asset inventory record. This is especially important for companies with assets at a variety of locations.

C. Establish a preventive maintenance program, with the responsibility for compliance charged to the employee who is responsible for the asset.

D. For assets representing relatively major portions of capital, maintain communication with parties active in the resale market for that asset, in case sale or lease of the asset becomes desirable. That contract may save valuable time and help assure full price.

Full Utilization

A. Consider the options outlined previously for upgrading, downgrading, converting and refurbishing assets in place of purchases.

B. Coordinate maintenance schedules to minimize downtime during production.

C. Consider additional shifts instead of a larger production line.

D. Keep an index of machine capabilities, so that these capabilities are not overlooked when new kinds of demands surface.

E. Set out written contingency plans to deal with breakdowns and other circumstances of unanticipated availability.

Performance Appraisal

A. Audit asset performance at least yearly.

B. Audit both operating statistics and the subjective evaluation of the asset by polling users, including especially the person assigned to the asset.

C. In considering operating statistics, perform a variance analysis against the originally anticipated results.

D. Recompute the Time Matrix Statement against replacement alternatives, especially if the a machine is substantially outperforming or underperforming.

E. Check the resale market for assets on a spot basis and consider the profitability of a sale as an alternative to retention.

Chapter 9

Maximum Value
From the Banking Resource

Few business relationships are as important as that maintained with your bank. Without external cash availability, many opportunities would be lost and few crises survived.

In this chapter we'll analyze that relationship, with particular attention to its formation and cultivation. We'll explore a variety of advantages that relationship can foster in addition to ready cash. We'll examine ways of minimizing the cost of funds and making the most of funds availability. Throughout the chapter we'll see how attention to your company's role in the relationship can actually improve the company's operations, crystallize its plans and clarify its objectives.

CHOICE OF BANK

Never in the history of civilized society have so many sources of external funds been available to businessmen. One hundred years ago, it would have been ludicrous for a medium-sized Kansas City company to do some of its banking and borrowing on a regular basis with a Swiss, Japanese or Middle Eastern bank. Today such relationships are increasingly commonplace. Despite the letter of the law, interstate banking is reality. More and more major cities are becoming national money centers. More and more banks are involving themselves in increasingly complex kinds of transactions and offering the newest kinds of services.

With so many bankers generally eager to develop new banking business, how should a company choose its bankers? These factors are frequently cited as considerations, although their relative importance will vary with company objectives and circumstances:

The Human Link

Knowing someone at a particular bank provides a great starting point. Whether a relative, close friend or nodding acquaintance, the banker's previous knowledge of your existence gives you a leg up in the establishment of banking ties. Computers, electronic transfer systems, automatic tellers and monstrous skyscrapers notwithstanding, the banking relationship is, as much as ever, fundamentally based on mutual trust. If you've already established the kernel of a relationship (or a whole cornstalk) that gives the bank reason to trust and respect you and your company, you're beyond square one.

Furthermore, while many managers may be subconsciously complacent about their bank's ability as a safe repository of funds, there is much more to trust than the simple confidence that the bank will not go belly up or abscond with your funds. The ability to move money, acquiring and spending it, is the essence of economic power. The bank that is less efficient in handling your account, a whit slower than others in getting the money where you want it, when you want it there and in the form you need it, a dram more brusque with your customers, vendors or employees, or a bit less accommodating regarding special requests, is not earning the trust (or deserving of the profits) you have placed in it. Thus, your knowledge of the bank and its people gives you a second leg up.

If no such "human link" exists, the customer should conduct a few interviews, based on the other factors relevant to his situation. References from other business relationships, trade associations and personal bankers (who may well be the appropriate choice himself), all are useful in developing a list of banking prospects. Where information is meager, the direct approach for making inquiry is the most effective. Bankers will understand that you need to size them up as they do you.

> **Word of Caution:** *In closely held businesses, it may not be the best idea to use the same banker for both business and personal needs, as problems in one area may then carry over into the other. Practically speaking, however, the mixture may be unavoidable, in which case the owner should make the most of the relationship by bringing his full economic weight to bear in transactions and negotiations with the bank.*

Location

For the small business, branch or division, location is often a matter of what bank is closest to the office. That's not an altogether foolish criterion. Employee time for bank deposits and other business counts. So does convenience for employees in cashing paychecks. It's easier to maintain communication and visibility with a bank around the corner instead of around the world. And, in a pinch, proximity may come in handy. While meaningful in this sense, however, location should carry more decisional weight in a different context.

That context is community, political, regional or national presence. For a company just getting started or attempting to establish itself in a new market or new area, a relationship with a local banker can become an important reference and contact if properly orchestrated. A new outlet opening in the rural heartland is not going to impress local townspeople with its money center banking connections, but they probably will be somewhat pleased and impressed to know that the company has put a lot of money into the local bank and the outlet manager and bank president (who's almost certain to be a leading citizen) are on a first name basis. On a grander scale, but similar in impact, the company that's dickering for tax concessions and regulatory breaks on a new facility may well get a better deal by bringing the local bank (which in foreign lands may be the state bank) into the picture as a business ally.

> **Point to Remember:** *Dealing with foreign banks is essentially the same as dealing with domestic ones. While language and regulations may differ, the fundamentals of trust and the identity of goals are still there. Consequently, it is virtually essential, and by no means very difficult, to establish a good banking relationship in each country in which a company plans to do business. The bank's knowledge of customs, economy, currency, etc. will all make the operations function more smoothly from the outset.*

Size

Size and safety often go together, but that does not mean that the biggest bank is always the best for your needs. It may be that a "big fish in a small pond" is the better way to go. If you're not president of a stock-exchange listed company (and, often, even if you are) the chances of your going to the president of a multinational money center bank to back your loan or special request (if you know the president in the first place) are nil. But, on the local banking scene, it may both be possible and make all the difference in the accomplishment of your objectives. Finally, when it comes to size, a company should be certain that the bank is large enough to accommodate its needs. However else it may fit, there's obviously no sense in seeking a hundred-million-dollar line of credit from a billion-dollar asset bank.

Specialization

Some banks are known to specialize in certain areas, while others are known to be unfamiliar with certain kinds of transactions. The obvious example is international banking. Any company dealing regularly in the international arena should have a money center bank among its relationships, though such a bank does not have to be the lead bank. That statement used to mean that the company had to have a New York bank or a San Francisco bank in its corner. Today, the term money center is much broader, embracing Atlanta, Philadelphia, Houston, Chicago, Los Angeles and Boston among others.

Some banks develop expertise and familiarity with certain industries (e.g., Pittsburgh banks and steel), which, it you happen to be in that industry, may be not only an understanding source of funds, but also an excellent source of information.

Some banks are regional specialists. Their dominance of the financial life of a geographic area may be an important fact of life when operating in that region. Their knowledge of the structure, sociology, economy and politics of a region may be as important as their financial assistance.

Services

Decide what the things are that you want the bank to do and then be sure the bank has the capability to handle the requirement. A partial checklist of potentially important services includes:

BANKING SERVICES CHECKLIST

Account Analysis and Reporting	Leasing
Appraisals	Letters of Credit
Automatic Reconciliation	Lines of Credit
Bankers Acceptances	Lock Box Processing
Business Consulting	Merchant Banking
Checkwriting and Bookkeeping	Money Management
Computer Service	Money Market Investment
Correspondent Services	Mortgages
Credit Insurance	Non-Fed Clearing
Daily Balance Reporting	Offshore Services
Economic Analysis	Overdraft Loan Privileges
Electronic Funds Transfer	Pension/Funds Management
Employee Check Cashing	Pre-Authorized Checking
Executive Personal Financial Planning	Remote Disbursing
Export Financing	Securities Transactions
Factoring	Specialized Financing
Faster Check Clearing	Special Form Drafts
Foreign Currency Denominated Accounts	Swiss Banking
Foreign Exchange	Syndicate/Consortium Formation
Forward Market Transactions	Tax Deposits
Government Sponsored Programs	Transfer Agent
Imprest Account Services	Trusteeships
International Branches	Wire Transfers
International Services	Zero Balance Account Disbursing

Efficiency

An important part of the trust reposed in the bank focuses simply on the bank's ability to handle transactions expeditiously. Banking is a service business. Efficient delivery of services is the essence of such a business.

The only sure way to gauge the efficiency of the bank is to have some direct experience with it. Until experience can be obtained, however, one must go on the basis of reputation, just as in the choice of any other vendor. Information about banks and their reputations can be obtained from these sources, among others:

Trade Associations	Competitors
Suppliers	Customers
Dun & Bradstreet	Robert Morris, & Associates
Chamber of Commerce	Comptroller of the Currency
Better Business Bureau	State Banking Regulators
Accountants	Attorneys

Cost

While cost usually looms large in the selection of most vendors, cost in terms of direct payments to a bank is somewhat less significant in the general choice. It will become more important in individual transactions, where the company's leverage and negotiating skill will come into play as in any other "purchase" transaction.

Where cost is more important is in the indirect impact on overall operations, as a function of the bank's servicing, efficiency and cooperation. The bank that minimizes indirect costs and saves money for its customers by providing the best cash handling, the most favorable loan terms (which embraces far, far more than just an interest rate) and the most effective execution of requests, especially the provision of information, is the most desirable bank to do business with.

ONE BANK OR SEVERAL?

As activity proliferates and varying banking requirements arise, chances increase that additional banking relationships need to be established. Geographical expansion, entry into new markets, new ventures, changes in technology and just plain old growth all promote the need for multiple banking ties.

The sum of the parts of such multiple banking relationships will often be greater than the same activity as a whole concentrated in one bank. More rapid cash collection and net higher aggregate cash balances are possible. More sources of credit and very probably a greater dollar availability of funds will accrue with multiple relationships. A wider range of expertise is at hand to call upon.

Nonetheless, multiple ties are not for everyone, nor should expansion of banking be engaged in recklessly. Each relationship requires a certain amount of attention, time and administrative input. There are no economies of scale. In fact, the burden tends to expand geometrically, for each demands a new measure of control and coordination. Each absorbs its own precious management time.

An improperly handled relationship, or one that deteriorates from neglect, does far more harm than one never ventured. Credibility and reputation may suffer. Few industries, if any, enjoy the tremendous degree of competitor cooperation and exchange of information as banking. Thus, a failure with one institution can conceivably have a chilling impact on many others, including older and more solid relationships.

In using more than one bank, care need be taken that conflicting bank requirements not arise, or if they do arise, they not confuse operations. For example, one bank may insist on a particular percentage for a compensating balance, whereas another may require a flat figure. When planning cash uses and availability, these differences must be taken into account.

Another danger to be on the lookout for is simultaneous cleanup of short-term credit. (For the uninitiated, banks often require that short-term lines be paid off in full and remain unused during a portion of the year — usually a month.) If more than one bank requires a cleanup at the same time, a sudden cash flow crisis may develop.

One should also recognize that when a variety of banks place requirements on a borrower, the most conservative bank will set the tone for the others. Thus, if three of four banks do not restrict dividend payout, but the fourth does, payouts are restricted. Under such circumstances, the time is ripe for reconsideration of relationship number four.

Such reconsideration does not necessarily mean a cancellation of the relationship. It may merely mean a discussion with the offending bank. A substitute for the dividend restriction may have to be accepted, but if it's one that is already in force under terms from the other three banks, it is not an unworthy sacrifice. Alternatively, the offensive loan might be refunded elsewhere, while the company continues to take advantage of other services offered by the bank. If the loan is refinanced, the other three banks may each be willing to pick up a piece of the loan, demonstrating an advantage of multiple ties.

Properly handled, such a change in the relationship should not be resented. Often the banks will suggest it. Frequently they will welcome it. They will be pleased with the dilution of risk and glad to find that their confidence and trust in the customer have been confirmed by others. The two things they will resent however are playing the banks off against one another or the disregard of past favors. In that sense, they are much like most suppliers and most human beings.

ESTABLISHING THE RELATIONSHIP

Once the need is identified, introductions made and initial confidence established, the first transactions should usually not be too complicated. Opening of a clearing account, say, for payroll or imprest funds, or participation in some foreign exchange or other specialized transfers are the best ways to get the business relationship underway.

The first transactions involving extensions of credit by the bank should usually take one of five forms:

1. A short-term note (e.g., 90 days), best being sought for a specifically identifiable purpose that will clearly be "self-liquidating." For example, the receivables generated from a specific contract with a completion date leading maturity of the note by 30 to 45 days (so that payment will arrive as the note falls due) is the textbook case. Of course, the note will be payable out of general company funds if the contract is extended or late in payments. However, it may be that the note can be renewed.

2. A secured loan for a specific piece of equipment (e.g., computer, vehicle, material handling equipment).

3. An equipment lease for the same kind of item.

4. A line of credit for working capital.

5. A letter of credit, which is a form of transaction particularly common for initial overseas dealings.

In other words, the initial transaction should be a simple and fairly discreet one in terms of tracing cash flow. First impressions being lasting impressions, the opening shot is designed to be one in which little can go wrong and complex or extended negotiations are avoided.

As the credit record is strengthened with the bank, and as the relationship flourishes, more intricate and longer-term credit arrangements can be made. From the simple and discreet borrowings above, it is not a long journey to revolving credit lines, floor plan financing and even long-term financing.

Of course, if the company's needs are not the kind that fit into simple and discreet patterns, go forward with confidence and candor, recognizing that a more complicated transaction may be more difficult to sell to the bank. Even so, rare will be the banker who will turn you away cold.

LOAN ARRANGEMENT TACTICS

Banking is perhaps the only business in which the customer sells the supplier. The customer sells credibility. The best way to establish and maintain credibility is to provide a timely stream of accurate and relevant information. When seeking a loan, the best way to go about it is to prepare a *written* prospectus for each transaction. Such a prospectus not only will keep the bank up-to-date, but like many a written plan, it will:

1. Clarify the company's own objectives and plans
2. Raise issues that cause management to prepare for contingencies that might otherwise become crises
3. Provide continuity of purpose within the company
4. Provide a basis for firm administrative control
5. Yield a historical data base for analysis
6. Give the company a storehouse of ideas for future transactions

The prospectus will include these documents:

1. *Introduction*: An introductory statement about the borrower. If it's a first-time loan, a more detailed description of the borrower is in order. For subsequent borrowings, a brief capsule is enough, complemented by a verbal statement of recent developments, new undertakings, major plans, etc.

Avoid being too "blue-sky" about the company in these statements. If there are real problems, do not hide them. But don't give a negative picture or be too modest. Strive for accuracy. Shun apologies.

> **Point to Remember:** *Your request will likely go before a loan committee, not all of whose members will be as familiar with you as your loan officer, to whom you'll be presenting the prospectus and request. Hence, don't be afraid to be repetitive, transaction to transaction. Too much information is certainly preferable to too little.*

2. *Rundown of Management*: A thumbnail sketch of each officer (and sometimes the Board of Directors or its Executive Committee) is appropriate. Include education, career background and history with the company and industry. Just give facts. Do not use subjective descriptions like "This handsome and effective Vice President. . ." Facts, not PR. Where a loan is sought for a particular project (e.g., the launching of a new division or the funding of operations on a major contract), a sketch of the lead personnel, perhaps including data on special skills exceptionally relevant to the project, is a valuable inclusion.

3. *Professional References*: Attorneys, CPA's, insurance agent or broker, consultants and other professionals of importance used by the firm ought to be listed. Even if the bank does not use these for direct reference, their presence says the company has the necessary competent assistance in technical areas. This section is also recommended for use in listing trade association memberships.

4. *Credit References*: Four or five solid references are enough. Landlords, mortgagees and utilities should be left out, as it is generally accepted that every company will let those credit relationships go bad at the very last. Consequently, if they are listed, the inference

may be drawn that there are no other good references left, to the detriment of the company. If you have relationships with other banks, these should be included in this section.

5. *Customer Listing:* A list of the company's major customers (unless the borrower is a retailer) will help to show both stability and credit-worthiness of the company's receivables. The best references are blue chips to whom the company makes a material amount of sales. Consider yourself fortunate if you can list a bank as a customer. Avoid listing blue chips that are occasional buyers, small-order buyers or long-ago customers, as their presence on the list, if checked out, may smack of puffing in tacit violation of the atmosphere of mutual trust. A list of twenty to forty customers representing at least twenty percent of sales is a reasonable barometer, with the approximate aggregate sales percentage stated in the description of the sheet. It is probably not necessary to show the precise dollar or percentage sales of each customer on the list.

6. *Balance Sheet:* Include an up-to-date balance sheet. If it's late in the year, it may be a good idea to include the previous audited year-end balance sheet and the most recent unaudited interim one.

The format for these statements need not be overly detailed, although the complete balance sheet should be available to the bank. A sufficiently expository statement would be laid out like this:

Assets	**Liabilities & Equity**
Cash and Equivalents	Current Liabilities
Net Receivables	Notes Due Within One Year
Inventory (state how valued)	Long-Term Debt
Other Current Assets	Total Liabilities
Total Current Assets	Capital Stock
Net Plant and Equipment	Retained Earnings
Other Assets	Total Equity
Total Assets	Total Liabilities and Equity

Tip: *If the company typically reports on the cash basis, it may make sense to show the statements on both the cash and accrual methods. While exact accrual accounting will likely be too time-consuming to execute, a rough accrual statement can be developed by factoring in receivables and material accruals such as payables, payroll and taxes. Include as backup data for the balance sheet an itemized list of accounts receivable and an itemized list of accounts payable, both of which ought to be aged, and, of course, tie in to the balance sheet lines. A similar schedule of corporate debt is also useful.*

7. *Operating History:* Show at least a five-year history, regardless of the term of the loan. If the loan being applied for is eight years or longer, use a ten-year history. Companies less than two years old use a month-to-month history. In some cases quarterly data is acceptable. Even for older outfits, if data throughout the year is not consistent, or if a few recent months or quarters deserve highlighting, they can be broken out separately in addition to the five- or ten-year history.

The statements need not be certified, but if certified statements are available, they should, of course, be used. Do not be afraid to mix audited and unaudited data (say the last few years against the last few months) so long as the distinction is clearly identified.

Statements need not be extremely detailed. Try this breakdown:

X COMPANY
OPERATING HISTORY

	Year 1	Year 2	Year 3	Year 4	Year 5	Latest 6 Mos.
Revenue						
Direct Expense						
Gross Profit						
Indirect Expense						
G & A Expenses						
Operating Profit						
Interest						
Net Pretax						
Taxes						
Net After Tax						

8. *Cash Flow:* Use the same time frame as operating history. A good format would be:

X COMPANY
CASH FLOW HISTORY

	Year 1	Year 2	Year 3	Year 4	Year 5	Latest 6 Mos.
Opening Cash Balance						
Cash From Operations						
Net Borrowings (+ or −)						
Net Change Current Accounts (+ or −)						
Other Cash Flow						
Net Change						
Closing Cash Balance						

9. *Projections:* Income and cash flow projections, both corporately and for a loan-related project are included. Projections should match the loan period and assume that the loan is made in exactly the form requested. It may be effective to combine the projections with the operating and cash flow histories.

> **Try This:** *Instead of a set of exact predictions, show a range of expectations. Such a "min-max" approach prevents charges of misrepresentation and shows a nice degree of sophistication. Use Best/Most Likely/Worst.*

10. *Footnotes:* Financial statement footnotes should be kept to a minimum. Auditors' footnotes can be referred to by a statement like:

> "Additional footnotes to the expanded financial statements were made by our auditors and are available separately."

Too many footnotes will be confusing and tend to detract from the salability of the document. Hit the highlights, not the whole spectrum.

11. *Insurance:* A schedule of major liability and casualty policies, showing carrier, deductible, co-insurance and limits of liability demonstrate to the bank the extent of the company's protection (and the protection of its security) in the face of abnormal occurrences. Include keyman, buy-sell and umbrella policies, especially when the borrower is a closely held concern.

12. *Attorney Opinion Letter:* A letter from an independent counsel stating that there are no pending lawsuits or other actions expected to have a material effect on the company is a standard ingredient. If there is the danger of a material problem, so that a "clean" opinion cannot be obtained, then the opinion ought to include a description of the potential outcomes and impacts on the company. Have the attorney tell specifically whether such results would be likely, in his opinion, to encumber the company's ability to repay the loan. If possible, have the attorney also give his assessment of the likelihood of each outcome.

13. *Intangibles Assurance:* Where the loan or operations will be especially dependent on the continuation or existence of a contract, copyright, patent, franchise, license or other intangible, evidence thereof might well be included in the prospectus. If such an intangible is in process (e.g., patent application filed) an expert appraisal of the situation may also be included.

14. *Loan Request:* A generalized verbal description of the loan sought will include the purposes for the loan, the benefits it is expected to generate and the impact on the company if the loan is denied. Also include a description of how the loan will be repaid, stating the source of the cash expected to be used for payoff.

15. *Terms:* Show the company's recommendations for the structure of the deal. A punchlist format like this may do the trick:

Loan Amount: $2,000,000
Loan Type: Equipment Collateral
DOWN PAYMENT: 20% per unit within 30 days of unit delivery
SECURITY: Vehicle Fleet (50 Tractor/Trailers)
FUNDING: Over next six months as equipment is delivered and accepted
REPAYMENT: Direct Reduction Loan Monthly Payments
MATURITY: Eight Years
PREPAYMENT: 2% Penalty Year 1; 1% Penalty Year 2; None thereafter
RATE CALCULATION: Fixed at 1½% Over Current Bank Prime
RENEWABILITY: None
FEES: ½% Commitment Fee
RESTRICTIONS: Company to carry casualty insurance at least equal to outstanding loan value for each vehicle.
SPECIAL TERMS: Company has firm purchase commitment for 30 vehicles and option for up to an additional 20. Company to draw down loan on a pro rata basis for vehicles accepted, without penalty if entire loan is not funded.

Obviously, such a set of terms requires a detailed knowledge of the bank's lending practices, so that the proposal is neither extremely unpalatable to the bank nor missing an opportunity for the company. Naturally, the list is subject to negotiation.

Propounding a list that is known to contain unreasonable terms in the hopes of obtaining bargaining leverage will risk inconsistency with the concept of trust. Negotiations should generally center on the amount funded and the rate. Occasionally a compromise will be needed over restrictions. The borrower should know the bank's policies on collateral and not monkey around with it. The only issues raised over security ought to be the appraisal value on which the parties should not be too far apart in the first place. For smaller companies, it is not unreasonable for owners to try to avoid personal liability, although, until certain size and operating parameters are met, chances for success are small.

16. *Budgeted Uses:* Tell how the money will be put to use. In this example:

15 Replacement Vehicles:	$ 600,000
25 Expansion Vehicles	1,000,000
10 Backup/Contingency	400,000
TOTAL LOAN	$2,000,000

17. *Personal Data:* Where a loan is to be personally guaranteed, the personal financial statements of the guarantors are included. Also include data on personal casualty, liability and life insurance.

> **Point to Remember:** *The data you provide will not be the only information the bank obtains. Most bankers will use Dun & Bradstreet reports or reports from Robert Morris & Associates. Therefore, it's a good idea to try to get hold of these before submitting your material, so you can defuse any contradictions.*

CONFLICTING PERSPECTIVES

In making its loans, the bank is ultimately concerned with just one thing: repayment with profit. From that single goal emerge other issues such as adequate security, rates and repayment schedules.

The bank wants assurance that the loan will be repaid from one of three sources:

1. Ideally, funds generated from the profitable application of the loan will nicely cover the payback. Where the direct generation of funds may not be identifiable (e.g., overhead items like refurbishment of a headquarters), overall operations have to carry the burden.
2. In the event that operations fail to meet expectations, the bank wants to be able to obtain repayment from the sale of assets, especially those that are the object of the loan.
3. If cases 1 and 2 are still insufficient, repayment must come from another legally obligated source, such as a guarantor.

In one form or another, these concepts guide the banks in reaching their decisions about the creditworthiness of a borrower and his loan proposal. If the customer can qualify, the banker prefers to make the loan, as that is the real source of bank revenue and income.

Meanwhile, the borrower's principal goal is not merely repayment of the loan, but a profitable return on the loan. The customer has a limited array of security sources to offer while the funds for repayment are being generated. The greater the security given on one loan, the less there is to go around for future needs, and, theoretically, the more stringent the constraints on the company's growth, profitability and future. (Remember, for instance, the cash constraint on inventory funding.) The shorter the payback period, the less opportunity to compound the earnings on the funds and the greater the strain to earn the adequate rate of return.

Within the framework of these conflicting perspectives, customer to bank, the shrewd borrower can employ several strategies to mold a loan structure that fits the borrower's goals and to coax that larger amount of funds from the reluctant lender.

LOAN MOLDING STRATEGIES

The longer the term of the loan, the less of a strain its repayment places on the borrower, not only because there's more time to generate the funds for the repayment, but also because each scheduled repayment (e.g., monthly) will be lower. Particularly when inflation is rampant, the borrower should seek to stretch the period of repayment as much as possible, as it is attractive to pay back a loan with less valuable dollars in the future. Getting one $10,000 four-year loan is also better than getting two consecutive two-year loans of $5,000 each, all other things being equal, for these reasons:

1. Uncertainty about funding of the second loan is eliminated, making planning easier.
2. Uncertainty about the terms (especially the rate) on the second loan is likewise eliminated, again providing stability.
3. The company has a contingency reserve, at least in the early term of the loan.
4. There is a saving in administrative time and cost in dealing with just one borrowing transaction.

The factor mitigating against larger and lengthier loans is the risk that the capital cannot be profitably employed. If a company is not in a declining market, that should be an unusual occurrence. Hence, the incentive to stretch payment time is usually there and might be accomplished with some of these concepts:

1. *Balloon:* By structuring the loan so that payments are lower over the life of the loan with a lump sum due at the end of the term, as opposed to higher payments that will entirely amortize the loan, the company has the same advantage during the life of the loan as if it were on a longer repayment schedule. When the balloon is due, it can often be converted into a new loan, refinanced with another lender or absorbed as part of a larger loan, if the company cannot pay it off entirely.

2. *Automatic Renewability:* If the bank will agree to renew the loan at the option of the company, the company has the assurance of capital availability for the longer period of time. This feature is most desirable when dealing with a note that is not being amortized (e.g., discounted note) or where a balloon is involved.

3. *Collateral Substitution:* By using longer-lived collateral, the borrower provides a rationale to the leanding institution for a longer-term loan.

4. *Longer Collateral Writeoff:* By slowing down the write-off time for the collateral, the same rationale applies. Essentially, longer write-off means stretching the life of the collateral.

> **Potential Pitfall:** *Longer period must be reasonable and cannot be so inconsistent with tax and financial reporting as to jeopardize tax status or credibility.*

5. *Uneven Payment Terms:* Structure the payment schedule for lower repayment in the earlier part of the schedule, with higher amounts due in the later part, averaging out to essentially the same payment as if a level payment plan were used. This tactic gives the company more time to make the application of funds productive.

> **Warning:** *This strategy will also increase interest paid over the life of the loan. If the schedule is too "deep" the company also runs the risk of being too tightly constrained toward the end of the term.*

PREPAYMENT

It is always wise to include prepayment rights in any loan agreement. Being able to prepay a loan affords these benefits:

A. It permits the company to avoid being saddled with debt that cannot be profitably employed.

B. It permits the company to take advantage of changes in the capital markets, such as a reduction in interest rates relative to the loan rate or improvements in the equity market that yield a relatively lower cost of capital.

C. It permits the company to restructure debt with a minimum of obstacles, in such situations as a debt consolidation.

D. Where the cost of debt capital is high and the company does better than anticipated, reduction of debt may be the most effective investment of the cash, which would be prohibited without prepayment rights.

Even where prepayment will involve a penalty, the company is frequently better off having the option to prepay with a penalty than to have no right at all. If prepayment becomes viable, the cost of the penalty can be factored into the calculations of the overall transaction series of which the prepayment will be a part.

Wherever possible, avoid prepayment tied to the "Rule of 78's" which some lenders will erroneously claim is not a "penalty." The Rule technically provides the lender with extra interest, which is arguably not a penalty. In any event, the Rule is conceived on the theory that the lender will be entitled to a total amount of interest over the life of the loan. If the loan is prepaid, a pro rata share of the unpaid interest is charged to the borrower as consideration for prepayment. In the early stages of a loan, prepayment can raise the effective cost of the funds employed to an uneconomic level. Had the borrower understood the full size of the penalty early in the transaction, the loan might even have been reconsidered.

From the bank's standpoint, the logic for a penalty embraces these points:

A. The bank has incurred certain administrative costs in making the loan, which the bank had expected to recoup ratably over the life of the loan. It is foreclosed from so doing if prepayment is made.

> **Point for Counter-Argument:** *If there is a loan commitment, origination or discount fee, that should be compensation for the administrative costs.*

B. The bank has predicated its own capital and debt structure on certain assumptions and projections including the current state of its loan portfolio. If prepayment occurs, the mix of its loan portfolio changes accordingly. The bank is entitled to compensation for the disruption of its carefully laid plans.

C. When a loan is prepaid, the bank has the opportunity cost of lost future income. While it seeks another lender for these same funds, it deserves to be compensated on a theory similar to that of a landlord who keeps a security deposit when the tenant vacates before the end of the lease term.

D. In accepting the prepayment and closing out the loan early, the bank incurs some new administrative costs it deserves compensation for.

E. Money has its market price like any other commodity. If the marketplace for money is able to get the higher price for its money through such a penalty, the bank, as a rational business entity seeking to maximize its own profits, ought to take advantage of the market situation.

Despite all these points, the borrower may still have some negotiating room. One alternative is to seek a declining penalty, so that prepayment can be made later in the loan term (when it is more probable anyway) without a penalty, or at least a lower one. Later in the term the bank has recovered more of its administrative costs and faces a smaller opportunity cost.

A second negotiating stance is to seek a waiver of the penalty (or a reduction) if the loan is refinanced by the same bank. Arguing for this approach can be especially effective when the penalty waiver is based on a new loan at a higher rate. While it may seem momentarily foolish to accept such a proposition, as the borrower may wonder why he ought to refinance at a higher rate, the concept makes more sense when the higher rate is lower than the effective rate on the old funds if the penalty is paid. This argument prevails when the new loan, for an assumedly larger amount, will be conditioned on elimination of the old one.

Third, prepayment is just another bargaining chip in the overall bank relationship. Where a loan is being sought with the likelihood of prepayment relatively high, other bargaining chips such as higher compensating balances or higher commitment fees might be economically substituted.

GETTING LARGER LOANS

While a company may not always draw down the limit of its credit and might even never draw it down, the larger the loan line, the more power and confidence the company can have in its own operations. In negotiating a loan package or line of credit, these approaches may make the difference between a large enough line and a niggardly one or even between an extension of bank credit and none.

1. *Unbundling:* Make a series of transactions, rather than one. For example, if a borrower already has a general line of credit, rather than asking for an increase therein, the borrower leaves the general line unchanged and instead seeks a separate specific purpose loan, such as an equipment collateral loan.

2. *Bundling:* Conversely, the consolidation of a number of smaller loans into one package will often improve the appearance of the balance sheet and will improve cash flow if the term of the "bundled" loan averages out longer and/or the interest rate is lower than the weighted average aggregate rate of the replaced loans. Consequently, the capability of the company's cash flow to support a net higher level of debt is improved.

3. *Tax Benefit Passthrough:* By structuring a loan in the form of a lease, the lessor-lender, who takes title to the new equipment, can keep the tax benefits, such as depreciation and investment tax credits. Consequently, the lender can accept a lower interest rate as part of the lender's return as derived from tax savings. With a lower rate, the loan can be for a higher amount and still be within the company's repayment ability. For example, assume a $100,000 loan request, that the bank will fund for a five-year term at 12% to cover new equipment costing $125,000. Monthly payments on the loan on a level payment full amortization basis will be about $2,225. If the transaction can be structured to give the bank title, depreciation and tax credits, the bank is willing to make a 9 3/8% loan. If the monthly payment is held constant, the loan amount it will support at 9 3/8% is about $106,250, giving the company an 85% loan instead of an 80% one. The bank also has the added security of title superior to a lien. Such a structure is particularly attractive for the borrower when there is doubt that the company can use all of the tax benefits.

4. *Funding option:* The company obtains the right to draw down additional funds if some contingency is met. For example, the company's line of credit will be X% larger if the CPA's audited statement due within the next thirty days shows a net worth of $A, sales exceeding $B and net income over C% on sales.

5. *Collateral Substitution:* While mentioned earlier to support stretched repayment, higher valued collateral used on a specific loan will also support a larger amount.

> **Point to Remember:** *During inflationary times, reappraisal of collateral may well show a higher value than expected by the company. Additionally, an independent appraiser may be able to suggest steps that can be taken (e.g., refurbishment of a vehicle) that will yield higher value above the investment to accomplish it.*

6. *Pledge of Future Collateral:* A guarantee to the bank is made that as additional assets are acquired, they automatically become collateral on which the bank has a lien. This concept is most useful when increases in current assets like accounts receivable and inventory are anticipated in line with greater sales.

7. *Guarantees:* Personal guarantees from owners, or corporate guarantees from other affiliates, are equivalent to an increase in collateral.

8. *Subordination:* Arranging for a new loan to have legal priority over older loans gives the lender stronger collateral. Usually, subordination is automatic where stockholder and affiliate loans are outstanding. Sometimes, other lenders (e.g., venture capitalists) will subordinate. It is also possible to arrange limited subordination whereby specific collateral is segregated as pledged to older lenders. However, as to all other assets, their claim for any

deficiency (i.e., shortfall in value in the collateral against the loan in the event of default) will be subordinated.

9. *Restrictions:* Promises by the company to take or not take certain actions prevent the company's worth from deteriorating and collateral value from being impaired in the eyes of the bank, as the restrictions reduce risk. For example, the company may be required to retain insurance of a certain kind or size, may be forced to limit salaries for top officers or even all employees, may be prohibited from otherwise encumbering certain assets or may be required to limit dividends.

10. *Multiplied Entities:* By establishing subsidiaries and affiliates, it may be possible to acquire an aggregate of debt greater than could be obtained if all activities were under one corporate umbrella. This is frequently the case when a company is engaged in a number of different businesses, as certain kinds of activity are viewed as inherently more credit-worthy than others. When all are rolled into one package, the least credit-worthy will often be viewed as the lowest common denominator for making loan decisions. Included in this concept are captive finance companies.

11. *Demonstrations:* While not precisely a financing technique, product demonstrations, plant visits, systems demonstrations, physical asset displays and other person-to-person communications that provide tangible evidence of corporate growth, capacity and expertise, may be the crucial link to prompting the extra measure of banker's confidence that permits the new or larger loan.

Amidst the technicalities of the transactions, do not lose sight of the nature of the relationship. Continued efforts to strengthen the relationship will often ease the technical transactions and make the banking relationship a multidimensional corporate asset.

Chapter 10

Prime Sources
And Uses of
Bank Debt Alternatives

No matter how successful a company is with its banking relationships, there will always be a ceiling on the amount that can be borrowed there. Circumstances will also arise in which a company needs additional capital, but doesn't want to wear out the welcome mat at the bank. And, of course, there is always an underlying desire to obtain as many sources of capital as possible, because capital sufficiency provides many opportunities and cures many ills.

This chapter offers a panorama of bank debt alternatives geared to funding short- and intermediate-term needs. Unlike permanent capital, which is the foundation of business activity, these alternatives are designed as lubricants to operational activity.

OBJECTIVES

The search for this additional capital encompasses one or more of these objectives:

1. *Cash Need:* Something needs doing and needs cash to fund the doing. There may be an outright cash shortage or the funding of a more complex requirement, but it boils down to wanting cash.

2. *Diversity of Funding:* Prospectively, a diversity of sources with which a company is experienced gives wider future opportunities to draw more cash for differing needs. Current diversity is also attractive, because no single provider of funds can then exercise too much power over the company's activities through exercise of its lender's rights.

3. *Least Cost:* The lower the cost of the funds, the more profitably they can be employed and the lower the risk in accepting them. A search among alternatives must naturally consider comparative costs.

4. *Custom Design*: Specific loan terms, from drawdown to maturity, are as much a key to profitability as any other aspect. Flexibility in terms translates into ability to seize the operational opportunity. This is a point worth some attention. Too many managers concentrate on the pure quantitatives of cost and yield. Yet, financing is a prospective endeavor. Whatever plans exist for the capital once obtained, these plans are just that—plans. Contingencies, detected or unexpected, can best be met when a company has the chance to respond with a minimum of third-party restrictions. As we examine these alternatives, we'll see ways in which terms can be shaped to provide that flexibility, save money and reduce risk.

Whatever the objectives, know them in advance of launching the search. Decide which can be compromised and in what priority. The clearer the searcher's idea of his needs, the easier it will be to match the capital source to the capital need.

> **Point to Remember:** A *carefully spelled-out plan, presented with confidence and evidencing a management atop its business will itself be a powerful persuader of lenders.*

CONCEPTS

The root concept of these alternatives may be summed up this way:

"Banks fund the general; Alternatives fund the specific."

In other words, the opportunity to be found in these alternatives lies in relating capital to a specific need, specific use and specific security for the lender. The bank's view is over the whole corporation. While the entire corporation's credit will always be at issue to every lender, the alternative source will and should be focused primarily on a single area of endeavor involving discreet assets and delimited expenditures.

Through such an approach a company will find that the sum of the parts of its capital searches through alternatives will be greater than the whole financed through the singular banking link (even if the link is forged with a consortium of banks).

There are a few reasons why this concept applies:

A. Some alternative lenders are willing to accept more risk, usually because they are demanding a higher return on their invested capital.

B. Some alternative lenders are in a better position to take advantage of certain kinds of security than a bank would be, and, accordingly, are ready to offer more funds for the identical security.

C. The expertise of some alternative lenders permits them greater insight and, hence, greater confidence in certain transactions than a bank might have.

D. In some cases, the alternative lender has an additional axe to grind, such as the consummation of a sale. That is not the concern of the banker.

E. In yet other cases, special relationships, such as the obvious one of parent to subsidiary, or perhaps, the more subtle one of takeover candidate to predator, may offer unusual opportunities.

F. Sheer market power coupled with a different business perspective than the banking industry's may be the key to yet another set of sources.

G. Last, but of substantial import, alternative lenders are much less likely to be constrained by the plethora of regulators and regulations surrounding the banking industry, and, thus, are likely to be much freer to innovate and speculate.

The ability to analyze the planned transaction for the conceptual links born of special circumstances will permit a company to find the necessary source. Coupled with proper cultivation, a company will find itself with much stronger financial resources.

APPLICATION—POSITION AND CAPTURE

Strategically, the acquisition of capital will not be accomplished in a vacuum. The use of these sources must be fitted into the corporate capital budget. Too many such loans, lenders and leverage are as damaging and dangerous as any other corporate excess. The building of the capital budget will be examined in a later chapter.

Given a certain potential level of such alternative funding, lead from strength. The stronger the specific project, the greater the chance of success. The weaker points of the company should be conceptually pooled for consideration via bank funding. As an example, if the tangible assets to be acquired with the borrowed funds will tend to have markedly lower resale value (and therefore lower value as security) and these assets are to be used in servicing blue chip customers, look to the receivables as the principal security, not the tangible assets. That decision will lead to certain types of lenders as prime targets and certain types of loans as the likely kind to be considered.

Tactically, follow these steps:

1. Determine the project to be funded. Ideally, several projects will be selected and ranked by desirability. The term "project" is used in the broad sense of intended use for the funds acquired.

2. Determine the amount of funds needed. Set a range of acceptable funding, as rigid requirements may be both unachievable and unnecessary.

> **Beware This Pitfall:** *Don't set the lower end of the range at too bare a minimum in the hopes of capturing the money without appearing too demanding, as under-capitalizing any project is practically a guarantee of failure.*

3. Determine the terms desired. (The checklist in the "LOAN MOLDING STRATEGIES" section of the chapter on Banking is applicable here.)

4. Choose a limited group of qualified lenders as targets.

5. Prepare a proposal package. (Use the Banking chapter format, with appropriate modifications.)

6. Submit the package for negotiation.

7. Close.

With these fundamentals established, let's look at some alternative sources and their characteristics.

COMMERCIAL PAPER

In a sense, we begin with an exception. Commercial paper involves the issuance of unsecured debt in marketable form. Technically, and in fact from the market's viewpoint, it is used to fund general short-term working capital requirements of the issuer. Maturities of one year are long by commercial paper standards. Hence, there is a potential disadvantage. Commercial paper can be "rolled" (i.e., refinanced) but, of course, at the going rate when rolled, so that the use of commercial paper for funding long-term projects is to be avoided because of the dangers of interest rate variations.

Being unsecured, paper also has the deserved reputation of being available under most circumstances only to those with near impeccable credit. Its attractiveness at any point in time is largely a function of the prime rate, as short-term bank debt and commercial paper are generally considered interchangeable to the borrower, the preference being for the lower cost. Commercial paper has more often commanded the lower rate.

Nonetheless, for larger companies, commercial paper is worth considering. If a company is publicly traded or preeminent in its industry, it is a candidate for commercial paper borrowing. The key to cracking the market is the dealer.

The dealers, the investment bankers, become the tactical target for the potential offeror. If the dealer is willing to attempt the sale, chances are the financing can be accomplished. The dealer will be willing if confident that the company's credit standing is sufficient to warrant a particular rate. Comparing the dealer's proposed rate to market conditions and the prime is the acid test.

For the larger company already in the commercial paper market, there may come a time when the company is able to consider direct issuance of paper without a dealer. Market power, a long and strong track record and a sophisticated staff with ample connections to buyers are the minimum prerequisites for such an attempt. The savings in cost can be substantial, though the exercise is certainly not for the occasional borrower.

In breaking new ground in the commercial paper market, the rating of the paper becomes the levering factor. Ratings are determined internally by the dealers themselves and publicly by agencies, the most well-known of which is the National Credit office, a subsidiary of Dun & Bradstreet. Such ratings are based on typical financial standards, with concentration, naturally, on attributes most likely to be salient in the short-term.

RECEIVABLES FINANCING

Discounting, factoring and pledging receivables are all well established methods of alternative short-term financing. They all rely, of course, on having "marketable" receivables.

The definition of "marketable" will vary with the kind of receivables financing sought. The basic theme of this kind of financing is that the lender may ultimately depend on the receivables themselves to repay the loan. Variations on the theme include:

1. Simple collateralization of receivables. This concept is closest to bank financing, substituting a commercial lender for the bank. The loan must be repaid like any other and

the lender does not deal directly with the receivables, except in the case of default. Normally, a financing statement will be recorded as a condition of the loan.

2. Discounting. Discounted receivables are assigned to the lender, without notice to the customer. Normally, the amounts lent are less than the face amount of the loan—hence the name. Payments made to the borrower are forwarded to the lender to liquidate the loan. Receivables not paid by the customer within a certain time limit (varying by industry and custom) must usually be "repurchased" by the borrower. Lenders may require their borrowers to purchase credit insurance (see the chapter on collecting Accounts Receivable).

3. Factoring. The receivables are sold directly to the factor on a nonrecourse basis. The factor has the right to approve customers before the goods are delivered. Ordinarily, customers are notified of the sale and directed to pay the factor rather than the seller-borrower.

Receivables financing may offer several advantages over bank financing:

The biggest advantage is that the receivables will be given a higher value by the lender than may be obtainable from the bank.

Second, the method of financing may improve receivables management and/or save collection costs.

Third, receivables financing is self-liquidating, for as payments are made by customers, the loans are automatically paid.

Fourth, it's a way to increase asset productivity. By permitting faster conversion of the asset into cash, resources are available for greater sales expansion.

The greatest disadvantage is that receivables financing is useful only for the short-term need. The funding of long-term assets or activities is, we note once again, playing with fire.

Outside of industries like textiles, which have traditionally used receivables financing, its use may be interpreted, rightly or wrongly, as a sign of financial weakness. Discounting receivables is often viewed as a last resort. This stigma is due in large part to the high rates usually associated with this kind of lending. The theory assumes that anyone willing to pay such high rates for money must be close to desperation.

That stigma should not be a barrier to using receivables financing, but it should not be ignored. Therefore, when embarking on a receivables financing program, take care to maintain creditor, especially bank, relations to dispel any injurious rumors or suspicions.

INVENTORY FINANCING

Because inventory is a short-term asset, financing secured by it is also short-term. Unlike receivables financing which is designed to liquidate the asset, inventory financing is almost always used to underwrite the asset.

As with receivables, there are several variations:

Inventory as Collateral

Unless the inventory is a readily salable commodity, like coal, grain or silver, the likelihood of the inventory carrying a high collateral value is limited. Even then, the swing in commodity prices tends to depress collateral values, too. The more volatile the commodity's price history, the greater the depression. Nonetheless, there are two particular situations when such financing may be particularly attractive:

A. When overburdened with inventory, pledge that excess as collateral to ease cash flow problems. Inventory's use as collateral turns an idle asset into a productive one. The sell-off of inventory, as in most inventory financing, is designed to liquidate the loan. Thus, as inventory is brought back into balance, the level of indebtedness is simultaneously reduced.

B. When in need of inventory and able to buy with trade credit, the simultaneous pledge of the inventory can satisfy that need in spades. Take the following example:

A retailer is short on cash but knows additional inventory can be quickly sold at a 100% markup. Management buys a 4-month supply of inventory for a price of $100,000 on terms of 2/10, N30. At the same time, the retailer pledges the inventory for a 60-day collateral loan, under which a UCC financing statement is filed, with interest payable monthly. The loan is turned around to liquidate half of the payable, with the $1,000 cash discount retained as a contribution to working capital. During the first month, the company records $50,000 of sales. (Being a retailer, the company assumedly produces immediate cash from these sales.) At the end of that first month, $500 of the cash saved from the discount is paid in interest. The $50,000 of sales is used to pay off the other half of the trade credit payable, thereby eliminating it. The second month produces another $50,000 in cash sales, which is used to repay the loan. Interest for the second month is funded from the other half of the cash discount. At this point, the company has paid off both creditors, while having used but half the inventory. In the next two months, sales will yield $100,000 of cash.

While the mathematical precision of this example may be rare, it demonstrates that inventory can be the source of its own funding as long as loan liquidation is built into the planning, which planning includes pricing. Pricing that creates the cash flow is the engine that drives the financing mechanism.

Floorplanning

This method relies on specific identification of goods in inventory—i.e., on an item-by-item basis—and so is used almost exclusively in durable goods industries. The costs involved in such recordkeeping, the expenses of lien recordation and removal and the exceptional communication needed between borrower and lender do tend to limit the use to "big ticket items." However, even a seller of penny candy could use floorplanning, as long as large enough specific lots were identified, inventoried, maintained and sold as cohesive units. Such a novel program would require careful coordination with the lender, but could pay off in greater collateral value and purchasing flexibility, which are the two big advantages of floorplanning.

The lender is assuming that the goods are readily salable at or above wholesale cost, the cost at which the borrower brings the goods into inventory. Of course, the borrower is guaranteeing the loan over and above the collateral, against which the lender has recorded a lien. As the liened item is delivered out of inventory, the loan is paid off.

It is a curious, but understandable, fact that floorplanning in its true form in certain industries, for certain products, is undertaken by a limited number of banks and other financial institutions. These lenders have specialized knowledge about the goods and industry, permitting them to appraise and lend with unusual confidence. Hence, once a company is considering floorplanning, it may be advantageous to look beyond its usual sources for these specialists. Trade associations and industry consultants are often an excellent source of information for locating the specialists.

To set up floorplanning, there are these prerequisites:

A. Inventory items reputed to maintain value with ready salability, to be used as adequate security.

B. Inventory items that can be liened, and, for the comfort of the lender, susceptible to easy enforcement of the lien in terms of taking physical possession and proceeding to liquidation.

C. Specific identification inventory recordkeeping so that the goods serving as collateral are properly accounted for.

D. Payment customary upon delivery so that the loan can be paid off when the borrower gives up possession of the goods.

E. Facilities and inventory amenable to lender audit for occasional confirmation of floorplanned inventory.

F. Strong communications and a strong confidential relationship with the lender.

Field Warehousing

Like floorplanning, field warehousing is an inventory financing method that fits a particular kind of situation. And, like floorplanning, it is theoretically subject to much greater use than currently enjoyed.

Conceptually, field warehousing gives actual possession of the inventory to the lender, providing an unusually high measure of security, and, hence, an expectedly higher collateral value for the borrower. This possession is accomplished by the engagement of a third-party warehouseman, who acts as agent for the lender. The warehouseman will ordinarily "lease" a segment of the borrower's premises, there placing the goods selected as collateral under lock and key. The warehouseman is bonded to assure performance. All of these costs are, of course, borne in one fashion or another by the borrower.

As inventory is needed, the borrower obtains it from the warehouseman on approval of the lender. The lender's OK is dependent upon the borrower satisfying lender conditions on the loan.

Field warehousing is especially common in circumstances where inventory builds up quickly and is drawn down steadily. Hence, agricultural products are prime candidates. Industries with sharply seasonal sales patterns are also attracted to field warehousing, for during the slow sales periods, production builds inventory that can be converted to cash by the borrower while the company waits for the busy season to resume.

The typical field warehousing arrangement will have these characteristics:

A. A fairly uniform inventory, permitting easy control for the warehouseman.

B. Facilities easily segregated to allow the warehouseman to carry out his responsibilities without undue cost.

C. A relatively large inventory (for correspondingly large loans) necessary to provide the economies of scale so as to cover the fairly high overhead that field warehousing entails.

D. Inventory usage and sales requirements that can accommodate additional scheduling requirements occasioned by the third-party involvement.

Field warehousing, therefore, makes the most sense when a company anticipates high
investment in inventory and desires to squeeze as much collateral value and cash out of that
inventory as possible.

Trade Credit

Ordinarily thought of as just a normal part of business activities and not considered a
financing alternative in the real sense, trade credit still deserves careful attention and
management. Properly used, it can be a valuable tool in cash flow management, providing
the edge needed to keep cash flow steady and balances positive. The choice of supplier and
the timing of purchases are the simple ingredients, although it is possible to also use trade
credit as a lead-in for something more than just ultra-short-term financing. A few ideas:

A. Negotiated renewals of trade credit, with or without interest, is a common practice
for avoiding the bank. The buyer with a strong market position may often find the interest
rate charged is better than that to be found elsewhere.

B. Establishment of a guaranteed purchase plan (i.e., contractual agreement to take
delivery of some minimum from the supplier), coupled with a periodic payment plan to
cover the purchases, can turn the supplier into a form of lender, if the deliveries are drawn
faster than the payments are made. For example, assume a buyer will want the following
deliveries in the coming six months:

	July	Aug.	Sept.	Oct.	Nov.	Dec.	Total
Goods	3,000	3,500	3,000	1,000	500	1,000	12,000
Cost	$30,000	$35,000	$30,000	$10,000	$5,000	$10,000	$120,000

Instead of ordering piecemeal, month by month, and paying N30 after deliveries, our
buyer goes to the supplier and offers a deal: A big order of 12,000 units and $120,000 over
the next six months, with a guaranteed payment of $20,000 per month and an agreement not
to take more than 1/3 of the deliveries in any one month. The financing benefit looks like
this:

	July	Aug.	Sept.	Oct.	Nov.	Dec.	Total
N30							
Payments	$30,000	$35,000	$30,000	$10,000	$ 5,000	$10,000	$120,000
Guar. Pay.	$20,000	$20,000	$20,000	$20,000	$20,000	$20,000	$120,000
Savings	$10,000	$15,000	$10,000	−$10,000	−15,000	−$10,000	$-0-
1%/mo. PV	$615.20	$765.15	$406.04	−$303.01	−$301.50	−$100.00	$1,081.88

In other words, the savings in the first three months have a present value over the life of
the contract that offsets the extra outflow in the last three months, so that a company with a
1% per month cost of money ends up ahead by $1,081.88, which is like saying the company
receives an extra 1% discount in the cost of its goods.

The supplier-cum-lender may be equally attracted because of the certainty it brings to
his production planning. Added advantages for the buyer include the possibility of negotiating a larger quantity discount and the chance to lock in a price without fear of inflation. The

big danger for the buyer comes if his expectations of usage turn out to be too high and he's stuck with more deliveries than desired.

Consignment

While not commonly thought of as a financing technique, consignment represents a way to build inventory with minimal capital investment on the part of the consignee. Although consignment arrangements are frequently limited to small retail operations, they need not be so limited. Whenever the potential buyer-consignee has the market advantage vis-à-vis the potential consignor-seller, consignment should be a viable option. Such options and advantages are often found where a supplier is seeking to introduce a new product or break into a market previously untapped.

The term "consignment" may be anathema to the seller, as it may psychologically indicate weakness or desperation. By restructuring the arrangement to one of extended trade credit with the right of unlimited return, the same goal is accomplished. Even if the right of return is limited, the buyer may still have a satisfactory consignment-in-disguise if the limit permits the buyer to return a large enough portion of the delivery, so that the buyer is accepting not more than the amount that will equal minimum expected sales.

> **A Word of Caution:** *Consignment is rarely cost-free, as the consignee will usually remain responsible for care and security of the merchandise, and must account for all deliveries when settling out. Consequently, consignment is best arranged in writing with all duties and rights spelled out in advance.*

LEASING

Leasing has been the financing star of the postwar era. Its expansion has been mightily fueled by taxation developments, by the proliferation of lessors and lease brokers, by creative marketeers and by a broader understanding and acceptance of leasing by the business community.

There are a number of lease sources and types, each of which has certain goals and advantages. General categories include:

Straight Third Party Lease: Purely designed to get the necessary capital to permit the asset's use, a third party, such as a bank or finance company buys the chosen asset and leases it out.

Leveraged Lease: For those seeking low payments, tax benefits are ascribed to the lessor-owner to compensate for the lower payment. Leveraged leases frequently involve a broker who will locate and engage the high-tax-bracket capital.

Related Party Lease: Usually designed for maximum tax benefits, but sometimes to limit liability exposure, assets are sometimes purchased by related parties (shareholders, subsidiaries, affiliates, etc.) and leased to the intended user. Beware that ultimate tax treatment depends on a variety of factors, and special care must be taken in the structuring of each deal.

Seller's Lease: To promote sales, some sellers will offer or arrange lease financing for customers.

Guaranteed Lease: SBA and other government agencies offer lease guarantee programs that operate just like loan guarantees. These programs ought not be overlooked by qualifying companies.

The lessor looks generally at three benefits in varying combinations to produce an adequate return on capital:

1. Cash Flow — coming from the lessee's lease payment, which may sometimes include a "kicker" representing a part of the lessee's return from the employment of the asset.

2. Tax benefits — Depreciation and investment credit (if applicable) accrue to the owner of the property. Note that the lessee also sees certain tax benefits discussed below.

3. Residual Value — Sale of the leased asset at the end of the lease produces additional cash for the lessor-owner.

A fourth contribution to lessor return can be obtained from the sale or assignment of the lease contract, much in the way that any receivable Chose in Action might be sold for the present value of its payment stream.

However, that fourth return factor tends to be a function of market forces and not readily subject to the influence of the lessor or lessee. Moreover, it is economically equivalent to a sudden realization of the entire return for the lessor accomplished by the substitution of one transaction for many. The character of that substituted transaction will be determined in large part by the attributes of the first three return components in the individual lease.

Given the first three components, the lessee may look to orchestrate them so as to satisfy the lessor's craving for an adequate return while accomplishing a number of secondary lessee objectives. As long as the lessor ends up with the desired rate of return within a reasonable range of risk, the lessee can orchestrate. Knowing the applicable prevailing market rate, the lessee has the intelligence about the lessor's basic objectives.

Payments

The lessee can choose from a shopping list of terms in presenting a package to the lessor:

Accelerating payments: Payment increase during the lease, giving the lessee time to build up income generation from the asset.

Decelerating payments: Payments decrease during the term of the lease, which may allow a better matching of income to outflow where the leased asset is subject to diminishing returns as a function of age. Additionally, higher payments up front can save imputed interest costs.

Flexible payments: Lessee is provided with the option to increase or decrease payments (within calculable limits) allowing the lessee to adjust lease costs in concert with inflow generated by the leased asset.

Varying payments: Payments change with the market rate of interest, which may "float" within a range or against a ceiling or a floor or be totally unrestricted.

Chosen Period Payments: While the most common payment term is monthly, advantages might be perceived in using quarterly, semiannual or other periods.

Delayed Payments: Payments do not begin until after a brief shakedown period or until some minimum inflow is achieved, allowing the lessee time for installation and start-up.

Taxes:

Investment Credit: Under current law, if an asset qualifies for the investment tax credit, the credit will be available to the lessor. However, by agreement, it may be taken by the lessee. Logically, the lessee should prefer the credit be taken by whichever party realizes the largest saving. If the lessor takes the credit, the lessee can get lower lease payments or count on a lower buyout price at the end of the lease. If the lessee takes the credit, the tax benefit should offset other costs.

Financing Lease: If the lease is deemed to be merely a financing mechanism, the lessee is treated as the owner. The lessee may take advantage of that situation by claiming depreciation, which may bear little resemblance to the lease payment. For example, assume a transaction wherein a 50% (combined federal and state rates) tax bracket company has a $10,000 level payment financing lease on a piece of machinery, at 12% annually for 60 months.

Compare first year tax benefits:

True Lease	Financing Lease	
12 payments @ 222.44 = 2,669	Interest	1,116
50% bracket exemption = 1,334	DDB Depreciation	4,000
	Writeoff	5,116
	50% Bracket savings	2,558

Financing lease savings	2,558	
True lease savings	1,334	
Extra F. L. Savings	1,224	
% Savings Increase	91.7%	

In circumstances such as these, the lessee may want to "ruin" the lease to get the greater tax benefits. To be sure of the ultimate outcome, a full 5-year analysis must be completed (here assuming a 12% cost of capital).

Yr.	True Lease Writeoff	Tax Benefit	PV Tax B.	Financing Lease Writeoff	Tax Benefit	PV Tax B.
1	2,669	1,334	1,191	5,116	2,558	2,284
2	2,669	1,334	1,063	3,318	1,659	1,323
3	2,669	1,334	950	2,138	1,069	761
4	2,669	1,334	848	1,528	764	486
5	2,669	1,334	757	1,245	623	354
Sum	13,345		4,809	13,345		5,208

Note that although the gross write-offs are identical, the present value under the financing lease treatment is far superior for tax purposes.

To achieve financing lease status under present law, any of these actions is likely to be an effective trigger:

1. Acceptance of risk by lessee for ultimate disposition at the end of the lease; i.e., lessee guarantees a fixed price in advance.
2. Title to the property held by lessee.
3. Lessee's equity increases in the property as lease payments are made.
4. Lessee has a fixed option to purchase for a fixed price at the end of the lease, without regard to fair market value of the property at that time.
5. Part of each lease payment is designated as interest at the market rate.
6. Payments approximate property value after a period much shorter than useful life.

> **Point to Remember:** *Change in tax status for a lessee will also affect the lessor's tax status and may have adverse consequences under the terms of the lease.*

Fixed Sale: Lessee may purchase at a fixed price at the time of termination. If materially different from FMV, this may change the tax status.

Guaranteed Sale: Lessee guarantees that lessor will receive a minimum price at sale. In the event of sale above the guarantee, lessee may receive part or all of the overage. A guarantee may also threaten true lease status.

Renewability: Lessee has the right to renew the lease at the same or a different rate. If the new rate is very different from the market rate, tax status may again be endangered.

Early Cancellation: Under some conditions, a lessee may prefer to terminate the lease before the asset's useful life or contract term has expired. Under some leases the lessor may receive a cancellation penalty.

> **Note for Negotiation:** *Eliminate the penalty if the cancellation is the result of a casualty, Act of God or specified event (cancellation of income-generating contract for which asset is specifically leased) beyond your control.*

Trade-in: Lessee may be entitled to credit in purchase or leasing of another substitute asset. Trade-in may also be used in the form of a waiver of penalty as long as another asset is substituted.

Restrictions

The following terms may be of concern to various parties and may deserve consideration that is not easily subject to quantification:

Subleasing	Insurance	Indemnity	Place of Use
Maintenance	Inspection	Reporting	Type of Use

(For other related terms, see checklist for bank loans in the Banking chapter.)

SUMMARY — CHOICE OF FINANCING

Conceptually and ideally, every financing alternative is entitled to consideration for every financing need. Practically speaking, the cost to do that would outweigh the benefits.

However, a shortcut approach using a matrix technique can be employed by the borrower to test any particular need for the best financing package.

Step 1: Rank the financing objective achievability against the different methods. Depending on the nature of the needs, the methods may be analyzed by general category (e.g., inventory) or specifically (e.g., floorplanning).

Step 2: Rank the methods not eliminated in Step 1 according to terms and non-quantifiable characteristics.

Step 3: Having narrowed the choices to one or two in the preceding steps, proceed to rank the individual sources according to the characteristics of the financing offered.

Step 4: Having chosen a limited number of sources, restructure their package proposals to your best anticipated advantage and seek to negotiate as much of the restructuring as possible.

Step 5: Repeat Step 3 and choose a source.

In following this format, keep in mind that a Step "0" might precede all, consisting of a comparison by objective of the different categories of financing covered in various chapters, including Banks, Bank Alternatives and Capital Market Funds.

Chapter 11

Mastering Five Critical Capital Objectives

Permanent funds are the foundation of every business. Whether piloting a new or seasoned organization, few chief executives will ever concede possession of a surfeit of capital. New horizons, potential acquisitions, broader activities are always under consideration. Coverage of losses, the financial strength to hang on until demand improves, the economy turns around, advertising takes hold or the learning curve learns, may all make the ability to attract more permanent capital the difference between corporate life or death.

At the same time, capital that is too costly creates more problems than it solves. Capital at the right cost in the right amounts can be the saving grace of otherwise marginal operations. Refinancing with the right package may be the step that propels an average outfit to extraordinary performance.

This chapter concentrates on capital structure and the necessary analysis of the building blocks for putting that structure together.

CAPITAL STRUCTURE ELEMENTS

Land, labor and capital are the classic elements of business entities. Capital is ordinarily evaluated as composed of four types:

1. Current liabilities
2. Long-Term Debt
3. Preferred Stock
4. Common Equity

Hybrids such as convertible debt and quasi-capital such as warrants also exist and will be discussed, but the enumerated four elements are the bedrock of structural development.

Current Liabilities: Because current liabilities are "soft" as a source of capital, in that they are rapidly depleted, some might argue that their inclusion in the capital structure tends to be misleading. Such a viewpoint is entitled to credence, but practically speaking there is generally a minimum level of current liabilities that a company will always carry on its balance sheet and that will always provide some of the corporate funds.

Calculations of that minimum are merely a question of how far back a company wants to look or how accurate its forecasts of future activities are believed to be. The lowest level anticipated within a given time period (generally advised to be no more than two years in either direction) is the easiest calculation. Means, averages and standard deviations can be applied, but the relative differences are usually not material. Additionally, the lower the current liabilities included in structural considerations, the more conservative the management's plans, as current liabilities typically carry a very low cost.

Of concern in current items is the projection of potential change in their level as business conditions fluctuate, for constriction of the liabilities if the company is counting on their use. To estimate the impact, consider current liabilities in relation to other forecasted items. For example:

Accounts Payable as a function of Inventory levels.

Sales Taxes Payable as a function of Sales.

Payroll Taxes payable as a function of Payroll.

Customer Deposits as a function of Sales.

Commercial Paper as a function of Accounts Receivable.

Finally, a principal argument in favor of inclusion of current liabilities, particularly in the smaller or undercapitalized operation, is to highlight their importance in providing working capital, thereby tending to add incentive for their careful management.

Debt Term: Long-term Debt is of relative definition. As accounting convention treats debt due within one year as a current liability and all other debt as "Long-term Debt" or "Debt due in more than one year," it is convenient to adhere to that distinction.

Refinements: Some additional definitional refinements to our four elements:

A. Leases are capitalized as debt based on their present value, per accounting standards.

B. Convertible bonds should be treated as debt until converted, because their cost is based on their debt status.

C. Similarly, convertible preferred stock deserves the same logic: treatment as preferred until converted.

D. So-called "preference stock" which has preferred status, but no yield other than increases in conversion value to common stock are treated like warrants and rights as below.

E. Warrants and rights are valued at the price paid for them, i.e., the capital that flowed into the company as a result of their issuance. If issued without additional direct consideration (e.g., warrants issued as a "sweetener" to debt), no amount is included for purposes of determining capital structure, until exercised, at which time the securities issued will be valued independently based on funds flow at that exercise point.

F. Retained earnings are a part of common equity, but evaluated independently in some circumstances.

G. "Loans" from stockholders in privately held companies and inter-company debt among related entities may be treated as equity if unsecured, subordinated and created with that intent.

Warning: *Such treatment by the company may also result in similar treatment by the Internal Revenue Service, resulting in characterization of interest payments as dividends and repayments liquidating dividends or ordinary dividends, leading to higher taxes.*

CAPITAL STRUCTURE OBJECTIVES

Of course, the essential objective of capital structure is to fund the corporation's activities. That fundamental objective can be analyzed, however in terms of five sub-objectives:

I.   Capital Sufficiency

II. Capital Stability

III. Capital Flexibility

IV. Cost of Capital

V.   Leverage

Capital sufficiency is simply enough capital to take profitable advantage of business opportunities. Capital sufficiency can be further analyzed in much the same way as cash sufficiency discussed in Chapter 2. Capital sufficiency is closely related to cost of capital, as profitability is obviously a function of cost as well as gross returns.

Capital stability refers to a measurable, dependable capital base, not subject to sudden recalls of capital (e.g., on demand). Capital stability does not mean capital stagnation or a static level of capital invested in the firm. Obviously, capital levels and sources have to be adjusted to changing needs.

Capital flexibility is the capacity to make those adjustments without undue cost. Access to additional capital on call, the right to prepay or repay and the opportunity to refinance or modify existing capital terms are all aspects of flexibility, as is the prerogative to employ the funds without constraints, such as might be imposed by indenture agreements, regulations or shareholder agreements.

The last two objectives each require extensive discussion.

COST OF CAPITAL

Cost of capital is the cost associated with each of the components of the capital structure and the aggregate of these components. There are actually three variants of the cost of capital, each of which has its own significance:

1. *Component Cost of Capital*: the cost of each block of capital; e.g., a particular issue of debt or preferred stock. The importance of component cost is twofold. First it is important as a constituent of total cost and average cost. Second, it allows comparison among the components.

2. *Average Cost of Capital*: the cost of each dollar of capital in the firm based on a weighted evaluation of all the capital invested at one point in time. Its significance lies in being essential for evaluating the overall performance of the company and its profitability.

3. *Marginal Cost of Capital*: the cost of obtaining the *next* dollar of capital. Marginal cost is the best standard for assessing plans and projects.

COMPONENT COST OF CAPITAL

The component cost of capital can be mathematically defined in general terms in all situations as:

$$\frac{\text{Payout} + \text{Servicing Expenses}}{\text{Net Capital Availability}}$$

Payout includes expenditures such as dividends and interest (but not principal) required or desired on account of the continued retention of the capital by the firm.

Servicing Expenses are the costs of maintaining the capital in the firm, such as transfer agent fees, checkwriting costs, etc.

Net Capital Availability is equal to:

Gross Capital — Capital Acquisition Costs — Repayments

Gross Capital is the total stated amount of the capital block acquired.

Capital Acquisition Costs include such things as SEC registration fees, legal costs, investment banker fees, loan commitment fees and compensating balances.

Repayments are ordinarily applicable only to debt and include principal payments of direct reduction notes, leases, sinking fund requirements and other redemptions. Preferred stock redemptions and purchases of common stock for treasury shares or retirement represent the rare circumstances when repayments do occur in relation to securities other than debt.

The time span in which the component's cost of capital is analyzed is usually a one-year period.

To illustrate how component cost is calculated, here are two examples:

A common stock issue of $100,000; and

A $100,000 3-year Note with a 12% interest rate with monthly

payments of $2,160.72 and a balloon payment at the end

of the third year of $50,000.

Payouts on the common stock are annual dividends of $6,000. Servicing costs consist of $2,000 per year. No repayments are made and the $100,000 figure was the net realized at issuance; i.e., there were no capital acquisition costs. The company tax rate is 50%; which is applied to deductible costs, like servicing, so the after-tax cost of capital is shown:

$$\text{Cost of Capital} = \frac{6{,}000 + 1{,}000}{100{,}000} = 7.0\%$$

Many academicians argue that the true cost of capital of common stock is determined with reference to opportunity cost. This opportunity cost is the highest rate of return that could theoretically be earned if the same funds were invested elsewhere. From the stand-point of the *shareholder*, opportunity cost is indeed a real measure of capital costs. However, from the standpoint of the *corporation*, the imputation of a theoretical and necessarily speculative element of cost is likely to be unworthy of consideration.

Proponents of opportunity cost argue that the corporation has a duty to return to its stockholders that portion of capital that can be more profitably used by the stockholder elsewhere, as the penultimate duty of the corporation is to satisfy its equity holders for whom it theoretically exists. Practically speaking, though, there are at least seven problems with that position:

1. Capital returned in the form of dividends will be taxed to the shareholder, effectively cutting the opportunity cost by raising the capital acquisition cost.

2. Capital returned as a "return of capital" may still be taxed under a variety of tax statutes and regulations. Even where the relatively stringent requirements to escape taxation are met, the *in terrorem* effect of audits and potential liability is a potent deterrent, particularly if recurrent distributions are contemplated. These risks are of prodigious concern in the closely held firm.

3. Opportunities may not be available on an equal basis to all shareholders, or, because of differing risk patterns, may not be acceptable to all shareholders. Yet, they must usually receive identical treatment where distributions are concerned. If disproportionate payouts are accomplished through such strategems as redemption or borrowing against corporate stock, other questions arise, such as the omnipresent tax considerations and corporate control among differing shareholder groups.

4. Bond indentures and bank loan agreements, and in the case of some industries, regulations, prohibit or seriously constrain returns of capital.

5. Even if not prohibited, diminution of equity capital will likely limit the ability of the corporation to attract debt (that may be needed as replacement capital) and may raise debt's cost, as ratios and assets for security, both dear to the lender's heart, deteriorate.

6. Capital sources are not a "faucet" to be turned on and off at will. The lack of high profit, immediately available capital employment alternatives may not necessarily mean that capital ought not be "inventoried" until sufficiently attractive opportunities are located or created. Casual and repeated withdrawals of capital because of perceived opportunity cost differentials may so destroy capital stability as to render the corporation incapable of capitalizing on its real potential.

7. For publicly held companies (and for many privately held ones as well) the shareholder has an open-ended right to recover his capital (albeit with both risk of shrinkage and chance of reward) by sale in the open market. Theoreticians would almost certainly point out that buyers in the open market must perceive the company's shares as the currently paramount market opportunity, even though the company's capital balances will be unaffected by the transaction.

If there is a cost factor not represented by the payment of real dollars, it is the company's present (or next anticipated) return on the presently existing equity. It is the group of present shareholders to whom the company owes its highest loyalty, and their position can be diminished by dilution of their earnings through the addition of common stock that earns less than the old common stock, even though it adds to overall aggregate net by earning a return in excess of the payouts required to support it. Elaboration of the dilution subject follows shortly with examples, but in the meantime, the general formula of cost of capital may be adjusted for equity to:

$$\frac{\text{Return on Equity + Servicing Costs}}{\text{Net Capital Availability}}$$

Note that the Return on Equity (usually equal to net profit) will ordinarily include dividends paid out. If dividends are paid out in excess of the return earned, the formula to be used would be the original, with Payout in the numerator. Such a result must necessarily be short-ranged, as the continuing payout of dividends in excess of earnings must eventually result in the bankruptcy of the company.

The denominator of Net Capital Availability also deserves a closer look. Our example has utilized Net Capital Availability as reflected in the books of the company. This book value reflects the actual dollars that are originally received at issuance of the securities.

However, when securities are publicly traded or some other basis of establishing a fluctuating value exists, the current market value of the securities may be plugged into the denominator as Net Capital Availability to reflect the cost the company would incur were it to venture into the capital market today. That present market cost is a meaningful criterion, for it signifies the level of profitability the company must earn if it is to continue to grow, as growth will require additional capital.

The distinction between Cost of Capital on Book versus Market can be conceptualized this way:

Book Value Cost connotes actual minimum return; i.e., the rate of return the company *can* achieve and break even. A return in excess of that level will mean the company is profitable.

Market Value Cost connotes the appropriate minimum return; i.e., the rate of the return the company *should* achieve as a theoretical break-even point.

If Market is above Book, it is the proper standard of evaluation of performance if the company is to remain competitive for funds. If Book is above Market, the company should refinance to obtain the lower cost at the present Market rate. Until such refinancing is accomplished, performance must be measured against the higher standard of Book Cost, because a rate of return above Market, but below Book, will result in a loss — which may be defined as a negative real rate of return. Hence, the performance standard is the higher of Market or Book, although both rates should be determined to find all the implications inherent in the two figures.

One other point to note about common stock is that the balance of retained earnings might also be included as a part of Net Capital Availability, as these retained funds accrue ultimately to shareholders. Alternatively, as in our example, they are not included. Instead, retained earnings are considered as a separate component with a cost of zero. This second alternative is favored to prevent distortions in historical costs that could develop as profits fluctuate. These distortions would be particularly egregious in a company with a negative retained earnings balance, as the denominator of the Cost formula would be reduced to a point so low that the overall cost would reach an astronomical level. While the prior losses would arguably be a part of the capital cost, it should not be incumbent on the company to recover all of those losses at one time, which would be the effect of using the loss adjusted equity. Of course, immediate recovery is desirable, but attempting to force it might brand all potential operations as losers because their rate of return cannot accomplish one-time recovery, even though they are profitable in a real sense as would be seen if measured against Book or Market cost unadjusted for past losses.

As to the debt portion of our examples, we'll examine the first year of the Note. Monthly payments of $2,160.72 break down as follows:

Principal	$14,720.83
Interest	11,207.81
Total	$25,928.64 which reconciles to 12 × $2,160.72

Assume that our lender also requires a $2,000 compensating balance. Legal and administrative costs expended in the acquisition of the capital totalled $1,000. Servicing expenses are $500. The company tax rate remains 50%.

$$\text{Cost of Capital} = \frac{(\text{Interest} + \text{Servicing Expenses})(\text{Tax Rate})}{\text{Face Value} - (\text{Issue Cost})(\text{Tax Rate}) - \text{Comp. Bal.} - \text{Prin. Repaid}}$$

$$\text{Cost of Capital} = \frac{(\$11,207.81 + 500.00)(50\%)}{\$100,000 - (1,000)(50\%) - 2,000 - (14,720.83/2)}$$

$$\text{Cost of Capital} = \frac{5,853.91}{90,139.59} = 6.494\% \text{ After Tax Cost}$$

Note that the principal repayments of the Note are end-point averaged $(14,720.83/2)$ to reflect company use of those funds during less than all of the year. Monthly calculations can be more precise:

Repayment #	Opening Loan Balance	Principal Repaid	Closing Balance
1	100,000.00	1,160.72	98,839.28
2	98,839.28	1,172.33	97,666.95
3	97,666.95	1,184.05	96,482.90
4	96,482.90	1,195.88	95,287.02
5	95,287.02	1,207.85	94,079.17
6	94,079.17	1,219.93	92,859.24
7	92,859.24	1,232.12	91,627.12
8	91,627.12	1,244.45	90,382.67
9	90,382.67	1,256.89	89,125.78
10	89,125.78	1,269.47	87,856.31
11	87,856.31	1,282.16	86,574.15
12	86,574.15	1,294.98	85,279.17
Totals	1,120,780.59	14,720.83	

Average loan outstanding = 1,120,780.59/12 = 93,398.38

Plugging into the formula, for Face Value and Principal Repaid:

$$\text{Cost of Capital} = \frac{(11,207.81 + 500.00)(50\%)}{93,398.38 - 2,000 - (1,000)(50\%)} = \frac{5,853.91}{90,898.38} = 6.440\%$$

AVERAGE COST OF CAPITAL

Once the Component Cost of Capital is found, the average is calculated for the company by aggregating and weighting all of the components, and dividing by the total amount of capital weight. For example:

Capital Item Name	Net Capital Available	Annual After-Tax Cost	Weighted Value
Current Liabilities:			
90-Day Note	$ 75,000	6.0%	4,500
Accounts Payable	115,000	3.6	4,140
Customer Deposits	41,000	2.5	1,025
Total Current	231,000	Av. = 4.2	9,665
Debt:			
Bond 1	75,000	4.5%	3,375
Bond 2	50,000	5.3	2,650
Debentures	50,000	4.7	2,350
Mortgage	200,000	3.5	7,000
Total Debt	375,000	Av. = 4.1	15,375
Preferred Stock:			
Series A	50,000	8.2	4,100
Common Equity:			
Common Stock	125,000	6.1	7,625
Retained Earnings	75,000	0.0	-0-
Total Common Equity	200,000	Av. = 3.8	7,625
Total Capital	$856,000	4.3%	$36,765

Corporate After-Tax Average Cost of Capital is 4.3%.

A few of the fine points of this particular example:

1. Component Cost is stated on an *Annualized* after-tax basis. Assumed here is a 50% tax rate. On the 90-day Note, 3% of the capital will actually be paid out on a pretax basis as interest, which annualizes on a 360-day year to 12% [(360/90)(3%)] which equates to 6.0% after tax.

2. The cost of Accounts Payable was calculated as follows:

One-half of payables offer terms of 1/10 N30.

The 1% discount is missed in 40% of those cases (20% of all payables).

1% for 10 days is an annualized rate of 36%.

20% of all payables at 36% equals 7.2% cost pretax.

With a 50% tax rate, 7.2% yields 3.6%.

3. Customer Deposits in this business by contract earn 5% in pretax interest, or cost 2.5% after tax.

4. Costs of each of the four types of capital are shown as subtotals (Preferred Stock with only one component is not repeated) which are themselves weighted by individual components, to provide additional perspective on capital costs.

5. Weight does not equal after-tax cost paid out, as the weight is calculated on an annualized basis. If all of the components were paid for on a yearly basis, weight would equal cost. This point is mentioned because some businessmen use actual expenditures to measure the cost of capital, which will yield misleading results if not time adjusted.

6. Average Cost of Capital is calculated at a specific point in time. Like any calculations derived from balance sheet items, the degree to which it will be representative of the company's true average cost during the year will be a function of how representative the balance sheet itself turns out to be. Consequently, the astute reviewer will verify and adjust the figures if the chosen statement is momentarily skewed, as when a company makes a concerted effort to reflect an annual short-term debt "clean-up" in the year-end statement, or when management otherwise controls the objectivity of the statement.

7. The same methodology is employed to show Market Average Cost, using the Market Cost of Components. After-Tax Cost and Weight will differ from those shown in the Book example.

8. Use of the method as a simulation tool to assess the impact of changes in the capital structure on average cost is advised to guide capital planning.

MARGINAL COST OF CAPITAL

With Component and Average under our belts, Marginal is an easier concept to deal with, but one that still holds very complex subjective implications. Marginal Cost is the cost of obtaining the *next* (not the most recent) unit of capital.

Speaking in purely mathematical terms, Marginal Cost is calculated just like any other component and will probably vary depending on what type of capital is under consideration.

But pure mathematics is not very helpful here. In broader terms, the addition of new capital will almost certainly have impact on the cost of precedent capital and subsequent capital.

Continuing increases in current and debt liabilities will reflect unfavorably on the company's image of financial stability. Higher risk perception ultimately demands higher payouts in interest and dividends. Substantial increases in liabilities can even threaten the company's ability to obtain *any* further credit.

Increases in preferred stock place greater stress on common earnings, because of the priority of preferred dividends, without the benefit of deductibility as interest enjoys. Consequently, preferred stock often has the highest after-tax cost from the perspective of the company.

Additions to common stock involve especially crucial issues:

1. Dilution of book value may occur. Dilution is the allocation of net worth (book value) to a larger number of shares. Dilution of value will occur if shares are issued for consideration less than present book value per share. For example:

	Total Book Value	# of Shares	B.V./Share
Initial Status	$1,000,000	100,000	$10.00
New Issue	250,000	50,000	5.00
Total After New Issue	$1,250,000	150,000	$ 8.33

In effect, each of the new shares takes $1.67 from the previously existing shares to achieve parity. This will generally not be pleasing to the old shareholders.

2. Similarly, dilution of earnings would occur if the return earned on the newly acquired capital is less than that otherwise achievable on the old capital, as in this example:

	Total Earnings	# of Shares	E.P.S.
Initial Status	$100,000	100,000	$1.00
New Issue	35,000	50,000	0.70
Total After New Issue	$135,000	150,000	$0.90

Why, one might ask, would the company bother raising such capital if the return is going to penalize the older shareholders? The capital may be required to meet expenditures required by regulation or committed for. The shares may be issued in a merger, the benefits of which may not be readily realizable. There are other situations, but the more important issue is often the understanding of the risk of dilution if the earnings anticipated from a new issue are not achieved.

Note too that the earnings are assumedly a return on the capital employed and are further assumed to be discreetly allocable to particular issues. These assumptions may not be necessarily applicable or verifiable, as capital is fungible. It might be worth adding that the appearance of earnings dilution can be erroneous, as the additional capital might be absolutely indispensable if the company is going to be able to achieve even the diluted level of profitability.

3. Ownership control of the corporation is a function of common stock distribution. (Exceptions exist for classes of common stock, but there is always some bedrock stock that carries the voting power.) The smaller the number of preexisting shareholders, the larger the issue of control looms. The *value* of control, both practically and psychologically, means that new shares threatening control entail a higher subjective cost, as the loss of control must be justified by a higher return on the capital so employed.

4. In the privately held outfit, the inclusion of new shareholders is of extraordinary import and may effectively preclude issuance of new shares. Not only is ownership involved, but the chemistry and personalities of additional owners in a small group can have repercussions that affect every aspect of management, operations and profit.

5. In the public company (and some private ones, too) the prospect of a takeover must be considered in wider distribution of shares.

6. In the small corporation, common stock issuance can affect the firm's eligibility to elect or retain Subchapter S treatment under the Internal Revenue Code, whereby the corporation is not taxed as a separate entity. Instead, its earnings are "flowed through" to common stockholders in proportion to their ownership.

7. The initial public issuance of stock not only involves a fundamental change in the company's control, but introduces new regulatory burdens, responsibilities and costs.

Recall that Marginal Cost of Capital is the best standard for project evaluation. The decision that the marginal capital whose cost will serve as the benchmark will be one sort of capital (e.g., debt) or another (e.g., common) may well be misleading.

Assume that the marginal capital for a firm, based on ratios and the state of the capital markets, will be preferred stock with an after-tax cost of 9%. The project under consideration will return a comparable 8%. Because the return is below cost, the project would be rejected.

Shortly thereafter, conditions change and the marginal issue becomes debt with cost of 6%. Another project is now under review with a return of 7%. Since return exceeds cost, project accepted.

But such a result is ludicrous: An 8% return is preferable to 7%.

Therefore, the highest marginal cost among all capital alternatives is the better measure. It is also okay to use an average of present market costs, preferably weighted with the company's ideal capital structure. However, if the ideal structure differs substantially from current structure, some adjustment to cost may be necessary.

Some managers use the firm's present average cost of capital, but if the firm has an excess of old capital at rates far different from current market, a disservice is done if the company might acquire new capital.

There is ordinarily a great deal of leeway in picking this marginal target, and the judgment the financial manager uses can have far-reaching effect. Exercising that judgment within a well-defined range of possibilities, with a firm grasp on the facts of the situation, is most likely to lead to goal achievement.

LEVERAGE

Leverage may be defined as the employment of fixed cost capital in pursuit of an unfixed return. The fifth objective of capital structure is an important influence on both profitability and aggregate cost of capital.

Leverage is most easily explained by example.

Assume two firms, each with identical sales and cost profiles and the same amount of invested capital, but differing capital structures:

	Firm I	Firm II
Capital Structure:		
10% Debt	50,000	-0-
Equity	50,000	100,000
Total Capital	100,000	100,000
Sales	500,000	500,000
Operating Expenses	− 450,000	− 450,000
Operating Net Income	50,000	50,000
Interest Expense	−5,000	-0-
Pretax Net	45,000	50,000
50% Tax Rate	−22,500	−25,000
After Tax Net	22,500	25,000
Return on Equity	45%	25%

Firm I's shareholders realize a substantially higher rate of return, because fixed cost debt provides half the capital needed at a cost below the average operating return on total capital:

Operating Return = Operating Net/Total Capital

Operating Return = 50,000/100,000 = 50%

Point to Remember: *In comparing the rate of the fixed cost capital to operating return, be sure that both rates are calculated on the same (either pre- or after-) tax basis.*

When the fixed cost capital earns an above-cost return, the leverage is favorable, but earnings below cost will cut the return to shareholders:

	Firm I	Firm II
Capital Structure:		
10% Debt	50,000	-0-
Equity	50,000	100,000
Total Capital	100,000	100,000
Operating Net	6,000	6,000
Interest	−5,000	-0-
Pretax Net	1,000	6,000
Taxes @ 50%	−500	−3,000
Net Income	500	3,000
Return on Equity	1.0%	3.0%

And will magnify the effect of losses:

	Firm I	Firm II
Operating Net	(5,000)	(5,000)
Interest	−5,000	-0-
Pretax Net	(10,000)	(5,000)
Taxes	NA	NA
Net Income	(10,000)	(5,000)
Return on Equity	(20%)	(5%)

Therefore, the greater the leverage, the greater the risk.

Some degree of leverage is generally desirable to magnify earnings. The point at which leverage becomes too heavy is a part of determining the optimum capital structure.

OPTIMUM CAPITAL STRUCTURE

Let us define Optimum Capital Structure as that combination of invested capital that produces the highest SUSTAINABLE net return to common shareholders. "Sustainable" means that our view is a long-term one. While it may be possible to show enormous profit in one year, if those profits are achieved through massive overextension that will bankrupt the company in the next year, the overextended structure is clearly not optimal.

As long as the sustainable rate of return on additional capital will exceed the cost of that capital, it is desirable to acquire the additional funds. Furthermore, the more capital *profitably* employed, the higher the return. (Remember, we are basing cost of equity capital on current return to existing shareholders, so that the return must exceed that cost to be "profitable.") Hence, the optimum capital structure is one that will allow us the greatest amount of capital at an acceptable cost.

Recalling our initial objectives, that greatest amount must be

1. *Sufficient* for our needs;
2. *Flexible* in its terms;
3. *Stable* as far as our ability to retain it is concerned.
4. Acceptable in *Cost*; and
5. Entails acceptable risk, as evidenced by the extent of *Leverage*.

All of these objectives implicitly postulate a known rate of return on which our capital decisions can be based. At the same time, we can visualize units of capital standing at attention to be summoned forth to duty in order of the cost associated with each.

Graphically, this scenario of capital availability reflects the environment in which the structure decisions are made:

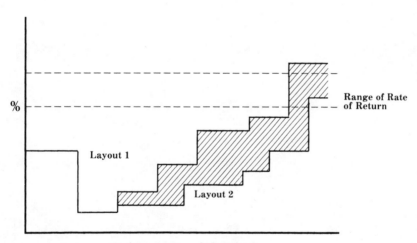

$ Amounts of Capital

Initially, capital cost is relatively high, as start-up capital tends to be more expensive because of the risk associated with it. As more capital is added, it is initially cheaper, rising in cost as supply diminishes and investors grow warier of overextension.

What the firm seeks to do is to go as far rightward as possible in acquiring capital (i.e., greatest amount) while keeping the cost at or below the range of the rate of return. Moving the capital cost configuration from Layout 1 to Layout 2 adds the profits in the shaded area.

The steps to be taken to make that move while continuing to meet the five capital objectives are examined in the next chapter.

Chapter 12

Ten Proven Tactics That Provide the Right Capital At the Right Time

The tactical steps to be taken in satisfying our five capital objectives as outlined in the last chapter are the subject of this chapter. The steps that will make capital available affect the units of capital one at a time. The process of selling a stake in the company is like the process of selling almost anything. If the product is not at least as attractive as competitive alternatives, the product will not sell.

Each of the tactics adopted seeks to promote the achievement of one or more of our five objectives:

I. Sufficiency

II. Stability

III. Flexibility

IV. Cost

V. Leverage

and the whole fabric woven of these tactics must adequately clothe the company in capital tailored within the minimum tolerances of each of those objectives.

MARKET DEFINITION

In broad terms there are five markets from which capital may be attracted:

1. Individual Investors

2. Institutional Investors (Non-Corporate)

3. Corporate Investors

4. Lenders (Those only offering debt capital)

5. Governments (Federal, State, Local and Foreign and their agencies)

213

These labels are less than perfect, because some entities will have a presence in more than one market. For example, a commercial bank will be a lender, will have a trust department acting as an institutional investor, may from time to time be seeking an equity position for its own account (as a corporate investor) and will even act as a conduit or participant in government programs, such as SBA guarantee programs. And all the while, the bank's officers, directors and employees maintain their personal identity as individual investors (although insider trading rules and ethical considerations of conflict of interest must be mentioned in passing and strictly observed).

Nonetheless, it is convenient to think in terms of these broad categories to help identify the investor motivations to which various tactics will be more responsive and, hence, more successful. All five of these larger categories can be divided into investor subgroups as in this partial listing:

Individuals:

Present Investors	Previous Investors
Upper-Income Investors	Small Investors
Employees	

Institutions:

Pension Funds	Trust Funds
Mutual Funds	Foundations
Insurance Companies	Labor Unions

Corporations:

Competitors (Merger)	Vendors
Suppliers	Customers
Affiliates	SBIC's
Investment Bankers	Venture Capitalists

Lenders:

Domestic Banks	Foreign Banks
Finance Companies	Insurance Companies
Investment Bankers	Money Market Funds

Government:

Federal Programs	Federal Agencies
State Agencies	Municipal Agencies
Small Business Admin.	Business Development Agencies
Foreign Authorities	

While some of these subgroups may be unconventional (e.g., labor unions), none should be rejected out of hand. In fact, the location of unconventional sources is a major coup for the financial manager, so long as the funds derived fit into the firm's capital objectives and strategy.

INVESTOR MOTIVATIONS

Of course, the ultimate investor motivation is the highest net return free of risk. The components of these two standards — risk and reward — are the focus of these tactics.

Return Components

1. *Return on equity:* Overall profitability to the shareholder, the backbone of immediate reward, which may also be manifested as "interest coverage" for debt investors.

2. *Earnings Growth:* The promise of continuous increasing profitability and an indicator of potential worth of the firm and its shares.

3. *Cash Flow:* Hard dollar profitability, of particular importance in non-corporate operations such as real estate investment trusts.

4. *Dividends and Interest Payouts:* Reward in hard dollars as to each unit of investment.

5. *Dividend Growth:* The promise of greater hard dollar potential and another factor in worth.

6. *Equity Value Growth:* Increase in net asset value, either as a result of increases in book value, market value or both, brought about by increasing profitability or increases in asset values.

7. *Taxability:* Maintained at as low a level as possible and a function of the circumstances of the individual securities.

8. *Securities Value:* Increases in intrinsic worth because of the greater assets represented thereby, and/or in market value simply as a function of supply, demand, and market rates, although demand may well be induced by changes in intrinsic value.

Risk

9. *Stability:* Not in terms of remaining static, but in not being erratic.

10. *Predictability:* A cousin of stability, but encompassing opportunity for the investor to make plans in relation to the investment.

11. *Liquidity:* The ability to change from one investment to another, or into cash for expenditure.

12. *Convertibility:* The opportunity to swap for another investment without the intermediate step of cashing out.

13. *Control:* The ability to influence or restrain the company and its risks and opportunities.

14. *Security:* Sufficient net asset value to assure the worth of the investment.

15. *Reputation:* The history and character of the company and its principals.

16. *Self-Sufficiency:* Avoidance of the need to invest more to support prior investments. Not to be confused with the opportunity to increase the investment at will to reap a greater return.

INVESTOR MOTIVATION TALLY

An Investor Motivation Tally will help to match and mold securities to investors. The sheet subjectively appraises the investor group or subgroup motivations in the format shown in this example:

INVESTOR SUBGROUP: SBIC's/Venture Capitalists
Amount to Be Raised: $1,000,000
Security Type: Equity

Motivation	Priority	Level Required	Company Sufficiency
Return on Equity	7	20% per year	Possible
Earnings Growth	2	25% per year	Likely
Cash Flow	9	Steady; 2/1 Cur.Rat.	Yes
Dividends/Interest	13	None	Yes
Dividend Growth	8	Begin w/in 3 yrs.	Difficult
Equity value Growth	1	12% per year	Possible
Taxability	15	Not Meaningful	NM
Stability	12	No deficits 5 yrs.	No
Predictability	3	Close curve fit	Good
Liquidity	4	90 days to cash	Difficult
Convertibility	14	None required	Yes
Control	5	Contingent	Acceptable
Security	11	Equal Investment	Difficult
Reputation	6	Clean	Yes
Self-sufficiency	10	20% on call	Yes

Once the potential investor target groups are evaluated in this way, choose those where the company is sufficient and where the investor's higher priorities dovetail with the company's strengths. Then, to achieve the most favorable satisfaction of the capital objectives, undertake to structure the investment with tactical maneuvers that also improve the company's responsiveness to the investor priorities.

TACTICAL ALTERNATIVES — DEBT

All of the structural tactics listed in the chapters on Banking and Bank Debt Alternatives apply to debt and are relisted here for convenience:

Variable Interest Rates	Balloon Payments
Automatic Renewability	Collateral Substitution
Larger Collateral Write-off	Prepayment
Callability	Leasing
Tax Benefit Passthrough	Funding Options
Pledge of Future Collateral	Guarantees
Subordination	Indenture Restrictions
Multiple Entities	Residual Value Adjustment
Accelerating Payments	Decelerating Payments
Flexible Payments	Fair Market Value Buyout
Fixed Sale Buyout	Guaranteed Sale Buyout
Early Cancellation	Trade-In

Additionally, lenders, particularly where long-term loans are involved, may be enticed by "equity kickers" or an opportunity to participate in profitability while retaining the safer status of an assured return and prior claim on assets. The borrower may also desire an equity kicker to bolster, presently or potentially, the equity portion of the capital structure.

Such a kicker can take these forms:

Warrants/Options: The right of the lender to also buy equity. Several variations can be used, including:

A. Fixed Price — usually at or above the market value price at time of issuance, but below prices anticipated in the future.

B. Declining Price — If the initial price is set above current market, the price may be made to decline at fixed intervals so that the lower price will encourage eventual exercise.

C. Increasing Price — If the price is set to rise, the portent of that increase will encourage purchase early on.

D. Renewability — Right of the issuer to extend the time for purchase.

E. Contingency — Not exercisable unless certain events occur. This twist is usually used as a method for the lender to exercise control via ownership in the event of borrower default or shortfall in standards.

F. Cash Payment — Warrants may be exercised only by cash on delivery.

G. Debt Payment — Warrants may be exercised by payment in cash or by cancellation of debt. If debt is issued at high interest rates relative to historic and anticipated levels, the company may favor this alternative, as its ability to buy in the debt will be limited by the higher market price or relatively higher call price. Conversely, if debt is issued when rates are relatively low, this term is undesirable, as cash payment can be used to retire the debt at a cost below face value.

H. Repurchase — If warrants can be bought back by the issuer, it encourages exercise if called for purchase when market price is above exercise price. Alternatively, exercise can be permanently avoided if market is below exercise, and the issuer repurchases. Where stock is closely held and there is no market, avoidance or encouragement will depend on the holder's view of company worth.

I. Assignability — Allows the lender to sell or assign the warrants, thereby being able to realize a return on them without having to exercise.

Convertibility: The lender has the chance to convert to equity by cancelling the debt under these alternatives:

A. Fixed Conversion — A fixed number of shares for each specific amount of debt face value.

B. Decreasing Conversion — Fewer shares per specific amount of face value as time passes or events occur.

C. Increasing Conversion — More shares per specific amount of face value as time passes or events occur.

D. Revertibility — Lender must convert, it being the borrower's choice to demand it, and may be limited to certain circumstances. This term is rarely used, but instead most debt is callable and the holder will usually convert upon call if the value of the shares obtained by conversion will exceed call price.

E. Mixed Conversion – The debt may be converted into shares of another entity (i.e., not the debtor), such as that of a parent or subsidiary.

A third form of equity kicker is the direct issuance of shares along with the debt in the form of "units" where the face value of the debt plus the market value of the stock exceed the price of the unit. The interest rate on the debt may be below market rates, so that the market value of the debt may be below face value.

A fourth form of equity kicker is pure profit participation without actual equity ownership, through increases in the payments due on debt as a function of profitability. These payments may be in the form of "bonus interest" or the applicable interest rate may be changed to change the payment or the face value of the debt may be increased.

TACTICAL ALTERNATIVES — EQUITY

Because one share of stock must be treated like any other of its class, the initial issue of stock determines many of the attributes of future issues. Similarly, changes and decisions involving new issues also have a retroactive impact on the outstanding shares. Nonetheless, equity also may entail some tactical considerations:

Tandem Offers — Sale of equity together with debts, as in unit offers above, offers savings in issuance costs and should make both securities more attractive than either would be alone, as where a tandem offer permits maintenance of desired capital structure. (Sales of common with preferred stock are another form of tandem.) Such offers may allow investors to choose one or the other security or may sell only in unit form, depending on which approach is likely to be the most successful in the marketplace.

Classes — Common stock may be segregated into classes with the approval of state authorities governing corporate charters. The situation most frequently producing adoption of classes involves voting control without dividends in one class and limited or no voting with dividend preference in the other class. The second class is issued instead of preferred stock, because preferred's fixed dividends are not desirable. Two pitfalls of class usage:

1. In closely held companies, the issuance of more than one class of stock will prohibit election or retention of Subchapter S status for corporate income tax treatment.

2. Presently, the New York Stock Exchange will not list classes of common stock.

Options Market — Since the early 1970's, trading in listed put and call options has attracted substantial funds and attention.

A listed option is a contract to buy (Call) or sell (Put) a stock at a fixed price (usually a multiple of $5 or $10) by a certain date (usually within a year). The offeror (Writer) is paid for the option by the offeree (Holder) who can sell the option prior to exercise. Calls increase in price with the underlying stock, whereas puts increase in price as the price declines.

There are two schools of thought on options relative to the listed company:
Those opposed often cite these reasons:

1. Options attract funds that would otherwise be invested directly in the stock.

2. Options promote volatility in the underlying stock price by their operation and by fostering speculation.

3. Near the expiration time there is artificial activity in stock trading that tends to distort price and ignore fundamentals.

4. Options, being a strictly short-term investment, promote short-term management goals.

5. Options introduce another item of securities regulatory burden.

Those in favor usually point to these factors:

1. Options create interest in a stock that attracts additional investment.

2. With the hedge that options provide, institutions particularly are able to invest with less concern and able to stick with a stock in difficult periods, thereby promoting stability.

3. Options provide an additional dimension of the market's assessment of a company's prospects, useful for planning future securities marketing.

4. Options provide shareholders with a measure of liquidity that promotes share retention, as the holder need not sell off shares to obtain cash.

There is merit to both sides of these arguments, but on balance, options listing would be an attractive opportunity for most companies, as the "pro" arguments tend to be borne out by experience.

Options may also present one other opportunity, that of the company itself writing call options as an ongoing capital attraction program. There are a number of noteworthy legal hurdles to overcome, such as exemption from preemptive rights for some companies, and continuous SEC registration maintenance for all. There are also limits to the amount of such activity the company can engage in and such activity must be carefully calculated not to artificially influence the price or trading of either the stock or the option. Once these hurdles are overcome, however, a company can sell calls regularly, pocketing the premiums. Calls exercised can be satisfied out of new issues or treasury stock, capturing more funds when exercise occurs.

Here are three practical problems:

A. If the company writes too many calls it will drive down the option price, reducing the attractiveness of the sales. The options markets are frequently "thin" so that relatively few transactions can induce relatively large price swings.

B. Transaction costs are relatively high both absolutely and because the company must necessarily deal in small increments, increasing the cost of the capital so obtained.

C. Dilution can occur as with any other additional equity sales. Hence, a company is effectively foreclosed (or should be) from the market if contract prices are below book value.

Rights — Issuance of rights is much like listing options, except that rights offerings are generally completed within a short period, usually not over a month. Marketability of rights provides a way for shareholders to be rewarded with hard cash by the company. Similarly, they are also rewarded by the opportunity to acquire additional shares with less-than-average transaction costs while maintaining their relative control position within the overall shareholder community. At the same time, rights offerings can provide the issuer with savings over the cost of a straight issue, although the issuer is accepting the risk that not all of the rights will be exercised, and, therefore, not all the capital hoped for will be raised. Theoretically, that danger can be offset by increasing the number of rights, thereby anticipating a shortfall in exercise that will bring in the amount of capital desired. However, that approach may raise the prospect of dilution in relation to the price of the shares.

For example, assume 1,000 shares outstanding before the offering carrying a price of $20 per share, which happens to equal book value, but also reflects a price–earnings ratio of 10X on E.P.S. of $2. Assume the company wants to raise $20,000 with a rights offering in which it expects to succeed in selling 90% of the shares offered, and on which it anticipates a 10% return. If it puts out an offer of one right for one share at $20 per share and 90% are exercised, only $18,000 will be raised. If the company decides to offer 1,112 shares, on the theory that 90% of that number exercised will yield 1,000 new shares, the market will evaluate the offer on the basis that only $2,000 in profit is anticipated from the capital to be raised (10% × $20,000), but if all the shares are bought there will be 2,112 shares outstanding to split only $4,000 in profit, yielding an E.P.S. of $1.89 per share and a price of $18.90 if the PE ratio holds. The best solution to this problem is to offer the rights to purchase shares at a slight discount (say $19.50 per share) to encourage the exercise of all the rights, account for some limited dilution in profit and to imbue the rights with an intrinsic market value (in this case $20.00 − $19.50 = $.50 per right) that will place them in demand to stimulate exercise. Note, however, that this approach may drive the share price down to $19.50.

Stock Dividends and Splits — The technical distinction between stock dividends and splits is that the former result in no change in par value, while splits reduce par value per share. Stock dividends result in an accounting entry crediting capital stock and debiting paid in capital or capital surplus. In companies with no-par stock, the distinction is essentially semantic. In any case, there are four reasons for employing them:

1. To keep equity prices in a range believed likely to promote purchase. Many analysts believe this level is usually above $25 per share and below $100 per share. Price at too low a level may denigrate the stock by relating it to those with low prices that are selling down there because of poor quality. Prices too high take a round lot out of the purchase range of many individual investors, even though such investors are generally less of a force in the market than in previous times.

2. To increase the distribution by putting more shares in the hands of the public.

3. To provide shareholders with more liquidity as they can sell off a part of their holdings with greater ease.

4. In the closely held corporation, to permit sales to third parties (e.g., employees) without giving up large amounts of voting power.

To raise the price of stock and reduce the float (i.e., shares outstanding) some companies have resorted to "reverse splits" wherein a fewer number of shares are issued in exchange for outstanding shares. However, such a tactic can boomerang precisely because the smaller distribution, higher price, greater illiquidity and tighter control may make the shares less attractive.

Par, No-Par, Authorized Shares and Stated Capital — These concepts have lost a great deal of their old-fashioned importance and are now of interest in most cases only as a determinant of charter, qualification and franchise fees in various states and taxing jurisdictions. Nonetheless, in the closely held corporation, particularly as expansion requires qualification in more and more jurisdictions, a restructuring of capital accounts and share terms can produce material savings in the applicable fees and taxes.

Exchange Listing — Listing of shares on an exchange usually makes shares more attractive by providing holders with greater liquidity and by promoting awareness of the company. The formalization of listing may also add to the company's image of progress with stability. The value of listing even on a regional exchange should not be overlooked, particularly as the initial listing will give the company's stock national exposure through the financial media that it might not otherwise enjoy, thereby opening up new capital territories for potential conquest.

Employee Stock Ownership Plans — ESOP's were created by enabling federal legislation in 1976. They permit a corporation to recapture income taxes in the form of additional equity. There are two basic types of plans. Deduction plans involve a donation by the company to a trust qualifying for a deduction to the extent of the donation, thereby reducing corporate income tax. The trust then invests the proceeds in the company stock, returning the actual cash to the corporation, while leaving the taxes owed at a lower level. (See Figure A.) Credit type plans permit companies to also take an additional investment tax credit on qualifying property, so long as the additional credit flows into a trust. The trust uses the taxes saved to purchase corporate shares. Credit type plans may also encompass the mechanics of deduction plans, but need not. (See Figure B.)

In both types of plans, each employee's interest is a function of his salary. Plans are subject to essentially the same rules and regulations as other deferred compensation plans.

It is also possible to leverage these plans. In such circumstances, the company borrows from a bank or other lender, pledging its shares as collateral, with the company frequently guaranteeing the debt. The money borrowed is repaid by the trust's income from company dividends. The money borrowed is of course invested in additional stock. (See Figure C.)

In all plans, to the extent not used for administrative costs and to repay debt, dividends are reinvested in stock, which is distributed to employees when they retire or otherwise terminate their employment. Thus, ESOP's may also have a substantial employee relations benefit that rewards the employee with additional deferred income and, properly presented, increases motivation as the employee has a direct stake in the company's future.

In addition to the employee benefit value and the use of taxes as a capital source, ESOP's also provide an excellent estate planning tool for the closely held corporation, as the trust can become the beneficiary of "buy-sell" life insurance on the life of the principal owner, the proceeds of which it will use to buy the owner's shares on death.

The major disadvantages of ESOP's are:

1. A certain element of control is passed to employees via their shares.

2. ESOP's generate a certain amount of administrative expense like other deferred compensation plans requiring tax qualification.

3. ESOP's may create a "market overhang" in the sense that a large number of shares may be concentrated in one place. However, as these shares are generally distributed piecemeal to terminating employees, this disadvantage tends to be remote.

FIGURE A
CONVENTIONAL PLAN
(Unleveraged)

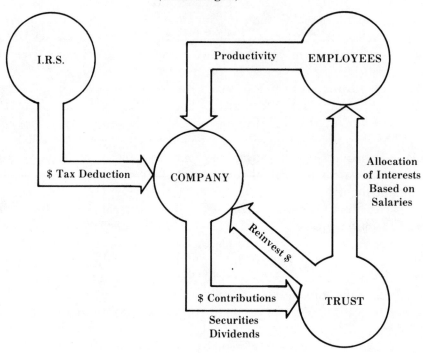

FIGURE B
TAX REDUCTION PLAN
(Unleveraged)

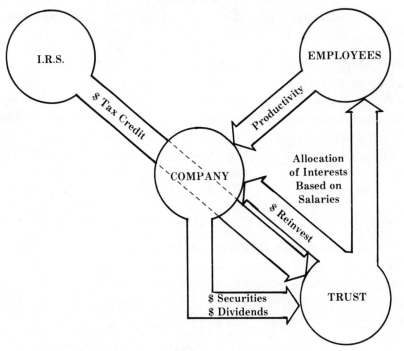

NOTE: Company serves as a conduit for the tax credit moneys.

222

FIGURE C
TAX REDUCTION PLAN
(Leveraged)

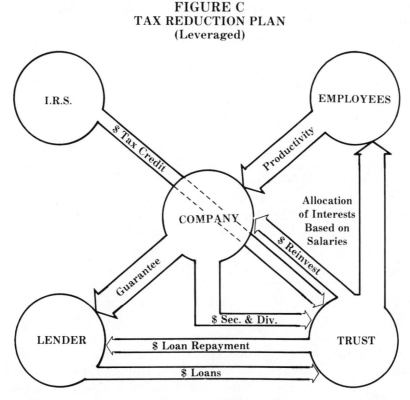

Dividends — Dividend policy concepts vary substantially with the corporation's circumstances. In the closely held corporation, because of double taxation, dividends are usually best avoided. These techniques are helpful for avoiding dividend declaration, but still permit compensation to shareholders:

1. Characterization of some equity as debt payable to shareholders. Payments against such debt will either be deductible to the corporation as interest or non-taxable distributions to the shareholder as a return of capital (repayment of debt).

2. Payment of bonuses and additional salary, which are deductions to the corporation.

3. Deferral of payout by establishment of a qualified pension plan, heavily skewed to the extent possible within regulatory limits, in favor of shareholders.

4. Purchase of business assets by shareholders. Instead of putting the cash into the corporation, which would then buy necessary assets, the shareholder makes the purchase directly and leases the asset to the corporation. Lease rates must be reasonable relative to the market, but still provide an opportunity for the owner to pick up additional income without double taxation. This method also has the advantages of safeguarding some corporate assets from corporate liability, allows the shareholder to pick up investment tax credit and avoids payroll taxes on the payouts that might otherwise be salary. Further, the IRS can question "excessive" salary payments to shareholders and elect to treat them as dividends to obtain the double taxation and higher tax revenue. While leasing will not provide an absolute safeguard against such a claim (e.g., the IRS can claim the transactions to be a sham among related parties getting to the double taxation point by another route), it is a

method that draws attention away from a single outstanding focal point, such as a high salary, and offers an additional legitimate business argument for higher deductible payouts to the shareholder.

5. While not an avoidance of dividends, election of qualifying corporations of Subchapter S status "collapses" the taxable entity into one, while dividends paid out are exempt from payroll taxes.

Warning: *Tax authorities may characterize transactions differently.*

In the public company, dividend policy is more complex because a plethora of factors conflict with one another. While double taxation and future internal cash needs merit caution in making payouts, the need to attract additional capital and the desire to increase stock price and shareholder approval incline toward ever-increasing dividends.

At the same time, stockholders themselves may have conflicting goals. Upper income holders may prefer that the company retain the earnings and that their stock increase in equity value accordingly. Others may desire the income in immediate form.

Yet, in determining if cash should be used to pay dividends, the basic business premise of rate of return still applies. If the cash can be employed in the business to earn a return higher than that which can be earned in the hands of shareholders, payment of dividends seems illogical.

There are three complications to this logic:

1. Pinpointing the rate of return of shareholders is at best an uncertain undertaking. As a reference point, however, one can assume that the company's shareholders are, more or less, a reflection of the market at large, and, as such can obtain the current rate of return available on corporate bonds or other fixed income securities. To further narrow the range and to equate risks, it would seem that the most appropriate bond rate to use would be that at which the corporation itself would currently borrow.

To calculate the alternative rate of return at which shareholders would presumably be indifferent, some tax considerations become important. Take the following example:

Assume the company has $100.00 it can retain or use as dividends. The company's after-tax rate of return is 7%, and shareholders are presumed to have a marginal tax rate of 30% (another tough item to pinpoint). Note that this rate is likely to be somewhat on the low side because of the limited dividend exclusion important to small investors.

If the company keeps the money, next year the shareholder's stock will be worth an additional $107.00 = ($100.00 + (7%)($100.00). If that were paid out as a dividend next year, the shareholder's after-tax portion would be $74.90 = ($107.00 − (30%)($107.00)).

If the company pays out the $100.00, the shareholder would have $70.00 available for investment which must yield $4.90 in additional after-tax income = ($74.90 − $70.00). Therefore, the shareholder's alternative investment rate must be at least:

$$\frac{(\$4.90/(100\% - 30\%))}{\$70.00} = \frac{\$4.90/.7}{\$70.00} = 10.0\%$$

Mathematically we can restate this as:

$$\text{Indifference Point} = \frac{\text{Corporate After-Tax Rate of Return}}{100\% - \text{Shareholder Marginal Tax Rate}}$$

Of course, the results will apply to the average shareholder, so that there can be no certainty that a particular dividend decision will be in the best interests of all shareholders. Note, as well, that there is an implicit assumption that all money retained by the company can be used to produce a uniform rate of return, which may not always be an accurate assumption.

2. One of the goals of dividend payments is to improve stock price, thereby rewarding shareholders and improving the company's prospects of attracting more capital in the future. Furthermore, increases in share price make the stock a potential tool in acquisitions. Accordingly, the impact of dividend declaration on share price has to be assessed.

The payment of a dividend reduces the company's worth and a stock is typically devalued in price when it trades ex-dividend. It is the prospect of future dividends that will increase the demand for shares, and, therefore, consistency of policy is to be prized. Such consistency can be in direct conflict with the concept of best alternative return. Therefore, the amount payable per year should be expectedly sustainable, as few events will do more to cause share price to nose-dive than a cut or elimination of dividends. Whether good practice or not, it has been customary in American industry to maintain dividends except in the face of the most grievous and dangerous financial reverses.

Three approaches to maintenance of consistency are:

a. Payout of a guideline percentage of earnings. This assumes steady or rising earnings and is therefore not useful for companies with erratic earnings.

b. Payout of a guideline amount of *cash flow*.

c. Setting dividends with reference to projections of future earnings and anticipated cash availability.

> **Try This:** *When alternative returns or other factors strongly suggest a payout, but its sustainability is questionable, make the dividend an extra rather than a regular one, so as to signal that this may be a bonus windfall, not necessarily an ongoing payout.*

3. There may be some legal and regulatory complications to making payouts. These include:

a. Double taxation as already cited, which grows more complex as more and more taxing authorities (states and foreign countries) enter the picture.

b. Loan or bond indenture agreements may restrict dividend payments.

c. Par values and minimum capital retention requirements may also constrain payouts.

d. The accumulated earnings tax, leviable by the IRS when it appears that a company is avoiding payout to avoid double taxation, may impel larger and more frequent payouts.

e. Certain business forms, such as real estate investment trusts and limited partnerships, may be in jeopardy as to their tax status or investment desirability if they limit payouts. (Essentially a factor for closely held firms only.)

One other aspect of dividend tactics is the initiation of a dividend reinvestment plan, whereby shareholders may elect that their dividends be retained by the corporation to purchase additional shares. These additional shares are obtained without commission and may even be offered at a slight discount from market. Essentially, this is another opportunity to build cash while still satisfying the demands of shareholders for an immediate cash reward.

Market Intervention — Subject to certain securities regulations, companies can influence stock price by open-market purchases and sales. Corporate purchases of stock sop up supply, thereby adding upward pressure to share price.

Nonetheless, cash used to shrink the outstanding claims on aggregate net worth must produce a higher return for the remaining shares than would be realized if the funds were used in some other way by the company and the repurchased shares had remained outstanding. The return on repurchased shares is reflected in three ways for the remaining shares:

1. Increase in book value:

	Before Purchase	Purchased	After Purchase
Shares	1,000,000	200,000	800,000
Net Worth	$5,000,000	$600,000	$4,400,000
Book Value/Share	$5.00	$3.00	$5.50

To obtain such an increase, purchase must be at a cost below book value per share.

2. Increase in Earnings Per Share:

	Before Purchase	Purchased	After Purchase
Shares	1,000,000	200,000	800,000
Total Earnings	$1,000,000	$120,000	$880,000
E.P.S.	$1.00	$0.60	$1.10

To achieve this increase, the earnings that could be obtained with the cash used for shares purchase must represent a smaller portion of the total anticipated earnings than the shares purchased constitute of the total outstanding.

In this example, the $600,000 used to purchase 200,000 shares would yield a 20% return of $120,000 in the next year, equaling 12% of total possible earnings, while 200,000 shares are 20% of all shares. Hence, E.P.S. is higher with the stock repurchase.

3. Increase in dividends:

	Before Purchase	Purchased	After Purchase
Shares	1,000,000	200,000	800,000
Earnings Available	$500,000	$60,000	$440,000
Dividends	$0.50	$0.30	$0.55

This concept is derived from the earnings calculation, operating on the theory that a fixed portion of earnings (here 50%) is committed to dividends.

Market Communication — As stock prices are a function of supply and demand, given a fixed supply, prices will rise if demand can be stimulated. These financial "marketing relations" techniques include:

1. *Advertising:* Ads that promote the company's image as an investment may produce results, although advertising results in this situation are difficult to validate.

2. *Media Relations:* News releases, interviews with company executives, articles and the like have a definite place in investment promotion. These activities must be a part of the company's broader public relations program. It does not make sense, for example, for a company to be claiming that its profits are unusually terrific to promote investment while simultaneously poor-mouthing its profits in the face of consumer charges of overpricing. A comprehensive program can, however, accomplish both results, but that cannot occur without adequate planning.

3. *Securities Firms:* The maintenance of credible relationships with analysts and principals of securities firms is an essential part of market influence. Communications with representatives of regional and local securities companies are particularly important for smaller and newer companies who cannot immediately command the attention of Wall Street. When money center firms have local branch offices, the branch manager can be a critical link to attract the attention of the main office, both as a source of market interest and a source of future financing.

4. *Institutions:* Major institutional buyers, such as mutual funds and insurance companies, also deserve the same kind of personal attention and cultivation of relationship as securities firms.

5. *Shareholder Relations:* Just as existing customers are valued for their loyalty, referrals and future sales, so, too, are present shareholders valued. Their retention of stock is tantamount to a continuing demand, and that retention must be encouraged, not just by high earnings and dividends, but by honest communications, timely reports in understandable format, efficient transfer and registration services, careful adherence to securities regulations and, where permissible, by grant of discounts and/or gifts of products and services. These communications, like all others, should be part of a comprehensive public relations program. Accordingly, the financial manager deserves the opportunity to provide input to such a program and to influence its output when financial matters are involved.

Chapter 13

Tailoring
The Budgeted Business Plan
To Fit Your Situation

Having examined in detail the disparate aspects of financial management, we will now pull all those aspects together in this chapter to combine and shape them into a comprehensive, achievable, sensible and tailored Budgeted Business Plan.

PLANNING THE PLAN

The strategic foundation of the Plan must first be laid by positing the principles for the Plan Development Process. Throughout the process, reference to these principles will help all of the participants to maintain the corporate cohesion that allows sufficient operating autonomy to each unit without units straying into unproductive or counterproductive postures.

These are the bedrock principles for development of the Plan:

1. Set measurable objectives.
2. Cultivate an organization with the ability to accomplish the Plan.
3. Develop a Plan that will motivate the organization to achieve its goals.
4. Require accountability.
5. Distinguish Variable Costs.

OBJECTIVES

The objectives themselves should conform to a subordinate set of principles:

A. Objectives must be comprehensive in the sense that all parts of the organization must have their own specified objectives that contribute to the accomplishment of the broader corporate goals.

229

B. Objectives at all levels must be reasonably achievable. If they are not achievable, and hence not achieved, the corporate plan cannot help but be compromised. Additionally, unreasonable objectives may demoralize the employees charged with fulfilling them, leading possibly to less than best efforts or abandonment of the corporate ship.

C. Quantify objectives to as great an extent as possible to make achievement measurable. Where quantification is speculative, at least make the completion of a tangible product the objective. For example, "Physical inventories will be taken at the end of each fiscal quarter."

D. Incrementalize objectives. Make them fit together in small, embraceable, understandable units that the employee responsible for a task can relate to. For example, instead of saying "Production output to be increased by 10% without an increase in working hours," the goal can be translated into "Minimum of 15 completed units per labor hour."

E. Set milestones and deadlines that signal progress (or lack of it) toward the objectives. Milestones should be close enough to one another in both time and magnitude to provide adequate leeway for correction, but not so close together as to yield repetitive data or create either a false sense of security through a quick series of apparent achievements or an unnecessary sense of crisis over a similarly quick series of shortfalls.

F. Consider the objectives in relation to the people and organizational structure charged with obtaining them. Without a capable organization, sufficiently staffed, properly motivated and adequately led, no objectives are achievable.

ORGANIZATION

Cultivate an organization with the ability to execute the plan with success. Developing such internal operating abilities requires a top management able to analyze the strengths and weaknesses, without bias, not only of its subordinates, but of itself, so that the right people are in place and in readiness to cooperate in the consistent execution of the entire undertaking.

Effective management styles and personnel policies are the essential foundation for a successful pursuit of all the objectives. Failure to attain them, or a vague feeling that objectives are being targeted below potential may well be a symptom of deficiency in management style and/or organization structure rather than in the managers themselves or in employees at large who are ready scapegoats.

Honest evaluation of management style is the initial critical step to rectifying any such shortcomings. Problems have to be identified before they can be solved. Toward that end, an unbiased third party, such as an outside consultant or perhaps independent members of the company's board of directors may be especially useful. Outsiders may also be helpful in promoting modification and education aimed at management behavior that will ultimately be helpful to plan development and achievement.

At the same time, organizational improvement should not become a goal in itself; normal operations cannot be "put on hold" while management takes stock of itself. Organizational skills and improvement are additional means toward the end of corporate profitability, and are best pursued not by crash cure but by a steady program concerned with management and organizational health, just as there is a steady program concerned with fiscal health.

MOTIVATION

Develop a plan that will motivate personnel to execute it with success. The whole plan is best accomplished when each segment of the company has its own subplan with its own objectives that employees can relate to. The constituent parts then mesh into successively larger subplans at each level of the organization.

Ideally, each employee's own program of goals, performance standards and responsibilities can be traced upward and through the chain of command to be reflected and understood at the corporate level. That permits top management to understand the role of each employee (not necessarily in the literal sense of John Doe to Jane Smith and so on, but by job description, such as welder to floor walker) and thereby assess what exceeding the plan or failing will mean. At the same time it permits a relative understanding of the worth of and return derivable from each position. Those elements, *worth* and *return*, are themselves fundamental to determining the appropriate rewards, both in the absolute sense and relative to one another, that are obviously an essential part of motivation.

ACCOUNTABILITY

Require accountability at all levels of the organization. Responsibility for each objective and sub-objective must be traceable in every case to a particular individual.

The concept of "Profit Center" is well known and its institution is a worthwhile step toward necessary accountability. But management can go one step further to "Performance Center" that covers *all* the objectives of which profit is undoubtedly the penultimate one, but by no means the only one. In these days of social responsibility, corporate stakeholders and an increasingly politicized world economy, a broader measure of achievement cannot be avoided.

There are three types of activities in particular that require Performance Center concepts and samples of at least one such activity are likely to be found in every unit of every company:

A. Extra-Profit (extra meaning outside, not additional) activities, such as Affirmative Action or Pollution Control programs. These kinds of activities are frequently mandated by regulation and arguably do nothing to contribute to profit and may even inhibit it. Accordingly, profit from them is exceedingly speculative. Nevertheless, there are real performance standards, including adherence to a money budget, that can be developed. For example:

A department with the responsibility for enforcing Equal Opportunity and Affirmative Action might be measured by such standards as:

1. Minimized variance from hiring and employee ratios.

2. Turnover rates uniform among all subgroups of employees, as an indication that substandard employees are not being recruited just to meet the variance standard.

3. A fixed target maximum of discrimination complaints and grievances.

4. A fixed percentage target minimum of timely and satisfactory (in terms of all parties agreeing to the outcome) resolution of complaints and grievances.

Similarly, a department responsible for pollution control might use:

1. Statistically significant reduction in pollution levels by type of effluent.

2. A fixed target maximum of citations for violations.

3. Obtention of negotiated accords with regulatory authorities limiting necessary investment in equipment to a maximum dollar amount.

B. Pro-Profit (pro meaning promoting) activities are those that are definitely meant to contribute to greater profitability, but specific dollar earnings cannot be traced to them, such as management development programs. Examples of standards for those responsible for such a program might include:

1. Fixed target maximum of employee grievances.

2. Fixed target maximum of management turnover.

3. Specific number of managers completing the program.

4. Specific minimum average rating of the program by those completing it.

C. Pre-Profit (pre meaning preliminary to profit) activities are those that have long-term value in yielding a profit, but the contribution to profit is not immediately measurable or even readily apparent. Product Research activities fit this definition and could use these performance standards:

1. Minimum number of patent registrations.

2. Minimum number of feasible product ideas.

3. Minimum number of test-marketable products developed.

4. Specific percentage of cost of production saving by improvement of product design or production method.

Note that the last of these objectives is a measurable profit standard. It is included here as a reminder that both profit and other-than-profit standards are appropriately applied to all activities.

> **Beware This Pitfall:** *Don't create a system of artificial measures to which people are slaves. Good management will ultimately judge performance by logical evaluation of contributions to corporate achievement.*

VARIABLE COSTS

Distinguish variable and fixed costs. Identification of which expenses will vary and to what degree, with given levels of sales, (but with other events as well, such as acquisition of additional equipment), is critical to properly anticipating the expense levels to be generated by and budgeted for each activity.

As an indicator of this importance, consider the basic business equation:

$$\text{Profit} = \text{Sales} - \text{Expenses}$$

Expanding the formula, we can consider expenses in the categories of fixed and variable, the latter being those that change with sales:

$$Profit = (Sales - Variable) - Fixed$$

If variable expenses will climb with sales, we need to determine their rate of climb in order to know the real contribution to profit value of each sale. Without that information, the general business tendency to ever expand and increase sales may be precisely the wrong policy. This may be so if sales increases force the company to a new plateau of built-in costs. The typical example is the expansion of a headquarters office, in boom times, because "people are crawling over one another." After the boom's peak, personnel may be trimmed, but the cost of the added space weighs heavily on cash and earnings.

Where many businesses go awry in planning in this area is in equating Direct Costs or Costs of Sale with variable costs. There is some level of activity at which overhead will increase, some level at which previously fixed costs become unfixed. (That is not to say that overhead and fixed costs are necessarily identical.) Recognizing early where those points are and evaluating them are central to successful planning.

Developing a "Fixed Cost Staircase" that relates sales increases (or other parameters such as production levels) to fixed costs is one effective way to promote recognition. Such a staircase might look like this:

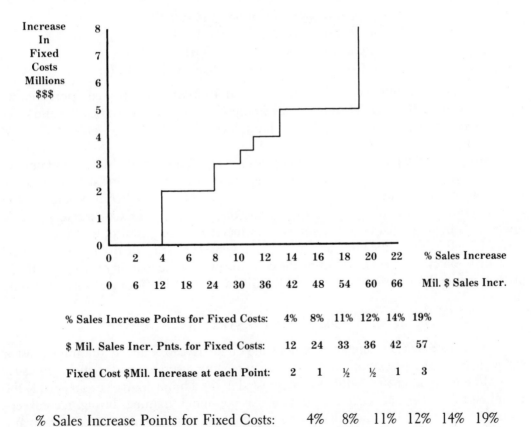

% Sales Increase Points for Fixed Costs:	4%	8%	11%	12%	14%	19%
$ Mil. Sales Incr. Pnts. for Fixed Costs:	12	24	33	36	42	57
Fixed Cost $Mil. Increase at each Point:	2	1	½	½	1	3

Forecast of these increases is best launched by purely statistical observations using techniques such as linear regression and correlation, where fixed costs are the dependent variable. The statistics should prompt refinement by judgment and analysis of isolated portions of the statistical continua. In developing the above staircase, assume that sales and fixed costs for the past ten years (time frame chosen as and tested for statistical reliability) looks like this:

	Millions $$	
Year	Sales	Fixed Costs
1	105	15
2	140	18
3	160	23
4	180	26
5	175	27
6	190	30
7	230	34
8	220	35
9	260	40
10	300	46

Computed using Linear Regression:

Coefficient of Determination = r^2 = 0.98
Coefficient of Correlation = r = 0.99
Fixed Costs at 0 Sales = a = -3.01
Fixed Costs rate of Increase to Sales = b = 0.17

Via r^2 and r the intuitive link between sales and fixed costs is confirmed. Moreover, we know that statistically, every $1 Mil. in sales prompts $170,000 in fixed costs. We also know fixed costs are not a pure linear function of sales as b's 0.17 would imply — otherwise, they'd be variable!

Now comes the judgment. Examining our present status at $300 Million in sales, we know inflation will add $6 Million to sales via a price increase, but that inflation's impact on fixed costs will be negligible, because such a large part of the fixed costs is composed of depreciation, lease and mortgage payments, and the remainder of fixed costs (e.g., headquarters staff) is expected to be prevented from increase by cost control measures.

At $300 Million, the company was operating at 98% of real capacity. (Theoretical capacity is somewhat higher, providing the company with some margin of error.) With the price increase, 98% capacity supports $306 million, so that 100% of real capacity would support

$$\$306 \text{ Mil.}/.98 = \$312 \text{ Mil.}$$

To increase capacity, another assembly line would have to be added, the annual cost of which, in terms of depreciation, capital cost, maintenance insurance and related overhead is $1.5 Million. Another $0.4 Million is anticipated in the administrative costs related to the operation of another line, covering such costs as personnel (training, hiring, recordkeeping). Yet another $0.1 Million in contingency costs are anticipated to cover start-up and "ripple-effect" fixed costs. Ripple-effect costs are those eventually required by incremental increases in operations. Larger computer systems are needed to handle the greater volume of work. More telephone lines are needed. More storage space must be found for more records until a microfilming operation is undertaken. While these are exactly the kinds of costs that the staircase seeks to identify, there must also be an acceptance of the fact that 20-20 foresight is rare, and some margin to pick up these oversights ought to be included. Some of that may also sound like "bureaucratic creep." Nonetheless, there will come a time at which more fixed cost lubricant is essential to the continuing function of the corporate machine.

The line costs, administrative costs and contingency costs are determined by additional analysis of historic and market costs for all the components and ramifications of a new assembly line. The subtopic information of machinery costs, personnel and so forth that build to the aggregate data is also developable by the same statistical plus judgment process.

PLAN COMPONENTS

There are seven basic components of the plan that are useful for organizing the basic data on needs and resources. These components overlap in many ways, but the overlaps are, in a real sense, the connecting points that create a comprehensive and cohesive plan. These seven components are:

1. Sales
2. Operations
3. Overhead
4. Facilities
5. Equipment
6. Personnel
7. Capital

A flow chart detailing the process for developing all the data and objectives into a logical sequence and relationship may be found on page 236.

BUSINESS PLANNING FLOW CHART

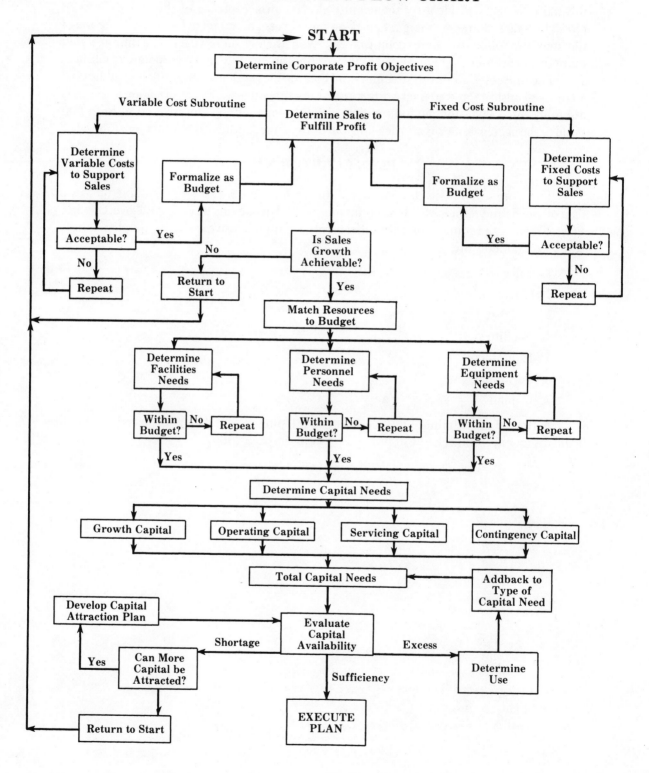

In practice, many of these activities will go on more or less simultaneously with adjustments being made as new data is uncovered, circumstances change, and new approaches are conceived. Yet, the formalization into a logically sequenced process will provide an internal discipline that mirrors well the company's progress with objectives, accountability, motivation, organization and cost control.

PLAN EXAMPLE — PROFIT AND SALES OBJECTIVES

A relatively simple example follows to illustrate the process. Our publicly held company has the following attributes:

Book Value = Present Market Price = $25.00

Price/Earnings Ration = 10X

Shares Outstanding = 10,000,000

Effective Tax Rate = 50%

Latest Current Annual Sales = $300,000,000

Latest Gross Margin as % Sales = 31%

Latest Present Fixed Costs = $46,000,000

Set Profit Objective

Increase profits so that the company's stock will sell at a price at least 20% over Book Value.

Assumptions:

A. Earnings are the principle determinant of our share price and will remain so for the immediate future.

B. PE Ratio, shares outstanding and tax rate are constants.

> **Point to Remember:** *Documentation of underlying assumptions permits their review, fundamentally safeguarding the integrity and construction of the plan.*

Profits Necessary:

    120% of Book Value = $30 Share Price
    Divided by 10X PE Ratio = $3 Per Share Earnings
    Multiply by 10 Mil. Shares Out = $30,000,000 Net Profit
    Divided by 1 − Tax Rate (1−.5) = $60,000,000 Pretax Profit Goal

Determine Sales to Fulfill Profit Goal

1. Go subroutine for Variable Costs to find Gross Margin.

Latest gross margin is 31%. Quantity discounts in materials purchases, together with progress along the learning curve, upgraded plant communications systems, avoiding a proportional increase in supervisors, and substitution of company trucks for common carriers will put downward pressure on variable costs. Wage increases, materials price increases, higher energy, supplies and inventory costs will put upward pressure on variable

costs, netting out to an anticipated decrease in variable costs from 69% to 67% yielding a
gross margin of 33%.

That improvement appears acceptable, pending further calculations. Discussion of
formalization into budget format will be momentarily deferred.

2. Go subroutine to determine Fixed Costs.

Here we will use the sample "Fixed Cost Staircase" developed earlier in the chapter. By
an iterative process, we will determine the sales level (having found the anticipated gross
margin) with reference to the changeable level of fixed costs. Watch as we "walk up the
staircase":

Pretax Profit Goal = $60,000,000
Add latest Fixed Costs = $46,000,000
Yields Initial Gross Profit = $106,000,000
Divided by 33% Gross Margin Rate = $321.2 Mil. Basic Sales Goal
% Sales Increase over $300 Mil. = 7.1%
Resulting Fixed Cost Increase = $2,000,000
Divided by 33% Gross Margin = $6.1 Mil. Additional Sales Goal
Stepped-up Sales Goal = $321.2 + 6.1 = $327.2 Mil.
Recomputed % Increase over $300 Mil. = 9.1%
Second Step-up in Fixed Cost Increase = $1,000,000
Divided by 33% Gross Margin = $3 Mil. Additional Sales Goal
Second Stepped-Up Sales Level = $327.3 + $3 = $330.3 Mil.
% Increase Over $300 Mil. = 10.1%
Resulting Next Step-up in Fixed Costs = 0.0
Therefore: Sales Goal = $330,300,000
% Sales Increase Goal = 10.1%

RECONCILIATION:	Sales	$330.3
	67% Variable Costs	−221.3
	33% Gross Margin	109.0
	Less Fixed Costs:	
	Initial	46.0
	Step-up I	2.0
	Step-up II	1.0
		−49.0
	Pretax Profit Goal	$60.0

A Useful Hint: *One can see that this process includes Break-Even Analysis that uses
the formula Sales = Fixed Costs/Gross Margin. Performing such analysis along
divisional lines, product lines, markets or other logical demarcations of activity, will
yield refined data and a window through which can be seen the order of return
obtained from each activity, thereby marking a trail for investment, expansion and
control efforts and decisions.*

Is Sales Growth Achievable?

This is a marketing question and we may assume that we get a positive response as a 10.1% increase is not inordinately high.

However, as a part of the earlier data collection process (inherent in the Variable Costs and Fixed Costs Subroutines) the marketing branch of the company would have supplied the maximum growth in sales achievable *and* supplied as well both the rates of variable costs (such as advertising and commissions) and Fixed Costs (reflected in the aggregate Staircase figures) generated by the sales and marketing efforts leading to each substantive increment to sales.

If the increase is not achievable, objectives will have to be revised or better cost and sales performance programmed to make the objectives achievable.

PLAN EXAMPLE — BUDGET FORMALIZATION

As a byproduct of determining the sales goal we have obtained the broad outline of acceptable variable costs and fixed costs. They represent the maximum aggregate expenses the company can incur.

This aggregate is generally built from the department level upward. A department is defined as a corporate unit charged with fulfilling a basic functional activity, for which the department manager has the front-line accountability and responsibilities. That manager, being closest to the details of the tactical battle for satisfactory completion of that activity, should be the party to initiate filling out the body of the budget within the broad outline drawn by top management. Of course, in different kinds of companies, "department" levels will be determined at different places. For example, in a restaurant chain, each store may be a separate department, whereas in a manufacturing operation, each shift or assembly line might be a separate department.

Each manager's budget should be more than just a justified recitation of what's to be spent. It should provide an annual forum for brief but intense evaluation of every aspect of the company, a chance to consider new initiatives and the blueprint of each department as a Performance Center.

It is the best opportunity for the finance manager to exercise his power to improve the corporation. Development and governance of the budget process can provide access to an understanding of the company dynamics that will influence its success in a way second only, perhaps, to the Chief Executive Officer (CEO).

Each department's budget should be a formatted document divided into nine sections. As an example, we'll use the company's Purchasing Department.

1. **Restatement of Mission:** A brief description of the essential purpose(s), the *raison d'être* of the activity.

Example: The Purchasing Department is responsible for acquisition of all goods, materials and equipment used by the corporation, such acquisitions to be of specified quantities and qualities ordered in timely fashion with incurrence of least net cost.

2. **Quantifiable Profit Objectives for Coming Year:** A listing of the concrete goals to be achieved in the coming year.

Example:
Raw Materials:

A. Hold raw materials costs to 28% of production costs.

B. Limit raw materials inventory level increase to 4% in face of 10% sales increase.

C. Find reliable second source of Material X.

Equipment:

A. Obtain all budgeted equipment within capital budget limit.

B. Revise manufacturing equipment and transportation equipment bid solicitation processes to reduce lead time by 25%.

Supplies and Miscellaneous:

A. Cut orders of less than $100 by 50% via consolidation and tighter screening to achieve minimum 2% reduction in expense (anticipating 8% inflation) by getting higher quantity discounts and lower shipping costs.

B. Achieve 3% reduction in shop supplies expense (anticipating 8% inflation) by standardizing companywide supplies used.

3. Other Than Profit Initiatives: Non-quantifiable procedures or activity goals to be undertaken.
Example:

A. Computerize mailing lists by standard purchase categories for bid solicitations.

B. Have all Purchasing Agents attend and pass a 2-week Purchasing Procedures Course offered at the local university.

4. Personnel: Provides data on departmental organization, personnel costs, number of personnel and personnel attributes.
Example:
A personnel data flow chart is found on page 241.

5. Facilities: A description of the area and facilities used by department, together with requests for any changes anticipated or desired.
Example:

Current Usage: Room #24 at Headquarters Building.
              3100 Square Feet @ $8.50/Sq.Ft. = $26,350.

Anticipated Usage: Unchanged

Changes Desired: Replace movable screens for Sr. Agents with permanent office partitions to provide greater privacy in negotiations. Cost: $3,600.

Business Plan

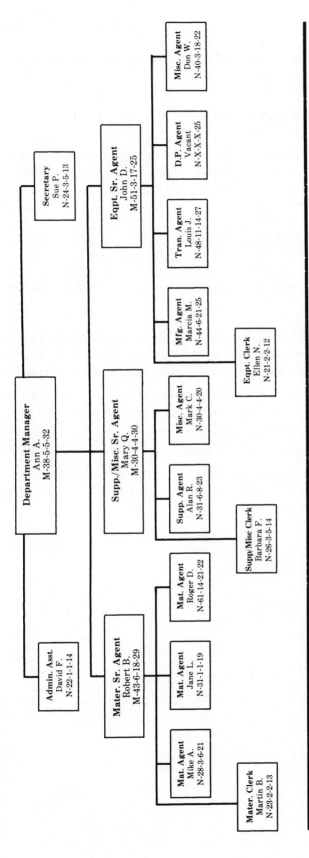

Code: Title
    Name
    M=Mgmnt/N=Non-Mgmnt — Age — Years in Position — Years with Company — Salary to nearest 000's

Summary:

	#	Avg. Age	Avg. Yrs. In Job	Avg. Yrs. W/Co.	Avg. Sal.	Total Sal.
Management Personnel	4	40.5	4.5	11.0	29,000	116,000
Non-Management Pers.	14*	33.0	4.2	7.7	19,290	270,000
Total Personnel	18	34.8	4.3	8.4	21,440	386,000

*1 Vacancy. Not used to compute average age (imputed for experience calculations). Budgeted salary of $25,000 used in salary calculations.

6. Equipment: Description and inventory of equipment used by department, together with requests and justification for changes anticipated or desired.
Example:

Equipment Inventory:

Current # On Hand	Items Description	Original Cost	Next FY Deprec.	Changes Request	Cost of Changes	Deprec. Effect
18	Furniture Sets	$18,000	$ 2,250	None	—	—
1	Conf. Rm. Set	$ 2,000	$ 250	None	—	—
2	Comp. Termin.	$10,000	$ 2,000	+1	$ 6,000	$1,200
3	Autos	$18,000	$ 6,000	+1	$ 6,000	$2,000
2	Photocopiers	$ 6,500	$ 1,300	None	—	—
0	Facsim. Trans.	None	—	+1	$ 2,500	$ 500
Totals		$54,500	$11,800		$14,500	$3,700

Changes Requested:

A. Additional computer terminal desired to complete mailing list computerization and to reduce time lag in order processing backlog resulting from three clerks sharing two terminals. Expected to save need for fourth clerk in the next two years.

B. Fourth auto desired to provide one auto per management employee, and eliminate scheduling conflicts. No net savings calculable. Expected to improve morale.

C. Facsimile transmitter desired to reduce contract and order verification time. Time saving expected to improve stockout record and cut inventory size requirements.

7. Expense Budget: Costs by expense classification according to the corporate Chart of Accounts, by month, with totals and averages. Changes relative to the year just ending are detailed as a second part of this section.
Example: See tables that follow.

Expense Budget — 000's

Expense:	Totals	Jan	Feb	Mar	Apr	May	Jun	July	Aug	Sep	Oct	Nov	Dec	Mo. Avgs.
Personnel:														
Management Salaries	116	9	9	9	9	10	10	10	10	10	10	10	10	10
Non-Management Sal.	270	20	20	22	22	22	22	22	24	24	24	24	24	23
Payroll Taxes	42	4	4	4	4	4	4	3	3	3	3	3	3	4
Fringe Benefits	58	4	4	5	5	5	5	5	5	5	5	5	5	5
Total Personnel	486	37	37	40	40	41	41	40	42	42	42	42	42	42
Facilities:														
Rent	26	2	2	2	2	2	2	2	2	2	2	3	3	2
Utilities	4	0	0	1	0	0	1	0	0	1	0	0	1	1
Maintenance	2	0	0	0	0	0	1	0	0	0	0	0	1	0
Total Facilities	32	2	2	3	2	2	4	2	2	3	2	3	5	3
Equipment:														
Leases	0	0	0	0	0	0	0	0	0	0	0	0	0	0
Depreciation	16	1	1	1	1	1	1	1	1	2	2	2	2	1
Repairs	3	0	0	0	1	0	0	0	1	0	0	0	1	1
Miscellaneous	2	0	0	0	0	0	1	0	0	0	0	0	1	0
Total Equipment	21	1	1	1	2	1	2	1	2	2	2	2	4	2
Operations:														
Supplies	12	1	1	1	1	1	1	1	1	1	1	1	1	1
Phone	12	1	1	1	1	1	1	1	1	1	1	1	1	1
Auto	12	1	1	1	1	1	1	1	1	1	1	1	1	1
Travel & Entertain.	16	1	1	1	1	2	1	1	3	1	2	1	1	1
Miscellaneous	12	1	1	1	1	1	1	1	1	1	1	1	1	1
Total Operations	64	5	5	5	5	6	5	5	7	5	6	5	5	5
Total Expenses	603	45	45	49	49	50	52	48	53	52	52	52	56	52

Expense Budget
Comparison to Prior Year

Expense	New Year	Old Year	Incr./(Decr.)	% Incr./(Decr.)
Personnel:				
Mgmnt. Salaries	116	100	16	16.0
Non-Mgmnt. Sal.	270	240	30	12.5
P/R Taxes	42	37	5	13.5
Fringes	58	51	7	13.7
Total Personnel	486	428	58	13.6
Facilities:				
Rent	26	25	1	4.0
Utilities	4	3	1	33.3
Maintenance	2	2	0	0.0
Total Facilities	32	30	2	6.7
Equipment:				
Lease	0	1	(1)	(100.0)
Depreciation	16	12	4	33.3
Repairs	3	4	(1)	(25.0)
Miscellaneous	2	2	0	0.0
Total Equipment	21	19	2	10.5
Operations:				
Supplies	12	10	2	20.0
Phone	12	12	0	0.0
Auto	12	6	6	100.0
Travel & Entert.	16	14	2	14.3
Miscellaneous	12	14	(2)	(14.3)
Total Operations	64	56	8	14.3
Total Expenses	603	531	72	13.6

Corporate Sales % Change v. Department Budget % Change:
10.1%   v.   13.8%

8. **Output Budget:** A statistical compendium, on a comparative basis to the previous year, of the principal measures of productivity. For a marketing department, this budget section would be expressed in sales measures (dollar sales, unit sales, sales per salesman, per territory, etc.). For a manufacturing department, production statistics (units of output, output per employee, per machine, per labor hour, etc.). For an essentially administrative or support activity, the measures may be somewhat more esoteric.

Example:

Item	New Year	Old Year	Incr./(Decr)	% Incr./ (Decr)
Total Mater. Purch. $	62,500,000	58,000,000	4,500,000	7.8
Tot. Mater. Purch. lbs	6,000,000	5,800,000	200,000	3.4
Tot. Eqpt. Purch. $	16,000,000	21,000,000	(5,000,000)	(23.8)
Tot. Eqpt. Purch-Units	4,104	2,243	1,861	83.0
Tot. Supp. Purch. $	8,000,000	6,000,000	2,000,000	33.3
Total $ Purchases	86,500,000	85,000,000	1,500,000	1.8
$ Purchases/Employee	4,805,555	4,722,222	83,333	1.8
$ Purchases/Salary $	$224	$250	($26)	(10.4)
$ Purchases/Dept. Bud. $	$143	$160	($17)	(10.6)
Budget $/Employee	33,500	29,444	4,056	13.8

9. Commentary: A descriptive summary of the budget proposal with concise explanations of the highlights.

Example:

As approximately 80% of this department's expenses are personnel related, recently granted salary and wage increases are primarily responsible for the rate of increase in excess of forecasted sales increases. There are no additional positions being created that fuel the personnel expense increase, although a recent vacancy created by a resignation at the non-management Purchasing Agent level is expected to be filled to maintain the department at full complement.

The companywide reduction in anticipated dollar equipment purchases is not a totally accurate indication of workload, as replacement of a large number of autos in the company fleet and plans to install word processing equipment in most departments will result in a higher number of unit purchases. The move to word processing will also cause a temporary spurt in office supplies purchases to be used with the new equipment. Inflation in the supplies is also expected to outpace inflation in general.

BUDGET EVALUATION

The aggregation of all of the departmental budgets should yield total expenditures within the previously defined corporate limits. However, the summation process is not a one-step affair.

Departmental submittals should first be made to divisional level and perhaps a second interim level (e.g., group) before final submittal to either the CEO or a budget committee under the CEO's direction. The Chief Financial Officer should also be a member of the Budget Committee. The competition for limited corporate resources may require more than one pass before final approval is given.

Zero-based budget procedures have been adopted in some quarters to promote more intense scrutiny of proposed expenditures. The process requires a conceptual rebuilding of each part of the company with justification for each block of expense used in the rebuilding.

The greatest disadvantage of zero-based budgeting is the enormous time and paperwork required by the process, which translates into an extraordinary administrative expense in the pursuit of lower overall expenses. The second disadvantage of zero-based budgeting is that it builds a budget from the bottom up instead of from the top down. This zero-based budget can become a case of the tail wagging the dog.

A more effective method for effective budget development is accomplished by setting corporate goals, communicating those goals throughout the organization and eliciting support from committed, trustworthy managers and employees for those goals. Incentives and effective management structure will help insure that those budgets are both established and adhered to within acceptable limits.

CAPITAL BUDGET

At this point, we've marched through the flow chart to the point where capital availability becomes the key to the plan's fruition. Insufficient capital requires the company to go outside using any or all of the techniques discussed in preceding chapters. If the additional capital cannot be raised at an acceptable cost, the only alternative left to the company is to scale back the plan to reduce capital needs.

Excess capital is also a problem, though not so serious. That excess can be invested or disbursed in a variety of ways, as also outlined in preceding chapters.

MONITORING RESULTS

Performance Center accountability is dependent on accurate and relatively frequent reports on performance. Development of a budget process is useless without a corresponding monitoring system to control adherence to the budget and alert conscientious managers to both opportunities and perils.

At the departmental level, right on up to the corporate level, the ideal format for budget monitoring reports use the headings and format shown on page 247.

Copies of these reports should be provided to the department head, his superior and on up through the chain of command, with the departments in each unit being added together, so that each division, group, etc. has its own totals for evaluation, backed up by the individual unit reports.

A report, possibly less than monthly depending on the subject matter, should also be issued on the statistical objectives. For example:

Purchasing Department
Output Progress Report
1st Qtr 19XX

Item	Year-to-Date	Annualized	Budget Total	% Accomplished
Tot. Mater. $ Purch.	19,500,000	78,000,000	62,500,000	31.2%
Tot. Mater. lbs Purch.	1,430,000	5,720,000	6,000,000	23.8%
Tot. Eqpt. $ Purch.	3,432,000	13,728,000	16,000,000	21.4%
Tot. Eqpt. Units Purch.	1,002	4,008	4,104	24.4%
Tot. Supp. $ Purch.	2,338,000	9,352,000	8,000,000	29.2%
Total $ Purchases	25,270,000	101,080,000	86,500,000	29.2%
$ Purchases/Employee	1,403,889	5,615,555	4,805,555	—
$ Purchases/Salary $	$285	$285	$224	—
$ Purchases/Dept. Bud.	$190	$190	$143	—
Budget $/Employee	7,395	29,580	33,500	—

Purchasing Department
Budget Compliance Report
April 19XX

Expense	Mo. Actual / Mo. Budget / Mo. Varia. / % Mo. Var.	Mo. Actual Yr. Ago Act / Incr/Decr / % Incr/Decr	YTD Actual / YTD Budget / YTD Varia. / % YTD Var.	YTD Actual / YTD Yr. Ago / Incr/Decr / Incr/Decr	Avg./Mo. / Avg./Bud. / Avg. Var. / % Var.	Mo. Annual. / Bud. Annual. / Annual Var. / % Ann. Var.	YTD Annual. / YTD Bud.Ann. / YTD Ann. Var. / % YTD Ann.
Management Salaries	10,300 / 9,000 / +1,300 / +14.4%	10,300 / 8,400 / +1,900 / +22.2%	38,400 / 37,000 / +1,400 / +3.8%	38,400 / 34,200 / +4,200 / +12.3%	9,600 / 9,250 / +350 / +3.8%	123,600 / 116,000 / +7,600 / +6.5%	115,200 / 116,000 / (800) / +0.7%
Non-Management Sal.	20,300 / 22,000 / (1,700) / (7.7%)	20,300 / 20,100 / +200 / +1.0%	81,000 / 84,000 / (3,000) / (3.6%)	81,000 / 79,600 / +1,400 / +1.8%	20,250 / 21,000 / (750) / (3.6%)	243,600 / 270,000 / (26,400) / (9.8%)	243,000 / 270,000 / (27,000) / (10.6%)
Departmental Totals	48,240 / 49,000 / (760) / (1.5%)	48,240 / 46,650 / 1,590 / 3.4%	181,350 / 188,000 / (6,650) / (3.5%)	181,350 / 174,560 / 6,790 / 3.9%	45,337 / 47,000 / (1,663) / (3.5%)	578,880 / 603,000 / (24,120) / (4.0%)	544,050 / 603,000 / (58,950) / (9.8%)

Abbreviations: Mo. = Month . . . YTD = Year-to-date . . . Avg. = Average . . . Annual. = Ann. = Annualized
Var. = Varia. = Variance . . . Incr = Increase . . . Decr = Decrease

Such reports are by definition customized, and their format and frequency are best developed in a joint effort among the department, the department's direct superiors and a representative of either the finance group or the budget committee or both.

This entire process is obviously very adaptable to data processing, which can augment the value of the process and the return derivable from it many times.

As these reports are received and evaluated, it is the responsibility of the managers at each level of the company to implement the appropriate strategies and tactics (from all of the preceding pages and elsewhere) to meet and exceed the goals and budgets these reports are designed to reflect.

PRACTICAL POINTER

The development and use of the Budgeted Business Plan is the strategic tool available to top management for profit achievement and cost control. By using it in conjunction with the tactical tools outlined in the preceding chapters and seasoning the entire approach with good business judgment and appropriate management skills, your company has the opportunity to embrace a SYSTEM for fulfilling its operational goals.

Index